An Essay on

NATURE

An Essay on
NATURE

By Frederick J. E. Woodbridge

New York: Morningside Heights

COLUMBIA UNIVERSITY PRESS

1940

TO THE READER

IN THIS ESSAY, Nature is considered as the domain in which both knowledge and happiness are pursued. I have not tried to write a theory of the universe, a theory of knowledge, or a theory of morals, but to analyze familiar and easily identifiable situations and follow the lead of the analysis. In doing this I have found it advisable to express radical opposition to the dualism which contends that the ways and means of acquiring knowledge and the knowledge thereby acquired warrant the conclusion that the familiar scenes we explore are but data whereby we ascertain the character and structure of a universe which somehow lies independently beyond and external to them. I am well aware that this opposition may be regarded as a willful flouting of the testimony of men of science, especially of those who devote their lives to the physical sciences. The essay is my defense. I do not think that it can be convicted of any disrespect for science even when it is caustic in view of popularizations which are misleading and productive of more confusion than clarity.

The dualism I have found important and arresting is that of the natural and the supernatural. It arises, however, not in the pursuit of knowledge, but in the pursuit of happiness. In that pursuit the dualism constantly appears and is not reconciled by increasing knowledge. We may, of course, speak of religious knowledge, and frequently do so. Science and religion are not, however, thereby reduced to a common denominator so that they can be added together as two fractions of one body. "To know" may signify "to be assured" without specifying ways and means of being assured. The assurances of knowledge are not like those of faith. The reduction of either to the other would rob each in turn of its own character. The dualism involved is reconciled by faith which, admitting that for the pursuit of knowledge Nature is primary, acknowledges that in any ultimate justification of the pursuit of happiness Nature is secondary. The assurance of faith rests on the fact that in a world wholly devoid of any desire for happiness, the advancement of knowledge would serve no purpose.

I have avoided a critical and historical comparison of theories of Nature because history is clear evidence that these theories find their initiative in familiar circumstances of daily life. We begin our reflections as animals living in a visible world around us. We do not start with an invisible world and then arrive at the vault of heaven above the earth. I have never found the visible world successfully generated by trying to build first an antecedent skeletal structure to be later veneered with visibility or clothed by it as with a garment or hung with occasional signs which advertise the hidden structure which supports them. It is available material for discovering the conservations which are characteristic of it and pervade it. No reader of the history of physics ought to be surprised at the course the science is taking today even if he is surprised at the pronouncements of some of its advocates and publishers of its news.[1] Bodies, living or dead, which come to be and pass away or move and change in the visible world, have been the initial subject matter of physics, and the discovery of that which is conserved has been its aim. In pursuit of this aim, the qualitative has repeatedly given way to the quantitative, for the latter is measurable and, above all, makes calculation possible. One may say that the history of physics is the history of the pursuit of a calculus adequate for whatever is in any way measurable, for one formula which would be the unification of all others. On turning from the formulas to their relevance to familiar things, there is the danger of being tricked by familiar words so that "waves" are pictured like ripples on a

---

[1] As I write, I note the title of an article condensed from *Scientific American* in the *Readers Digest* for February, 1940: "A Lamp That Freezes Motion."

pool, "rays" like beams of a searchlight, "quanta" like
tiny bullets darting about, and "the universe" like a
rubber ball expanding or contracting or just staying
put. Those formulas ought rather to make us see the
visible world more clearly in its unified spatial, temporal, and communicative character. By taking apart
and putting together, by adding and subtracting and
watching what happens, the calculus begins. Its progressive improvement does not give us reality as
against appearance, but greater effectiveness in adding
and subtracting.

It is not such developments as the calculus illustrates
that supplement the natural with the supernatural.
The calculus is relevant to conservations without which
Nature would be all flux, chaos, and confusion and
could be in no sense known. When authority is imputed to them as if they were creators and established
laws for Nature to observe according to their own design or, as it were, for their own glory, terms are then
borrowed from the pursuit of happiness. "Obedience
to the laws of Nature" is an expression with a tonic
effect very different from that of "illustrating Nature's
principles of conservation." The effect is to transform
the conservation of Nature into obedience to superiority. Thus it is that the dualism of the natural and the
supernatural arises out of the pursuit of happiness.
Could the dualism be reconciled by knowledge, the

superior would be discovered to be a natural principle of conservation and subject to formulation by a calculus. The dualism would persist. The reconciliation is by faith. The faithful confess that final happiness is worshipful participation in the obedience that pervades Nature. They have ceased to be slaves of despair.

In the first four chapters of this essay Nature is considered as the field of knowledge; in the final chapter, as the condition of the pursuit of happiness. Originally I had not intended to write a Preface for the reader. On the advice of friends and also because the essay in its present form is so radically different from what I planned many years ago and yet reminiscent of several unsatisfactory attempts at composition, I have found it important to advise the reader in a general way of what to expect in the following pages. I am unable now to rewrite the essay, and even were I able I doubt if I could do better. This is not an apology for a work which I think could be much improved, but rather a recognition of the fact that the more intensively I have worked on the subjects involved, the more I have been impressed by my own limitations and those of others. Philosophers' habit of writing as if they knew it all is ridiculous, but no more so than that of scientists who assume authority. In what I have written I have been deeply serious, but often I have had to smile at my professions of authority. I must add, on Nature's authority, that all this must be as it is so long as there are work and play, laughter and tears, life and death. A universe wholly without drama would offer no choices for anything it contained, no anxieties, no ideals, and no use for the possessive case.

Frederick J. E. Woodbridge

Columbia University
  January, 1940

CONTENTS

An Essay on

NATURE

γνόντες δὲ ὅτι ἔστι, τί ἐστι ζητοῦμεν

Chapter One ✱ KNOWLEDGE OF NATURE

Nature Identified

THE WORD "Nature" is used in this essay as a name for the familiar setting of human history. I like Sir Thomas Browne's picture of it in his *Religio Medici* as "that universal and publick Manuscript that lies expansed unto the eyes of all," because it is something evidently seen and like a book to be read with enjoyment and profit, a book which we are all engaged in reading either superficially or attentively. And I like Santayana's reference to it as "public experience . . . the stars, the seasons, the swarm of animals, the spectacle of birth and death, of cities and wars . . . the facts before every man's eyes."[1] His list of particulars could be much enlarged, but one would grow weary in the enumeration of them and be content to sum them up in "heaven and earth, the sea, and all that in them is." Such is the *familiar* setting of human history. It is

[1] *Scepticism and Animal Faith*, New York, Scribner's, 1924, p. x.

also the primary subject matter of all human inquiry. I would not have it displaced by any other, because when I try to displace it or consider what others do when they try, I find that a substitute for it cannot be found and that I am seeking ignorance instead of knowledge. In recognizing it as the setting of *human* history, I would not exclude other histories from it— neither that of living creatures other than man nor that of the stars—for I must think of it as expansed not only unto the eyes of all, but unto the eyeless also, for heaven and earth, the sea, and all that in them is make up a sum which seems to leave nothing out. "Nature" is here used as a name for that sum.

In so naming it, I have no intention of conveying information about it. So I spell the name with a capital letter to indicate that it is what we call a "proper" and sometimes "Christian" name. The heathen had in their languages somewhat equivalent words, suggestive of generation and decay, and that suggestion still influences our English use of the Latin word *natura*, as if Nature were once born of dubious parents and might later die, remaining meanwhile like a fertile mother who, in spite of never having had a husband, has had a prodigious offspring. I confess to some sympathy with the heathen in this matter. Personification is difficult for me to resist. I am afflicted with a sense of indecency whenever I refer to Nature as "it." My ancestors are all dead, but I feel like a child of Nature, cradled in her arms until my turn comes to die and to remain somewhere and somehow in her embrace. This sentiment I shall not resist. But I intend to be impersonal, since that which is here named "Nature" is evidently not a woman. Since, however, I am a man, my piety, growing as it does so spontaneously from a deep sense of intimately belonging to what is named, may be forgiven by those who dislike it. Let Nature's proper pronoun be "it" for those who like it better and would avoid all suggestions of personality. I would not have noun or pronoun lead the reader or me astray in what follows. I would not have the name informative.

The sacrifice of the common noun "nature" is, therefore, imperative, for its use could easily be misleading. I shall try to expose what Nature is as I think I have found her out by studying her character as best I could and beset by the limitations of my ignorance. Yet I hesitate to say that I am trying to discover *the* nature of Nature or to determine whether she is really nature or not. I accept her as quite genuine. Heaven and earth, the sea, and all that in them is are very real, so real that it is difficult to think of a reality in competition with them, especially when the all that in them is, is so far from having been discovered. The name "Nature" in this essay is not the noun "nature." The name as here used could be justified by much current usage. Not to poets alone does it call to attention the stars and life, but to farmers also, to toilers thinking of vacation, to explorers, and even to scientists and philosophers when they are off their guard. So I need not apologize for its use. Apology is needed only for what will be said about the named.

The adjective "natural" and the adverb "naturally" I need. They, like the noun "nature," are ambiguous. Let, then, that be "natural" which is characteristic of Nature and leads us naturally to expect this or that as a consequence. The behavior of adjectives and adverbs is, however, unruly and annoying. They will suggest opposites—the unnatural, the artificial, the supernatural—and tend to turn expressions which are ordinarily clear and sensible into a dialectical play of meanings. The context may save us from that. It is doubtless natural enough for a woman to paint and powder in order to make herself more good looking than she naturally is. We are all naturally artificial in many ways, of which the cited illustration is a sample. We are naturally artists, working with and upon Nature in ways that transform the natural into the unnatural. And the behavior of Nature, although all of it must be said to be natural, often exhibits the unusual and the astonishing, leading us to call these exhibitions unnatural and sometimes monstrous when they are not. Even the supernatural and certainly belief in it may be called natural in accord with the same kind of play of adjectives. Respect for context can save us from letting this play lead to confusion. When we let adjectives generate opposites or, by putting a "the" before them, new nouns, we ought not to forget what we have done. One travels a perilous road by going from finite to infinite, to the infinite, to arrive in infinity. I hope to keep respect for context.

So "Nature," a word with historical associations and redolent of meaning, is here used, not as a noun substantive in need of a definition, but as a name calling only for an identification of what is named such as has already been given. Although historical and current usage give point to its choice, I would keep the name free from unfortunate alliances. Sometimes I shall use the words "world" and "universe" as if they were partially or wholly equivalents of Nature. Of the two, "universe" is the more troublesome. We currently speak of the "visible world," "the social world," "the business world," and so forth without confusion of thought. "The natural world" and "the physical world" follow the same pattern. "Universe," however, has been lately so preëmpted by astronomers and physicists and sometimes allowed to have a plural, that its use suggests forgetfulness of much that I would wish to have remembered—the swarm of animals, the spectacle of birth and death—even if the universe, like a creature subject to mortality, is growing progressively colder, until all its heat is dissipated. Moreover, books about the universe have become increasingly mathematical and require considerable competence in mathematics to understand them properly. Translated into the language of daily use they often contain illustrations which seem more like fairy tales of a mathematical imagination than sober conclusions reached by men who work in laboratories and use instruments of precision. There is, for example, the tale of the remarkable twins, Peter the stay-at-home and Paul the adventurous traveler. When they were young men, Paul started out one day for a year's journey to visit distant parts of the universe. He traveled so fast that when he returned, still in the bloom of young manhood, he found his brother an old man tottering on the edge of the grave. I can take the tale as a myth indicative of a mathematical truth involved in the measurement of velocities, but not as an illustration of a possibly conceivable incident in the lives of a pair of twins; for it is not the requirements of measurement that beget children.[2] We are sometimes told what we would see if we traveled with the speed of light and are also told that only light can travel with that speed. Indeed, the universe seems to be generating a modern mythology surpassing the an-

[2] For literature on the subject see A. O. Lovejoy's "The Paradox of the Time-retarding Journey," *Philosophical Review*, XL. (Jan., Mar., 1931), 48–68, 153–67.

cient in extravagance. It gets into the papers and has a credulous acceptance such as the tales of Hesiod once had. But "universe" is a good word when used with caution. It suggests all things unified and whole however they turn and I shall now and then use it when emphasizing the comprehensiveness of Nature.

Knowledge

Having identified that to which the name "Nature" is given, and commented upon the use of cognate words, I would consider knowledge next. The literature on the subject is confusing. That there should be skepticism or doubt about much that we affirm and deny, and, consequently, a search for a criterion which would remove it, is natural. To affirm that knowledge is that criterion is also natural. To demand, however, a criterion for knowledge, although it may seem natural and sensible, may turn out to be the reverse. In Plato's *Meno* a slave is asked by Socrates to double a square and responds by doubling its side. A little knowledge of squares removed the absurdity. But what is the criterion of such knowledge? What would prove a proposition in a geometry like Euclid's to be knowledge? He proved many propositions which were difficult to prove and had criteria for doing so, but I have not found that he had a criterion for proving that the knowledge contained in those propositions was knowledge. It has been often affirmed that Euclid's geometry is knowledge of space. That is very doubtful, but its doubtfulness does not turn that geometry into ignorance. The demand for a criterion which will prove that knowledge is knowledge begins to look ill-advised.

It looks more so the further one pursues the matter. I have deliberately chosen an example from geometry because the search for a criterion for geometry as knowledge turns out to be an exposition of what a geometry is. I could have used other examples. That Napoleon lost the battle of Waterloo is historical knowledge. I can imagine one trying to prove that he did not lose it and succeeding in doing so; but I can imagine no criterion which will prove that historical knowledge is knowledge of history, nor can I imagine one that will prove that natural knowledge is knowledge of Nature. Trying to find criteria for knowledge irrespective of what it is knowledge of, appears to me ridiculous. It is trying to identify knowledge without anything to know. The end of such trying is skepticism absolute and complete. We may say so in words, but for my part I can make no sense out of it. I cannot identify skepticism without something to be skeptical about. Descartes lived in vain if subsequent philosophers have still to learn that a man cannot doubt that he doubts when he's doubting. The reason is not that if he did so he would contradict himself; the reason is that he can't do it.

The preceding paragraphs of this section are not exhibitions of acumen. That is their merit. Every child is vitally familiar with Descartes's principle *cogito ergo sum* without giving it expression in Latin, French, or English. Calling attention to it suggests asking why should a criterion for knowledge be ardently desired by anybody? I shall deal with that question later after having exposed what natural knowledge is. It is obviously knowledge of Nature. If what we learn by exploring heaven and earth, the sea, and all that in them is, is not knowledge, something else must be; and I look in vain for that something else. When a chemist tells me that water boils at 212° Fahrenheit, I understand what he says and do not think he is lying. I am quite sure I have at least that much chemical or physical knowledge and am disgusted if asked whether that knowledge is really *knowledge*. If it is not really knowledge, then I must ask for a sample of what real knowledge would be. Failing that I must do precisely what the chemist does, go to Nature, put questions to her, and accept her answers and refrain from trying to imagine what knowledge should be like before any knowledge is acquired.

That vital and intimate connection with Nature which we call our consciousness is not knowledge except in a sense gratuitous or beside the mark unless it involves curiosity satisfied or ignorance dispelled, and even then it may be knowledge only in a gratuitous sense. For not to know the taste of sugar means not to have tasted it or to have forgotten its taste rather than to be ignorant of anything. Tastes assist us to identify and to discriminate, but are hardly knowledge of that which is identified or discriminated. Were consciousness of Nature knowledge, the sight of the stars ought of itself to give us astronomy, and the mere memory of events ought to give us history. Knowledge is acquired, not given. If we ask, then, whence it is acquired, the answer is from Nature, not from our consciousness of her, even if that consciousness is indispensable. To equate it with her is like equating the reading of a book with the book read, like equating that universal and public manuscript expansed unto the eyes of all with seeing it. Even Berkeley, who held that there are no sights unless seen and no sounds unless heard, held also that neither sights nor sounds are knowledge. His basic principle of human knowledge that *esse est percipi* is not so foolish as it sounds, when construed as meaning that the *being* of objects of knowledge *is* what they are *perceived to be*, but that those objects themselves are neither knowledge nor perception. Trees are objects of knowledge but not knowledge of anything. The same is to be said of Nature. Natural knowledge and consciousness of Nature are not equivalent. When we say that we "know" that we are conscious, that we see, hear, taste, smell, and touch, and that we think, we are not laying down the foundations of that knowledge which it has been man's great ambition to acquire. We are giving expression to what our natural status is. To do more we leave that natural status to be just what it is and turn to Nature to explore her ways.

To be sure, our natural status can itself be explored. Both biologists and psychologists spend much time and labor upon it. We owe much to their researches. They do not, however, leave Nature out of the account. They cannot examine our natural status without her help. As for men called "philosophers," they often try, but are driven at last to admit, as Santayana does in the book from which I have already quoted, that Nature is the proof of their philosophy no matter how extravagant that philosophy may be. An appeal to the stars, the seasons, the swarm of animals, and the rest is an appeal to the ultimately supreme court of all knowledge. Setting ourselves apart is like setting anything else apart. It gives us "Nature *and* man" just as it gives us "Nature *and* the sun," "Nature *and* anything else" which can be so distinguished for purposes of study— this frog or this rock. Distinguishing man is not taking him out of Nature in order to secure for him a privileged position wherein he is fitted to receive Nature as a gift from an alien benefactor. Is it not time, I am forced to ask, to stop such nonsense and cease to think, as Hume apparently did, that what is called "human nature" is not only the source of knowledge but also the only thing that we know anything about? Is it not time to stop identifying experience with what we experience and trying to have philosophies of "pure experience"? Our natural status is as inseparably bound up with Nature as is that of the largest star or the smallest microbe.

Being the kind of beings that we are, living in and with Nature in a union intimate and profound, we profit by reading her signs and symbols. The candle may draw us when babies as it does the moth to be burnt by its flame, but it makes us even then cautious about repeating the experience. To be exceptionally teachable belongs to our natural status. The moth does not seem to learn that candles scorch. Its natural status is different from ours, for, even in our cradles we are quick logicians, turning the sight of a flame into an expectation of what may happen to a finger, into knowledge of the way candles behave. Soon we are using candles to lighten our darkness. Nature responds. Later we make candle-power a measure of how much light. Later we try to measure the velocity of light, and look, not to our ability, but to Nature for the answer. Such is the path to knowledge. We go from what Nature suggests in consequence of our intimacy with her and her intimacy with us to what we affirm Nature to be, distinguishing between her vital presence and something in that presence which we can express as knowledge of what she is—from what Nature is to what she is found out to be, guided by suggesting candles. Such is the way to knowledge. We find no other even when we turn around and retrace our steps, calling the forward way induction and the reverse of it deduction.

As we follow the way carefully, trying to avoid erring excursions which lead us off the track of our pursuit, we find ourselves more and more compelled to look upon Nature as a coherent and integrated system, an order, a cosmos, a universe which can find expression in language and, so expressed, be handed on from generation to generation and be from generation to generation improved. Much warfare, illusion, debate, and controversy attend the long tradition. A commonly accepted understanding is not always easy to obtain. But a good understanding is easy to define. Aristotle defined it by an illustration suitable for all purposes when he pointed out that a man without knowledge may be surprised that the diagonal and side of a square are not commensurable, while the geometer would be surprised if they were. Understanding is the elimination of surprise. We do not eliminate it; Nature does that. The man with a crowbar may be surprised at its effectiveness, just as many of us may be in seeing how easily great weights are hoisted by block and tackle. Neither is surprising to one who knows mechanics. We may be surprised that we have tuberculosis; the bacteriologist is not. Aristotle may be cited again in a somewhat cryptic statement to the effect that all knowledge proceeds from what is better known to us to what is naturally better known. It is as if Nature possessed without acquiring it the knowledge we acquire—possessed at any rate something inherent which can be translated into human speech, thereby eliminating surprise from anything that happens. Therein lies the power of knowledge. The airplane and the radio are surprising human inventions; but it would be more surprising, knowing what we do about Nature, if they could not be invented. And what but our ignorance makes it surprising that a spider can spin a web to catch flies in a world where the thing is done? Who would dare set a limit to Nature's symbolic power? From our ignorance we go to her knowledge, not only to Nature familiar but also to Nature understood.

The naturally effective symbolism which is developed by us into knowledge arises from natural events or occurrences or from what may well be called Nature's behavior. Our expectations, even when wayward, follow clues in the natural courses of events, as when changing weather comes with changing wind. But Nature—that universal manuscript, the stars, the seasons, the spectacle of birth and death, of cities and wars, heaven and earth, the sea, and all that in them is, the setting of human history—is not cognitively a symbol of anything. This I would emphasize. I do not mean that we never regard it as a symbol, for that would be to fly in the face of facts. It has often been looked upon as a symbol of God's glory, as the evidence of his creative power, as the justification of his ways to man. Sir Thomas Browne, in addition to calling it a manuscript, called it "God's servant" who can teach us much divinity. This I could readily believe. The spectacle of Nature does not diminish in grandeur the more it is contemplated. Its effect is overwhelming and can humble us to our knees, leaving even the hard-headed of us touched with awe. When face to face with Nature's sublimity and impartial indifference and free from taint of superstition, we must confess ourselves in the presence of our owner, confess no rights or privileges of our own, confess ourselves useless and needless unless we can justify our existence by a dignity it might attain. Otherwise we look pretty cheap, for all our cities and wars. The lilies of the field look a little better. To regard Nature as the symbol of God's glory is not at all strange or unnatural. It is very human. It is, perhaps, the thing we are ultimately led to do when, thoroughly sophisticated, disillusioned, and disenchanted, we take ourselves seriously in hand and ask what is our business here? Then we stand confronted by the Ancient of Days.

Yet this cannot be set down as an increment to knowledge even if we are now warranted in saying that we know that there is ultimately necessary existence if contingent existence like ours is to be, that we are dependent on it, not it on us, and that it holds us, as it were, in the hollow of its hand. But this is not knowledge of Nature. It is rather intimacy with Nature peculiarly and powerfully heightened, an experience of the loss of our selves, to find them again made or marred as that experience breeds aspiration or indifference. The experience may be studied. We may acquire knowledge of its power and operation; but we must take it for just what it is, a genuine natural experience from which important consequences flow for the lives and fortunes of men.

Nature's own evident being has sometimes been regarded as symbolic in an indirect and elliptical way which raises the question of a criterion for knowledge to which I have already referred.[3] No one needs to be told that unless we are affected by our surroundings we have no knowledge of them. If, however, we turn so obvious a circumstance into the question whether

---

[3] The literature on the subject is voluminous. The examination of it reveals how philosophers are often classified as empiricists, realists, idealists, monists, dualists, and the like. *The Revolt Against Dualism*, by A. O. Lovejoy, Chicago, Open Court, New York, Norton, 1930, is written in support of "dualism" and contains an expert presentation of the evidence for and against it. C. A. Strong's *Creed for Sceptics*, London, Macmillan, 1936, offers an ingenious solution of the problem in support of "critical realism."

our surroundings are in their own right what they are
to us when we are affected by them, we have a question which has frequently been answered by affirming
that what they are to us is symbolic of what they are in
their own independence or is a substitute for it. We
have now a strange problem of knowledge on our
hands which ought to be solved as a problem generally. It is not the problem of advancing natural knowledge, but one of finding an antecedent criterion which
will determine how far such knowledge *is* knowledge
or how far knowledge of our surroundings is *real* knowledge of what they are. Of course one may stoutly affirm
that our surroundings are the same in both cases, that
the garage into which we drive our car to let it remain
over night is the identical garage in which it actually
remains during that period, but one so affirming will
be challenged to demonstrate how that can be *known*.
I should like to avoid being embroiled in such controversy.

I have called this way of regarding Nature as symbolic, indirect and elliptical. That it is indirect should,
I think, be clear from the preceding paragraph because
it begins, not with an analysis of what our surroundings actually are in our dealings with them, but with a
hypothetical question about their status. It is elliptical
because it overlooks the fact that the question raised
cannot be answered unless it is possible to answer it in

one context. In other words, it cannot be intelligibly answered unless our surroundings when we are not affected by them and also when we are, are *both* somehow accessible to the questioner. If they are not, both question and answers are nonsense. That is something which, I hope, this essay will clarify without committing me to an answer. Nature, I find, does not pose the mooted question. She poses questions of a different sort: Since our surroundings are spatial, what is space? Since they are temporal, what is time? Since knowledge of them is expressible in language, what is language? So far as such questions are conceived, they are answerable only by an analysis of how our natural knowledge is actually built up. It is immaterial to me whether the analysis I shall attempt leaves me classified as idealist or realist. I hope it will leave me having told the truth in some measure.

Why is the mooted question asked? As I review the literature, I find that the answer is that the problem of perception is put before the problem of knowledge in such a way that the former becomes one of the validity and possibility of knowledge, not one of examining the mechanism of perception, in spite of the fact that such an examination is admitted to give us knowledge of what that mechanism is. But why is *this* done? The answer is best exhibited by citing illustrations like the following:

External objects are known not intuitively but through the medium of a substitute. This is proved by the fact that when a distant cannon is fired the flash is seen before the sound is heard. The seen flash and the heard sound are both, in different degrees, *later* than the real event, and, therefore, cannot be identical with it. In looking up at the starry vault, we see simultaneously objects that existed and from which light set out a varying number of centuries ago; these past objects are known by a single substitute which contains them all and is in the present. In double vision *two* substitutes are seen when there is but one thing—a clear proof that they are substitutes.[4]

In other words, peculiarities in what we perceive prove that what we perceive is a substitute for the known objects and events that produce those peculiarities. All this looks to me like relying on the validity of natural knowledge—optics for example—to prove that there are substitutes for its objects in order that we may know what those objects are. The habit of regarding what we perceive as knowledge of something else— as if two moons seen were knowledge of one moon existing, or one star, like Vega, seen, were knowledge of a double star—is a habit I regard as vicious. I shall, however, have occasion to refer to it repeatedly in the course of this essay. Knowledge is of what we perceive, and I have named that "Nature." I can find, however, no convincing reason for turning what we perceive into

---

[4] C. A. Strong, *Creed for Sceptics*, p. 1. I do not overlook the fact that Strong, who has spent his studious life on the problem involved, has dealt with it in this work with acumen. He impresses me, however, not as having solved it, but as having removed it.

a substitute for something else. I do not find Nature to be symbolic in that sense.

Limitations of Knowledge

That *we* are knowers of Nature carries the obligation of not overlooking the fact. Other animals and even plants may be knowers in their own fashion. There is abundant evidence that they are, even if we, in ignorance of just how they manage their affairs, flout the evidence and supply them with instinct instead of reason in order that they may behave without knowledge as we behave with it. The solitary wasp, without prior instruction, industriously provides for her offspring and then flies away, apparently unconcerned about the future, to die in ignorance of the consequence of her labors; her young follow her example. The dandelion abundantly scatters its seeds to the winds without making agricultural preparation for their planting and so yellows the field to the enjoyment of children and the dismay of the gardener. In instances like these, is there a display of greater or of less intelligence than our own? Let the answer be as one likes; the fact remains that Nature, to which *our* knowledge is addressed, is admittedly the common residence of such creatures and ourselves. We and they live together with interchanges of various sorts. Companionship is diversified both in association and in kinship, equipment, behavior, and achievement. The inanimate also belongs to Nature as acknowledged by us. Animation may be denied it, but joint residence cannot. Manifold and interrelated as her residents are, it is not likely that others of them that know, know her as we do.

Among ourselves, also, we must recognize differences in equipment and behavior. There are the maimed, the halt, the blind, the deaf, the dumb, the stupid, the insane. The problem of a standard which this situation suggests is solved by the pursuit of a solution. The question who is right and who wrong is answered by examining the differences involved. We would not ask the ever blind to tell us about the stars or the ever deaf to be our teachers in the matter of sounds. We may learn much from them and may teach them much they could not learn by themselves; but then we would have to have the ability to see and hear. In these matters we reach a norm in a quite different way than by computing averages or taking a vote. We rely on the exercise of discovered natural equipment and what follows from it. In other words, differences in natural equipment and in "human nature" are, through the recognition of them, progressively accounted for in the building up of our knowledge. The road to knowledge may wind and be marked by many a fruitless and painful excursion, but it has a beaten path.

Our knowledge is *human* knowledge, and Nature to

which our knowledge is relevant is *our* familiar residence. How far this fact sets a limit to our knowledge—as if there could be a kind of knowledge superior to it, more comprehensive, more complete, and more assured—is a question requiring a cautious answer. Knowledge is not identifiable or definable irrespective of the ability of a knower and the character of that which he seeks to know. Subject and object—a distinction long admitted in philosophy—are not determinable antecedently to the pursuit of knowledge, but are, as it were, found in that pursuit. The subject in seeking to know an object is not bringing to bear upon it a measure already secure of what knowledge is or ought to be. He does no more than follow the lead of the suggestions which the object makes to him, does his best to organize them in a manner consonant with the object, and names the result knowledge. A fish, but not the knower of it, except in terms of the latter's natural equipment for examining it, determines what knowledge of the fish is. Even the knower's method of organization has no antecedent rules to constrain him, for such rules as he finds necessary to employ are found in intercourse with what he is seeking to know. If these statements call for proof or validation, this is found in the process of inquiring itself. If, for example, I affirm that items of existence must be individually distinguished if they are to be counted, I certainly am not bringing an ante-

cedently prepared number system to bear upon existence. History refutes such a claim. All I am doing is to
develop a counting system out of distinguishable items.
That development, as history proves, can carry me
very far beyond countable things without, however,
becoming an antecedent matrix into which countable
things are forced to fit. That, in illustration, is what I
mean by saying that there is no antecedent definition
of knowledge which constrains us in considering limitations of knowledge.

That which constrains us is our ability and equipment on the one hand and Nature in which they operate on the other. We can entertain the supposition that
both might be different from what they are, even if it
turns out to be impossible to specify the differences in
a positive way. We can entertain the supposition because we are familiar with limitations of equipment in
other creatures. The sightless, for example, must be
limited in their knowledge of a visible world, for Nature does not lie expansed unto their eyes. Yet we do
not hesitate to affirm that Nature lies expansed around
them, that they manage to live in a world lit up and
visible, or that they can be taught much about the
visible world by those equipped with sight. The actuality of the more poorly equipped than ourselves suggests the possibility of the better equipped, who are
intimately familiar with a world they might name "Na-

ture," which would differ from our residence in ways which we, because of our limitations, cannot specify. But there is no sense in asking what Nature would look like were she not seen or sound like were she not heard. Limitations of our knowledge are senseless when considered after that fashion. If the actual equipment of the blind does not prove that a visible world does not exist, how could a suppositious equipment superior to ours afford the proof?

By virtue of our equipment we are daily familiar with sights and sounds in Nature. Optics and acoustics are resulting sciences. I can imagine an inferior, but not a superior, equipment without them. We do not bring sights and sounds into Nature by being equipped to study them; that is Nature's own work, not ours; although she lets us have, so to speak, some command of darkness and silence, for we can deliberately shut out sights and sounds after we have learned from her how to do it. Knowledge superior to *human* knowledge would be knowledge acquired by beings more elaborately fitted to acquire it and who might, therefore, have sciences we do not have; but imagination fails us when we try to imagine that the increase in the number of their sciences would deprive them of our own or give to their knowledge a radically different character.

Our equipment for acquiring knowledge is summed

up in the presence of our living bodies in Nature. They
are ingenious instruments, and we supplement them
with others almost equally ingenious, which often perform more effectively than our bodies do themselves.
Ordinarily we do not hear a man speaking in London
unless we are in his company there, nor have sight of
him. We have invented an instrument whereby we
hear his voice in our own distant rooms and are perfecting one whereby we shall see his face as readily.
Who dares set a limit to such inventions? Shall we not
one day, comfortably reclining, smell the perfumes of
Arabia and taste the honey of Hymettus, all for the
turning of a button? Let us not deny it; but let us not
forget after all the necessary interposition of the human
body. It is the ultimate instrument in all the miracles
of our invention. I lie in bed and turn on the radio to
hear the people of the world entertaining one another,
telling the news, and advertising their wares for sale,
turning the "air" into theater, university, and market,
putting a mechanical toy almost in command of our
lives—I at my ease. It is like a miracle—the ambient
air in control of the solid earth. When, however, I turn
to consider it and think of the thousands upon thousands of human beings at work from morning to night
and from night to morning to bring the impressive
ceremony about, then the miracle is, not the little box,
but the human body. No triumph of inventive art ex-

cels a tree growing from the ground or a child coming
to birth from its mother's womb. The great instrument
in the triumphs of art is the human body with its natural equipment, and the great miracle, if one wants one,
is the response which Nature makes when that instrument is employed.

To think, therefore, that products of inventive art
are indications of a possible improvement of our real
instrument or that our bodies, if naturally equipped
as they are supplemented by art, would give us superior knowledge, looks like an extravagant misreading
of the facts. Increasing the effectiveness of our natural
instrument by such supplementation is proof that there
is no break between Nature and ourselves, that intimate reciprocity prevails, and that we are interposed
in Nature rather than set over against her. The eye
uses the telescope because both are involved in an optical system of Nature's sights, and the ear uses the
radio because both are involved in an acoustical system of Nature's sounds. The use of invented instruments gives us more penetrating views of Nature. It
does not change the character of our knowledge nor
free us from the limitation—if we will have it a limitation—of ultimate dependence on our bodily organization. If our eyes were better than the best telescopes,
our vision would still be vision. Nature as optical in
character would not have changed. One can make
these affirmations with confidence.

We may, of course, imagine our natural equipment bettered, not by supplementation, but by addition. Here, however, we are beset by limitations of imagination. In the matter of our senses, for example, it is hardly prudent to affirm that we might not have had more, for there are living beings who evidently have less, and we may lose or lack some of our own or have them anaesthetized into uselessness. The difficulty in imagining more is one, not of number, but of quality. Sight, hearing, and smell may be called telepathic beyond the surface of our bodies; taste, touch, and pain may not. To have the latter like the former in this respect would be to suffer an intolerable inconvenience, even if we were supplied with gadgets, like eyelids, to turn them on and off at will. Additions to our natural telepathy are often dreamed of, sometimes desired, and sometimes believed in; I often wonder, however, how much the dreamers, the desirers, and the believers have seriously considered the conditions involved in the evidence they cite in their support. I am not arguing that a general telepathic sense might not exist. I have referred to inconvenience and lack of serious examination of conditions in order to suggest that Nature is apparently more provident and discreet than some of us in imaginative moments would be, knowing, so to speak, that, made up as she and we are together, conversation is better than reading one another's thoughts and working at a machine for television more profit-

able than trying to see without eyes. It is easy to refrain from asserting that there cannot be more senses
with appropriate organs than there are; it is far from
easy to imagine new kinds, for our senses do not come
first and what they sense, afterward. Their organs are
not instruments invented in anticipation of characteristics of Nature to be exposed to them. In supposing
that they are, both imagination and thinking are defeated. Only in the pursuit of knowledge are any limitations of its character discovered.

The Human Body

Limitations of knowledge appear, therefore, to be
limitations arising in the course of its development, as
when obstacles are met which have to be overcome
before progress can be made, or limitations arising
from our ignorance of its prime instrument, the human
body. Of the first sort history affords so many examples that it is hardly necessary to cite instances. Perhaps
the three most conspicuous and popular illustrations
are summed up in the expressions "the Copernican
Revolution," "evolution," and the "theory of relativity." All those expressions indicate the overcoming of
obstacles that blocked the progress of knowledge in
various directions. They have all raised themselves new
obstacles, not yet overcome. Yet none can deny that
they indicate an advancement of knowledge which has

been extraordinary in its rapidity. "Modern science" is the consequence. It so far surpasses that of the ancients that we have acquired the habit of belittling them and thinking them stupid, slaves to mythology, theology, and prejudice. That is unfortunate, for it convicts *us* of stupidity and of ignorance of history. I will not argue the matter, but simply point out that they, the Greeks in particular, used language to clarify what they had to say, while we—just as I am continually doing in this essay—having used it, try to explain what the words we have used mean. Every competent philosopher today is expected to make clear to his readers what he means by "meaning" and "making clear." So I, to exhibit my own competence, am trying to make clear what I *mean* by "knowledge" and its "limitations." But I confess I do not know how to make "meaning" clear except by using words which mean it. It looks very much as if language itself had become an obstacle to knowledge and that modern science and modern philosophy were responsible for it.

I have read about the human body, but am incompetent to increase our knowledge of it. My great admiration, let me confess, is for those who can. They cannot help being impressed by its greater importance as an instrument than any of their own invention. But the human body, in the study of it, is a very equivocal object. It is as readily identifiable as are the bodies of

other animals and, when studied as they are, presents
no other problems than those of its organization and
behavior. We cannot, however, escape the facts that it
is also what we call a conscious body and that its "consciousness"—a word that means no more than that it
can and does perceive, feel, observe, and think—is illu-
sive. Its behavior is, as we say, externally observable,
but its consciousness only internally or by introspec-
tion, with the consequence that the consciousness of
others is not accessible to me, nor mine to them. So far
as consciousness is concerned, each of us has his own
exclusively; there is no common consciousness, even
if the word "consciousness" has, as Hobbes long ago
pointed out, the verbal meaning of "knowing together." Nature seems to have made us inevitable
solipsists and in doing so has turned herself, as the
common residence of us all, into exclusive personal
experiences yearning for companionship.

> Yes! in the sea of life enisled,
> With echoing straits between us thrown,
> Dotting the shoreless watery wild,
> We mortal millions live *alone*.
> The islands feel the enclasping flow,
> And then their endless bounds they know.

This poetic presentation of our mortal status is in
key with that of some philosophers and psychologists.
We are isolated souls, feeling nonetheless that we are
not. I do not, however, attempt to solve the problem

of solipsism, preferring to leave it to the speculations of those who try to solve it. Problems of this kind, when stated this way, impress me as unprofitable, and so I try to avoid them. Returning to the study of the human body as a perfectly definite object of study, I must ask: What is it an instrument for? I do not see that it is at all obligatory on anybody to solve the problem of solipsism first in order that our knowledge of the human body may have a solid foundation, for that foundation is that body precisely as we are conscious of it in its surroundings. When we now ask: What is that body an instrument for? there is at least one positive answer which is beyond dispute: namely, that it is an instrument for coördinating our activities; and this is so quite irrespective of solipsism. And it is quite beyond my power to think or to believe that this coördinating produces Nature. It produces something that occurs in the natural world, as when I see what I touch or touch what I see, when I invent microscopes and telescopes in order to see better than I ordinarily do or invent a pair of scales to improve my estimate of weights. It is, in short, an instrument for better and more commodious living, for making a fire when one is cold, for building a house when one wants shelter, for spinning and weaving when one wants clothing, for having schools for teaching, churches for praying, hospitals for the sick, decent burial for the dead—where will one stop?

—and for discovering that all this is done because Nature and that body are inseparably and intimately bound together, even when that body is reduced to dust or ashes. I do not see how there can be any decent doubt about that positive answer. Like the fear of the Lord, it is the beginning of wisdom. Perhaps that positive answer and that awful fear are kindred. Contemplating that positive, obvious, but much neglected answer, I find it difficult not to be swept off my feet with wonder at the possibilities it opens. It makes Jacob's dream of a ladder the persistent and best dream of mankind.

But some will say—I see their heads and shoulders popping up to fire ignorance at me instead of knowledge—some will say that the human body is also an instrument of dreams. That must be admitted. But I cannot in sanity conclude that the human body and Nature are therefore, even possibly, dreams. That does not make sense. It overlooks the fact that dreams and waking moments are first so distinguished that the former are not the latter. To turn the latter into the former is only to make our ignorance of dreams totally abysmal. It is great enough as it is without making it so great that one is wholly lost in trying to begin to remove it. "Dreams within a dream" is not the pattern of knowledge. Clearly the human body is not an instrument for producing a dream named "Nature" or even the semblance of one. So, in addition to the positive answer to the question: What is the human body an instrument for? I would give a negative one. It is not an instrument for transforming the effects of its environment upon it into a visionary world. The supposition that such a transformation is made is often entertained by psychologists and philosophers, but is riddled by dialectic, by the evidence, and by the analysis of the procedure involved in making it and in identifying the basic partition involved: namely, a human body in its surroundings of which we are conscious and a human body in its surroundings of which we are not. And to make that first human body with its surroundings *the consciousness* of that second human body in its surroundings or, reversing the performance, to make the second situation a spatial projection of the first is to juggle with words and to produce endless controversy without increasing knowledge.

The student of the human body as an instrument is under no obligation to try to find in a head, in the interstices of a brain, or anywhere else—call it "in the mind" or "in consciousness" or "in intuition" or "in the immediately given" or "in us"—some semblance of an "external world" like the substance of a dream. Neither it nor its external world is composed of that sort of substance. If we want to know out of what sort of substance both are composed, physicists and chemists are the sort of knowers who give us anything like an intelligible answer. And if we want to know why the color blind see as they do, we will go to students of the eye and learn that it is not because they have different "sensations" of color but because their retinas are so constructed that their color-discriminations are limited. We may still use the word "sensations," but it will no longer mean a "mental content." Its use will be the recognition that the word has been restored to its natural status of indicating that the mental operation of *sensing* has been performed. The adjective "mental" is warranted both by its long usage and by the importance of distinguishing evidently different sorts of operations by different names. Seeing with one's eyes and hearing with one's ears—and in general what we call "feeling" or "being conscious"—are so different from rolling over, standing on one's head, digesting one's food, or breathing with one's lungs, that they merit a distinct classification. They are activities which so link us with Nature that we go on to knowledge. Hence arises the vocabulary of mind. Its words are names for what we do when we try to find out what we and Nature are and use knowledge as a name for the result.

The "mind" is not thereby dethroned. We have not by considering the use of words lost our "souls." We have found them. We have found that the more we learn about our human bodies, the more their dignity is enhanced; for we have found that through them our intimacy with Nature has no discovered parallel. We have found the source and whatever justification there is for that human egotism which regards man as the top of creation, the last thing made and although made out of the dust of the ground so made that he is in awe of a maker. We abuse our intelligence when we forget this. A candid mind must be sadly amused when noting how some people are scared by the word "materialism" and how others rejoice in the supposed justification it gives them for finding below the waist the bodily functions of supreme importance for an estimate of human life. The real shame of much of the sex literature with which we have recently been deluged lies, not in its indecency, but in its implied stupidity that our sexual constitution has only recently been discovered. I sometimes think that the remedy for this sad state is to require again the study of Greek and Latin literature as the foundation of a liberal education. If it was once a good preparation for entering the ministry, why is it not now a good preparation for going to the movies? But such things aside: if matter, if that which is made of the dust of the ground, can think and worship, could anything by any other name do better? If the discovery of our bodies is the discovery of our ownership by Nature, what then must that owner be? We mount together.

Nature can be put to many uses, and the human

body is the great instrument for that purpose. Again I emphasize the obvious because of its importance in understanding what the natural status of that body is. If we ask, as we often do, for what purpose we exist, and consult the way we live in Nature for an answer instead of imagining one, then the answer is clear and definite. We exist, not to reproduce our kind, not to enjoy life and love, and not to be happy, but to be provident and prudent in these matters through acquiring knowledge. And that, interestingly enough, is something most of us dislike; we would much prefer to reproduce our kind, enjoy life and love, and be happy, without any trouble. Our natural obligation to be provident and prudent haunts us like a guilty conscience. The natural purpose of our existence, however, is not altered by our preferences. We are born to improve. We find Nature usable. We grow better vegetables and fruits than are naturally produced, breed better animals, may breed better men, and exploit Nature generally to the best of our ability. In doing all such things the human body is the necessary instrument and thereby proved to be an instrument of co-ordinated activity. All the knowledge we can dream of acquiring would be useless and senseless were it not in the service of better living. So trite a remark becomes very pointed when the natural status of the human body is under consideration. It leads us eventually to ask: What must Nature be if she is amenable to dictation?

We can improve natural products, alter the natural courses of rivers, fly over the ocean, make the wilderness a garden, but we cannot improve Nature herself. Let imagination try its hand at it, only let it be sincere, thorough, and relentless. Then we end thankful that the task of making over Nature herself is not ours. We find that we remake after the pattern that we find, for anything else is unintelligible in the end. We find that what we like is so interwoven with what we dislike that we cannot remove the possibility of the latter without losing the possibility of the former. Strength and fragility, delicacy and crudeness, health and disease, pleasure and pain, good and evil—all the great opposites of our existence are rooted in a common soil. The more we learn, the more surely do we discover that this is so. We can improve products of Nature, but not Nature herself. Only sincerity, thoroughness, and relentlessness are necessary to find this out.

The admission does not imply that this is the best possible world. It implies that conjecturing possible worlds in which we might do better than we do here is not of much consequence. Certainly it is of no consequence when limitations of our knowledge are con-

sidered. It is easy to imagine Nature devoid of creatures at all like us and there is good reason to think
that she once was, but no limitation of knowledge
would thereby be discovered beyond the absence of
things like human bodies which could imagine such a
situation. Limitations of our knowledge are of little, if
any, importance compared with the extent of our
ignorance. Consideration of the former does little to
reduce the latter, but it does bring out the natural
status of the human body in the acquisition of knowledge. Our factual reciprocity with Nature is inescapable. She lets us live in this sense at least, that we are
naturally born residents in her domain. We may ask
for reasons why she should, with only conjectures for
answers. That sort of ignorance does not change the
fact that she lets us live as we do, on condition that we
study her ways, responding to her promptings with
questions put to her in expectation that she will answer
them if they are rightly put. Her silences may be
moments when intimacy with her is closest and
language fails us, but sometimes she speaks and her
ways are like the pages of an open book. We read, to
find more reading necessary. Although our ignorance
decreases slowly and we are often rebellious when confronted with what we read, we are fortunate if we find
with that decrease some portions of knowledge which
remain secure and some encouragement to obey.

Objectivity

Since knowledge is in the interest of better living, and since our success in acquiring it is measured by Nature's clarifying responses to our questions, knowledge should be disinterested or objective. A man who looks to Nature, not for truth, but for a confirmation of his own prejudices, is not highly commended. He is not disinterested. His intellectual integrity is under suspicion. We usually forgive mistakes when they are made accidentally and even when a man, sure that he is on the right track, overlooks facts which are evident to a less confident person. Suspicion of one's own conclusions is recommended. Willful distortion of evidence, however, and stubbornness in admitting it when adverse are hard to forgive. Truth is sacred, so much so that calling a man a liar, even when he is, usually causes him to appeal to force in his own justification. He prefers to be told that he may be mistaken. Then he is less irritated, content that a euphemism has avoided the nasty word. All this is a little curious— this obligation to be disinterested in our own interest, to accept truth even when it hurts, to put ourselves out of the way and let Nature alone decide, no matter what the consequences are. Yet we are under that obligation and under it naturally. We need neither schools nor parents to acquaint us with it. An in-

fant's first cry is proof enough. It has lost its familiar
world and cries for restoration of familiarity, finding it
at its mother's breast. Objectivity has then been recovered, recovered in the baby's interest.

The illustration is not fantastic. We are like babies,
content to be at Nature's breast so long as we are not
discontented and disturbed. We are born of her and so
enfolded that to be enfolded without disturbance is to
be at peace. Again I am emphasizing the obvious. I do
so because in this instance of it we find what objectivity is. It is far more a state of Nature than a state of
mind and is the latter only because something happens
to us as we search for it. Objectivity is Nature with or
without our crying, but as if we did not cry or as if we
had never been born. It is Nature undisturbed by our
presence, although our disturbances and presence are
among her events. Now, dialectically, there is an argument that objectivity is impossible for us to attain. It is
well illustrated both by Berkeley and by Kant and in
much the same way, although their idiosyncrasies in
the presentation of it obscure the likeness. Berkeley
argued that what perceiving beings perceive is objective to their minds because not of their creation; he
strangely concluded that God also perceives, but that
what he perceives he also creates. Kant argued that perceiving beings perceive the experienced world of space
and time and that the world is objective to them be-

cause experience makes it so; he strangely concluded that experience is not otherwise objective. With Berkeley *real* objectivity was an association of spirits; with Kant, an association of "things-in-themselves." In neither case could the association be delivered. In both cases it was assumed, and assumed to be capable of delivering the circumstances responsible for the search for it. When we search for Nature as if she were without our presence, how can our presence find her?

The dialectical argument does no more than leave us with the problem of creation on our hands, the solution of which is irrelevant to our knowledge. I use the word "creature" frequently and could readily believe Nature to be created, for she often does not seem to be wholly self-sustaining. But I do not see how this belief, if justified, could alter human knowledge of a created world or free us from the obligation of disinterestedness. So in considering objectivity I am not impressed by dialectical arguments. I do not have to be reminded that I cannot get myself outside of Nature. I turn, therefore, to an analysis of what happens when I try.

When we ask in our own interest what Nature is as over against ourselves, the sense of individuality is heightened. We are turned into persons each of whose personal histories has an absorbing interest of its own. We do not cease to be residents of Nature, but become

residents with the sense of possessing and being possessed acute. There is established a kind of trinity,
Nature and *you* and *I*, with these three in a dramatic
unity in which the fortunes of the *I* are at stake. Nature
becomes *my* world, yet you and Nature are there to be
taken into account. The consequence is that this very
circumstance forces us to take them into account ob-
jectively. This is not a matter of our own choosing, as
is sufficiently proved by the fact that we commonly
wish that all that is objective were amenable to our
wishes or our prayers. The story of Aladdin and his
lamp is not instructive. The story of Midas is. And a
common proverb warns us that we cannot have our
cake and eat it too. All this indicates a natural wisdom
which is forced upon us despite ourselves, the power of
which increases as we proceed. It drives us to consider ourselves and to be so ultimately reflective that
the bare fact of being reflective becomes the core of our
being and all else goes into Nature as a single integrated system demanding of us that we find out what
such an integrated system is. Our bodies have not lost
their own integrity. They are as passionate as they
were before, but they have become minds, looking as
it were through an open door at Nature going on of
herself.

That is the only meaning of objectivity I can find
that suits the character of our experience of Nature.
Too many who talk about Nature, explore her ways,

and try to solve the problems she suggests seem to forget that the universe of their discourse is none other than the universe at their door. They talk sometimes as if it were an alien universe which explains their own. They expect to be understood and convincing; but they pay little attention to that expectation, although it is the natural and compulsory admission of the commonly accepted and accessible world, in which the birth of minds is as natural as the birth of babies, the coming of seeds to fruitage, or the rolling of a stone down hill. Does the solving of a problem mean anything else than the discovery of its solution? Where then does one go for a solution—to his own mind or to Nature objective? Even those "brain-twisters" with which we socially amuse ourselves illustrate the answer. Given six matches, arrange them so that they will form four equilateral triangles the sides of which equal a match in length. How often have we seen even the acute and agile work at that problem, give it up as unsolvable, and even wager that it is unsolvable. How foolish they feel when they discover that Nature solves it by providing something more than the surface of a table. Going to Nature to discover solutions is something quite different from going to something else to discover Nature. The universe of discourse may change in language when we become scientific, but it does not change in objectivity.

That disinterestedness and objectivity are names for

the same natural occurrence needs now no further exposition. The failure to solve that match puzzle on the table's surface is objective in spite of our interest in trying to solve it there. Nature won't let it be solved that way. She is amused at the stupidity of one who tries. Personifying her thus, as if she laughed and cried, is an inversion of our own sense of detachment when objectivity is in force. We are then like onlookers at a play in which we have neither part nor responsibility, while the play goes on exhibiting its actors comically or tragically caught in their destiny in spite of their attempts to escape it. That "theater" and "theory" are verbally akin is more than accident. I often think of Lucretius theorizing about Nature in his poem *De rerum natura*, how, having glorified the spring as the work of Venus, he proceeded to instruct Memmius how all that glory and much besides came originally from tiny first bodies in the void, like motes in sunbeams, and would finally return to them. There they stood watching the vast panorama unroll before their imagination, as calm and aloof as that suave man of the second book of the poem who, safe and undisturbed on shore, watched another's great labor with the great and storm-tossed sea.

Objectivity has that effect upon us, giving us the sense of truth approached or attained, of something in Nature which is inevitable, without which Nature could not be what she is. That philosophical excitement of a few years ago known as "pragmatism" had the great merit of reminding us that Nature, not our wit, controls and evaluates all our definitions and conjectures in the use of them and that the internal logical consistency of a theory is not the ultimate guarantee of its validity or worth. All that was and is salutary. But truth is not "that which works" but something in Nature that is worked with. The facts that we have found little of it and have frequently to revise what we thought we had found are no proof to the contrary; for all inquiry proceeds governed by the principle that there is a way of an eagle in the air, of a serpent on a rock, of a fish in the midst of the sea, of a man with a maid, quite irrespective of our understanding it. Wherever we are lost, there is a way home whether we find it or not. That principle is misread when named a principle of "human nature," as Hume would have it, or a presupposition of all science, as some others affirm. It is a principle of Nature. Who in his senses can sincerely assert that a habit of man or the presupposition of anybody has anything to do with a river finding its way to the sea or our finding it out? We have our habits, and we make presuppositions as we go along, but Nature is the critic of them. Faith in her principles, if one will speak of faith, is not wishful thinking or an hypothesis that governs human understanding. There is an order in Nature which we flout at our peril. The many-times-quoted opening sentence of Bacon's essay "Of Truth" deserves repetition because those who do not jest, but stay for answer, are those who learn.

Objectivity is, moreover, a natural intensification of individuality. I have already suggested this when referring to Lucretius. It is like having the universe lie at one's door without entering one's house, or like a beholding of Nature which is both attentive and passive. The experience is not extraordinary. We have it every time we go sight-seeing. The more attentive we are to the scene, the more the scene isolates us from it as if it were pushing us out and we were passively submitting. In order to be calm, we are advised to relax; the advice is so good that relaxation is often prescribed as the best of medicines and often pushed so far that it is recommended as a remedy for all our ills, on the theory that if we relaxed completely Nature would do the rest and for our good. Striving and crying is what ruins us. We should stop it and let Nature take her course. "Why so hot, little man?" That question of Emerson's was asked, as I remember, to convince us of the Oversoul. It may be asked just as well to convince us of Nature. It is asking for our individual exclusion, although we are expected to remain in Nature. That is what I mean by an intensification of individuality. It is often regarded as something only psychological.

It is psychological, but I hesitate to add the "only." It looks to me too much like a natural principle which our knowledge does not escape. Why so hot, little atom? What can *you* do when "left to yourself"? Yet I must isolate you and even try to break you up in spite of your name. That is one sort of thing we are doing all the time—dividing atoms and trying to find the smallest. Every individual, whether large or small, is a challenge to divide it. It is an atom in its individuality. That is sufficiently proved by dividing a man in two or a line in two, for after the division that which has been divided is no longer the individual it was before. *An* individuality has been lost. The new individuals are less *intense*. There is obviously a loss of integrity when a man or a line is divided. An intensive effectiveness is lost. One need try no more elaborate experiment than that of retying a package after the string with which it was originally tied has been cut. Multiplying illustrations of trying to find *the* atom by division or breaking up may readily lead to thinking of Nature as a hierarchy of individuals with varying degrees of intensification, which have, for all that, a residence in common—from the atom of modern science, which does not build guns to bombard itself to pieces, to the human atoms that do and that sometimes deliberately commit suicide with a gun. Such a theory of Nature looks quite intelligible and compelling when we divide, but not so much so when we start putting the pieces together again, for then we find ourselves in need of some sort of glue. Yet if man can break up the atom in Nature, atomic theories ought to remove all surprise that we see and hear beyond our bodies or think of places and times remote from them. We ought not to be surprised that Nature seems comprehensible to some individuals in such a way that the universe lies at their door, which opens—opens out into its immensities and minutenesses —while they stay at home trying to see things without any refraction due to their own mode of living. They illustrate the intensity of individuality at a maximum or intimacy with Nature so intense that bodily individuality is lost in the consequent objectivity. "The union of the mind with the whole of Nature"—to borrow Spinoza's words—may sound like a grandiose expression, but it is illustrated, however limitedly, in every act of thought.

Although in objectivity we are passive in the sense I have indicated, the attainment of objectivity leads to the release of power. In objectivity we discover our freedom. I see no merit in trying to solve the "problem" of the "freedom of the will" or in arguing whether we are "fated or free." I always suspect some failure in analyzing what knowledge factually is or some confusing of the discovery of the necessary conditions under which an action can be performed with the performing of the action; as if the binomial theorem actually developed $(x + y)^2$. I dare affirm, quite confident that I am speaking the truth, that neither knowledge nor what is known *does* anything. I am sometimes tempted to wish that they did, trying to delude myself into believing that we should then live happily forever after. But, as I have said, the attainment of objectivity leads to the release of power. Then actions can be performed which were not performed before. Knowledge can be applied. What possible sense is there in discussing whether it can be or not when it actually is? We do not discover our freedom by futilely trying to break endless chains of causation. We discover it in the release of power through objectivity and in applying knowledge. That is why we hold objectivity sacred, insist on disinterestedness and that "teachers" especially should be left free to tell the truth even when it hurts and not be like those "politicians" who tell it only to please, to enrage, or to delude their hearers. That puts a heavy responsibility on teachers, forbidding them to turn "academic freedom" into a shelter for security of tenure, incompetence, ignorance, and political pressure. Objectivity is too sacred for that, and I could wish that the expression "academic freedom" had never been invented. It clouds too many issues. It fosters the habit of going to school to learn and stopping there for a diploma of some sort, instead of going through school to Nature which lies expansed to all and is the only place where truth is eventually found. She is the great teacher, and the proper aim of all human teaching is to get rid of other teachers as soon as possible and to turn children into adults who will not have to be under tutelage their whole life long. That is the road to freedom.

Knowledge and the Sciences

The principle of division of labor applies to knowledge as well as to industry. Inquiry becomes increasingly specialized, with a consequent multiplication of sciences. It is interesting to note in this connection that our current linguistic usage avoids a plural for knowledge, following thus a natural tendency to recognize that there is or should be a unity and integrity in all knowledge no matter what its subject matter may occasionally be, that Nature without disruption is the ultimate object of all the sciences, and that knowledge is like a tree with many branches. This tendency is a proof of wisdom, for a man would be obviously foolish who thought that any science says the last word about Nature. Philosophers, modestly uncomfortable when esteemed as lovers of wisdom instead of contributors to knowledge, have often sought for some specific subject matter which they might explore and so rank among scientists at their best, only to find that they fall under the suspicion of being trespassers in fields occupied by jealous proprietors and that they are sometimes brutally told to keep off the grass. Then, too, expressions like "philosophy of science," "philosophy of history," "philosophy of government," "philosophy of law," "philosophy of religion," and so forth creep into the language, indicating that after scientists, historians, statesmen, jurists, priests, and the rest have said all they have to say, there is still need of a special kind of knowledge to inform us what it is all about, as if every man should not be his own philosopher. Or, again, philosophy comes to be regarded as an extravagant super-science which, coming after all others, unifies them into a completed whole. The word "metaphysics" has had much to do with such a notion. It suggests something to be done after physics is over, although originally it had no such suggestion, being only an editorial device for convenient reference to a collection of Aristotle's writings.

Scientists are as culpable in this matter as philosophers, but they are usually more discreet, making a polite or ironic bow to philosophy and then leaving it in the air. I venture an illustration, because it delights me.

We conclude, then, at last, that no one can yet say how our system originated in detail, but that we may reasonably regard its birth as the merest incident in a far vaster process,—the shaping of the material Universe as we know it. What lay behind that shaping we do not know. Our searching has brought us no nearer the Power whence all things proceed than did Job's colloquy with his friends. But one who has attempted to set out in order what little we have learned or may surmise, may hope, at least, that his endeavors may seem less destructive and even perhaps more profitable than those of Browning's poet and philosopher, who had

> . . . Written three books on the soul
> Proving absurd all written hitherto
> And putting us to ignorance again.[5]

Just so! We explore the heavens and conclude that we have come no nearer to ultimate things than we were before, but when we try to go further we return to ignorance. Other scientists are less discreet. They admit that more might be said and then proceed to say it. Usually the result is that science becomes confused or misunderstood, although popular philosophical scientific books may delight or comfort the reader. Having been informed of wonders he never imagined before, he may exclaim, "Great is Diana of the Ephesians!" or go to church confident that religion and science are not opposed.[6]

[5] Henry Morris Russell, *The Solar System and Its Origin*, New York, Macmillan, 1935, pp. 138–39.

[6] I dislike giving examples after such an uncivil remark. I can name Professor Russell without distaste, because his ironic closing is very much to the point. Should I cite, however, books like Professor Eddington's *Nature of the Physical World*, I should be guilty, I fear, of making fun of his candid exposure of many misconceptions. Yet I must say that the two tables with which he begins do no more than amuse me. I think he wholly misunderstands their importance. He seems to overlook the fact that he never in his life wrote upon a "scientific table." And for the life of me I cannot see how an astronomer can look at "scientific stars." "Scientific objects" often impress me as the most amusing fictions ever invented, and "scientific truth" and "scientific method" often leave me bewildered.

I repeat that it is foolish to suppose that there is any science which says the last word about Nature. There may, however, be one that says the first words. It may be called philosophy. It has been repeatedly so called, even when attempting to say the last word. Here the history of philosophy as exposed in the books may be profitably consulted. Men in their efforts to say the last word have always been driven to try to find out what the first words are. Name great names—Aristotle, St. Thomas, Spinoza, Descartes, Locke, Kant, Hegel— every one of them was driven back to first words. Consider that unknown genius whose meditations are discoverable in the mélange of the opening chapters of Genesis. Sometimes I think he was the most penetrating of them all. He had the advantage of coming early, of being naïve, free from dialectical disturbances and the encumbrance of too much special knowledge. Consider his first words. I will not repeat them for they ought to be familiar not only to people who go to church or are brought up on the Bible but also to every searcher for knowledge. But I change my mind—God, inchoate matter, light, space, time, and, above all, words. Then, heaven and earth, the sea, and all that in them is. Then man and woman. Then murder and cities and wars. Then God again, continually surprised at the result, at what was done in his name, at profanity. Then man again, searching out what God's words were and are. Who has done better? What other

philosopher has had as great an influence—read in
nearly all the languages of mankind, convincing little
children and sophisticated adults alike in spite of the
fact that his words as the record of an historical event
are utterly incredible to a candid mind?

The thing is impressive. It makes me think of a remark of Santayana's, in the preface to *Scepticism and
Animal Faith*, to the effect that all that is needed to get
the hang of the world is candor and courage. Only
that is not quite true. Candor and courage can go far,
and one of the impediments to knowledge is the lack of
those virtues. It is not true, or at least it is very equivocal to hint, as Santayana does, that it makes no
difference under what sky a philosopher is born pro-
vided he has candor and courage. And candor and
courage compel me to say that it has made a great
difference to hi:n and to admit that it has made a great
difference to me. The difference between Greek and
modern philosophy is far more a matter of birthdays
and birthplaces than it is of virtue. What I suppose
Santayana means, and what I might also affirm, is
that the first words or, if one will, "the realms of
being" are always the same no matter where or when a
philosopher is born and that it takes only candor and
courage to recognize them; but in dealing with those
first words geography and the calendar are of equal
importance with virtue. We all ought to have the same

philosophy, because we all live under the same sky; but knowledge of the same sky is, in the acquiring of it, bound up with the labors of men like Ptolemy, Copernicus, Newton, Kant, and Einstein so much that it looks to me ridiculous to affirm that with all my candor and courage—which I rate high in philosophical matters—I could in ignorance of them write about the visible world as I shall in the next chapter. Convinced as I am that for knowledge of Nature there are things to be said first and of such importance that the intelligibility of what is later said depends upon them, I am equally convinced that the first sayings are profoundly influenced by the later. As a student of history I have learned that in all philosophical revolutions and disputes the same *first* science tends sooner or later to emerge; but it emerges either refined and clarified or debased and obscured, and alternating refinement and debasement depends very much upon new discoveries in special fields of knowledge.

Conceivably the first science might be written once for all and become wholly dogmatic like the multiplication table, to be learned rather than disputed; but it certainly has not been done in a manner that will never need revision. I could maintain that it is always the same philosophy, however written, but it has to be rewritten to be handed down from generation to generation and to be from generation to generation understood. It has to be translated from language to language, from words that are not understood to words that are, and this is no easy task. It has to be discovered much as a man discovers his birth, as something vitally experienced yet in a way forgotten. He knows beyond cavil that he was fathered, that his mother labored, that he left her body to be a new child of Nature; yet when he wants precision he must ask many questions. Socrates will doubtless remain in character so long as he is remembered as the typical philosopher—ignorance bringing half-remembered or wholly forgotten things to light by questioning the acquired knowledge of them, seeking man's first words and trusting the divinity in him to warn him about the last.

The division of labor in acquiring knowledge, although it begets new sciences, is yet a recognition of the unity and integrity of all knowledge and a challenge to expose it. This is a much different undertaking than trying to piece together as parts of a whole the specific results of specific sciences or using the results of one of them to shape the concerns of the others. Nature, not the wit of man, gives to knowledge its integral character. This suggests a science of nature which is neither physics nor chemistry and the like nor the social sciences and their like and which is, in a somewhat Hegelian way, a special science because restricted to what is, not specific, but general. Had the history of the sciences been kind in its preference for Greek words, this special science might well have been called "physics" and all others summed up under "metaphysics," subdivided in terms of specific subject matter. Then we might never have mistaken the one for the other. Then we might have detected in Newton's title to his great work, *Principia mathematica philosophiae naturalis*, a profound significance. Mathematical principles branch out from natural philosophy, they do not compose it. "Scientific" language branches out from natural language; it is not the source of the latter. Materials and machines come before atomic theories and mechanics. In the remainder of this essay I shall try to give significant illustrations of such coming before.

Chapter Two ✷ THE VISIBLE WORLD

Its Preëminence

WHEN HEAVEN and earth, the sea, and all that in them is are identified in their familiarly conspicuous union and named "Nature," Nature is at once recognized as preëminently the visible world. Only creatures gifted with sight may make that recognition and acknowledge that world to be their evident residence—the world in which they are present along with other creatures not so gifted. Those who do not see at all obviously do not find the visible world to be their evident environment. Since they do not see, we cannot in sanity imagine them making globular models of the earth with land and water colorfully displayed upon them or building planetaria wherein they may gaze at a mimicry of the wonders of heaven. The sightless are denied these privileges, and, although some of them may go to the seeing for instruction about the visible world, the seeing do not go to them to be taught geography or astronomy. Yet for the privileged seeing, the sightless, both animate and inanimate, have their residence in the same world as themselves. They share the same sunshine and weather, abide under the same sky, and find their way about with astonishing success, knowing their way, as it were, without seeing it. With the seeing, however, the better the sight the more the visible world controls their directions, from the direction of their feet to the direction of their thoughts. They do not find an invisible world an adequate point of departure from which to set out to discover how they themselves see or how others without sight are directed.

And if we speak of "public experience," what can it be if not an experience of that which lies expansed unto the eyes of all? It is the kind of experience which is shared in such a way that in that experience the sharers are identified as sharing in it, clasping hands, as it were, with other hands identified as not one's own and belonging to other bodies similarly identified, but not the kind of experience in which the clasp of another's hand is an alien pressure on one's own skin. "Public experience" and "visual experience" are well-nigh synonymous expressions. Publicity in any other than a visible world seems a little incongruous; if we could remain unseen and out of sight, our embarrassments would be different from what they are. Out of sight is refuge both from the policeman and the camera.

"Come and see" is the one generally public invitation, conveyed by the voice, the beckoning finger, the imprinted and pictured page. Other invitations, like "come and touch" or "come and taste," are invitations to come for assurances which sight does not afford, as when we are not sure by simply looking whether the heat is turned on or whether we are offered salt or sugar—invitations to private, not public, experience.

Genetically considered, organs for sight seem to be the last to develop, or at least they seem to lag behind the others, giving to these others an apparent historical priority. Kittens are "born blind," and the dog trusts his nose far more than his eyes for direction. Such illustrations are familiar. One should, however, go to the biologist to get the full impact of genetic history and to find how far sight has gained supremacy and what it has lost thereby. Sight suddenly given to one by an operation for cataract has bewildering consequences. Genetic considerations revealing, as it were, a pyramiding of the senses, with touch as the base, suggest a corresponding pyramiding of experiences, as if what sight reveals were added onto or grounded in experiences more basic and more solid. Visual experience, it is admitted, is not necessary in order to live or even to exist. A stone is normally accepted as existing without any sense experience at all on its part. It is, however, not disrespectful to genetic considerations to point out that the visible world, once experience of it has begun, begins to assume possession of all existence whatsoever. However late the arrival of sight may be, without it any reading of Nature's book is very fragmentary and with it a completer reading is inconceivable except in terms of a completer vision. That is why the verb "to see" becomes an ultimate intellectual term and why absolutely completed knowledge is likened to an intellectual vision or intuition of all things *sub specie aeternitatis*, a vision so penetrating and inclusive that nothing escapes it and the distinction between seeing and being seen vanishes. We seem to have a presentiment of it when, quite relaxed and untroubled by practical affairs, we look into the vault of heaven. Then there seems to be no *seeing*, but only *being seen;* it is Nature that looks, not we that see; transitive vision has become intransitive.

It is not important to debate whether completed knowledge would be like that or not. Ecstasy, even if admitted to be a kind of knowledge, is less like answers to questions than the absence of them. It may be the profound sense of truth possessed, but it is not the sense of truth possessed in utterable form. It may leave a song in the heart, but it does not replace a book before the eyes. It is, however, testimony that the visible world is the all-embracing world, the world wherein alternating light and darkness bid us come and see even the invisible.

In this all-embracing world alight in vision are

found the plants and animals we study in their habitats to discover how they live, subjecting them to selected and unusual surroundings, trying to isolate specific behavior and to find its specific mechanism. There are the stars at which the astronomer points his telescope, extending his vision to remote places in the sky, telling us how far away are the stars we see, and finding others normally unseen, measuring distances and magnitudes so vast and awful that we must be content with number symbols to express them and give up counting the miles. We do not see the violet's odor, but we find its source in the violet we see. The swinging bell we see, but not its sound; that comes to us from the bell, and by ingenious devices we photograph the airy disturbances it makes on its way. We see the smoke coming out of yonder chimney to disappear in the surrounding air and yet remain there in some invisible manner. It goes out of the chimney on a journey into the chimney's world. We see the steam from a boat's whistle and later hear its sound, but steam and sound are originally together with the boat seen upon the water. With our two eyes we often see two objects in the same world when only one is to be seen. We see the rails of a track converge in the same stretch of country in which we see an engineer superintending their laying down in parallel lines. Even what we call illusions are in the visible world exposed to sight, strange apparitions which elude other senses and which are, therefore, called unreal. Energies, powers, influences, tendencies, desires, aspirations, hopes and fears, pleasures and pains, emotions, love and hate, blessing and cursing, our thinking—all are somehow in the visible world even if unseen. God himself ought to dwell there, and like Moses we ask to see His face. Failing that, we build temples where His invisible presence may abide with all the earth silent before Him. Heaven ought to be reached as Jacob dreamed it—by a ladder with angels ascending and descending. Failing that, we project it into a place at present invisible, to be seen by and by, after we are dead, in all its shining beauty and with its chanting choirs. Or, baffled by such a picture of enchanted perfection and unwilling to let our immortality be no more than the indestructibility of matter or the uncertain remembrance of us by others when we are here no longer, we would have ourselves pure spirits, still somewhere in a world of light, but happily relieved of mortal bodies. The visible world is supreme in being the place of all that we try to understand.

Ordinary folk, and philosophers and scientists when not professional, have no doubt about all this, because the visible world is not a matter of belief. Descartes tried very hard to doubt it, sitting in a dressing gown before a fire. He even invented a deceiving demon to trick him into believing, he himself was so serious about not being deceived. The result was that he found himself sure only of thinking—*cogito ergo sum*. But just thinking with nothing to think about was a dead end. So he began to think about perfect and imperfect beings, found himself among the latter because he was trying so hard not to be deceived and not to let any being, perfect or imperfect, deceive him. Clearly he could not be deceived by a perfect being. That was as certain as his thinking about perfection and imperfection. He must be self-deceived in thinking that a deceptive demon could deceive him against his will, against such rigorous thinking as he was doing. So God, the Perfect Being, must exist, because Descartes was not that, and yet his thinking could not escape the distinction between perfection and imperfection. His own limitations could not be generalized. Thinking about the visible world, which he called "extended being" because he was awed by geometry, was not evidence of his limitations, because "thinking" and "extension" are so different that the latter cannot be derived from the former. So "extended being," "the external world," that which was expansed unto the eyes of all, existed, at least in its extension, beyond any possible doubt. Descartes had not invented it, nor had any thinker like him done so. If he were in any way deceived about it, that was due to his own carelessness in thinking about it. All he needed now was to be careful not to allow himself to be deceived. All he needed was a method of avoiding that unhappy consequence.

His contemporaries found all that very impressive. His book is still among the "required reading" for students of philosophy, and the tercentenary of its publication has merited the attention of an international congress. It has been much debated. It has divided philosophers into controversial sects. It is excellent discipline in philosophy. And yet, candidly, does it amount to any more than a proof that the visible world needs proof? "The extended world"— what is it as *extension* only and no more? As extension only what is there in it? Isn't it a little strange to be divinely happy at finding that the extended world is something inescapable when one is attentive to what one thinks about? Having discovered that the extended world is necessary for knowledge, some philosophers have, because "thinking" is so different from "being extended," devoted their time to discussing how it is possible to think about an extended world, and how it is possible that such a world can contain colors, sounds, odors, tastes, the hot and the cold, the hard and the soft, the heavy and the light, and how extension can be solid, move, become agitated, be public experience or like a manuscript expansed unto the eyes of all. It is not strange that other philosophers contend that the extended world, robbed of the visible, is itself a matter of belief.

In the interest neither of knowledge nor of action guided by it is the visible world a matter of belief. It calls in these respects for no proof of its existence either as dependent or as independent. In affirming this so positively I am not pleading a cause. I am not posing as what textbooks in philosophy call a "naïve realist." Like Descartes I am trying my best not to be deceived, only going about it in a different way. I am not beginning with doubt and trying to find certainty or beginning with belief and trying to support it. In this matter of the visible world considerations of doubt and belief, of certainty and uncertainty, are relevant to affirmations about what it contains, but not to its status as the field of knowledge and action. Its status irrespective of that field is a wholly different matter. This was indicated in the preceding chapter when the view that Nature herself is a symbol was considered. As the visible world, is she then a vision? We may frame the question in words, but how shall we proceed to answer it? What is she a vision of? In trying to answer that question problems of belief, doubt, and certainty are quite different from what they are when relevant to what the visible world contains. Even the problem of existence is changed, for that problem within that world is one we are constantly attacking and solving in ways familiar to us. Columbus, a hackneyed example, asked whether a westward route to India existed. Physicists ask whether the ether exists. With such questions we are on familiar ground. But does the visible world exist? There is no sea for a Columbus to sail and find out. There is need of a definition of "existence" uncontaminated by the visible world and freed from its embracing character. What *ought* that definition be?

Many pages could be written in reviewing the answers given to that question. The attempt to define "existence" free from contamination with the visible world is very desperate. Sentences can be framed which have an intelligible form but have no intelligible meaning. It is, I think, unnecessary to review them, for one may ask very simply and directly: If the visible world is not itself the residence of existence, where and when and how does anything exist, and where and when and how does the visible world itself exist? It's a tough question. Trying to answer it leads one to suspect that questions of that kind are questions about something else than existence even though the word "existence" is used. There can be a kind of doubt and uncertainty about the visible world which often may lie heavily upon us. That world itself is like a question, to which all our knowledge and all our action are no answer. We would have this all-embracing world justified for being what it so evidently is. We would have the existences in it explained, not simply in its terms, but in terms that would make clear to us why they are as they are and not otherwise and why they behave as they do and not otherwise. *Why is there a visible world at all?* We search that world for an answer and get none that is free from doubt and uncertainty.

I do not like to dismiss such a question as trivial. Too many wiser and more learned have asked it. I could jauntily dismiss it because I have learned the trick of doing so. A child asks me: What is the biggest number? The question habit has been carried out of bounds. What is an ax for? For chopping wood. What is Nature for? The question habit has been carried out of bounds. I have learned the trick and use it in this essay. The wiser and more learned than I know it just as well, and only little people, having learned the trick, think that there is nothing more to learn. Nature and Nature as preëminently the visible world does not need any justification. I dare say that. But I must also say that she asks for it. And I must confess that the little people who have learned the trick of crying "out of bounds" look amusing and often tragic when, stopped in their tracks by misfortune, they cry out: "Why should this happen to me?" Why it did happen may be seen clearly.

When, instead of identifying existences, examining them, observing them, experimenting with them in order to know more about them and to use that knowledge to our advantage, we ask whether they exist, and we push that question to Nature, we confuse the question of existence with that of justification. We do go out of bounds in that sense. I said above that I am not pleading a cause. That is not quite correct. I am. I am pleading that we do not deceive ourselves by confusing questions of existence with questions of justification. Failure to justify the visible world for being what it is, failure to justify why it is that, when vision arrives, be it late or early, then there lies the visible world expansed unto the eyes of all, there is experience publicly operating, there is a world commanding the direction of our feet and of our thoughts—failure to justify all that is wholly irrelevant to an interest in knowledge and in action guided by it. To make that failure relevant is to be deceived. Why should the stars be visible? I have never found any explanation of that, nor have I been able to invent one. That the stars are visible is not a matter of belief or disbelief, of certainty or uncertainty. If I should admit that it is, I should also have to admit that the visibility of anything is in doubt; and that means that I am crying to have visibility justified. It means that I am crying to be told why it should happen that with stars in the sky, with light in Nature, and with eyes on the earth, there should be astronomy.

This is not pleading the cause of realism as over against idealism. It is not pleading the cause of common sense. It is pleading the cause of intellectual clarity. It is pleading the fact that with the visible world made problematic, intellectual clarity has vanished, and the reign of confusion has begun. I repeat: the world revealed in vision is not a matter of belief or uncertainty unless we ask for a justification of why it should be. It is where we are, and it surrounds us. Why it should be is now of no consequence. Our vision of it may come late, but coming late or early does not apply to the visible world itself; for it is now a first world and a last world in the search for knowledge of what it contains. Here it is inescapable as our residence. It is, not a state of mind, but the sphere of existences both visible and invisible. The astronomer never looks at stars which it does not contain. The physicist never deals with forces or energies which do not operate in it. The chemist does not analyze substances which he finds elsewhere. The geologist does not find his materials somewhere else. The geographer does not make maps of another country. The biologist studies the living beings found in it. The historian tells the tale of its events in sequence. Poets write verses about it. In it mathematicians count and construct geometries. Artists paint and sculpture it and compose its music. Man talks about it, tells stories about it, writes fiction and fairy tales about it. The farmer tills its soil. There the workman works. There we eat, drink, make merry, and therein we are born and die. When the philosopher robs it of its reality and seeks another, he adds nothing to all those enumerated enterprises. He is seeking, not knowledge, but justification. He has good reasons for that, for Nature drives him to it. He is perhaps more sensitive than others to the fact that there is the problem of the good life, although we are all sensitive to it, and he knows that our living intimacy with Nature, the brute fact that our lives are lived out in the visible world and nowhere else, is responsible for that problem and no man ever invented it. But he makes a mistake when he turns the fact of the visible world into a problem of knowledge. He claims incentive for so doing, but Nature refutes him by making the visible world the justification of his claim.

Visibility

Ability words, although indispensable, are dangerous and tricky. I shall have more to say about that later. It is sufficient for the moment to note that abilities are prized and that they are not detachable from their possessors. Thinking of them as detached or detachable is a pretty sure road to confusion. If they could be detached, there would be a steady market for them and prices would run high. All the stories of selling one's soul to the Devil illustrate it. He will give you any ability you want in exchange for your soul. Nature is not the Devil. She makes you take a possessor along with every ability—the Devil along with his ability to provide, opium along with its ability to put you to sleep, and an elaborate optical mechanism along with the ability to see. But sight is more precious than eyes, or eyes are precious only because of the priceless treasure of vision.

Nature as preëminently the visible world is called "visible" because *we* can see her rather than because *she* can be seen. We see how she looks. If we did not, if no creature ever saw her, the adjective "visible" would not be attached to her. And obviously we should not see her had we not the ability to see along with the attendant optical mechanism. Visibility is thus in a sense imputed to her in consequence of an ability we possess. Similarly we say that she is tangible because we touch her, audible because we hear her, perceivable because we perceive her, thinkable because we think her. In the sense brought out by these illustrations we may say that all Nature's abilities are imputed. They are charged by us to her account, and she is expected to pay the bill. This circumstance, however, does not entitle us to conclude that because abilities are imputed to Nature in the manner just described she does not possess them. Such a conclusion is monstrous. It is like concluding that since *we ascribe* a dormitive power to opium because it puts us to sleep, it has not such power and, therefore, cannot put us to sleep. Visibility imputed to Nature does not mean that she is not visible. If we pursued such a meaning to the bitter end all existence would become imputed existence with nothing or nobody to impute it. The ascription of visibility to Nature means that our ability to see and her ability to be seen—can see and can be seen—are complementary and supplemental. Our ability to see would be ineffective were there not a visible world, and Nature's visibility unsupplemented by seeing creatures would not be effective as vision. This is elementary.

There is no error in imputing visibility to Nature, just as there is no error in imputing tangibility. If by arguments it is made hard or impossible to see her, the same kind of arguments make it hard or impossible to touch her. Her solidity is also imputed. That her visibility is not reducible to her solidity requires no proof. The supposition that we must either touch things or in some way be touched by them if we are to see them is like the supposition that Rome must touch us or we must touch it if we are to think about that Eternal City. That kind of supposition leads straight to confusion and to riddles which remain riddles only, and ending in riddles is not an increment to knowledge.

These remarks on visibility are in a way a restatement of the preceding section. There are abilities in Nature and in us and they are complementary. They cannot be reduced to tangibility without entire loss of the differences between them. If the word "ability" blocks the ability to think and if other words do better, let them be used—words like "energy," "power," "potentiality," "the dynamic," and the cumbersome expression "the can-be-done." I have just said that all abilities cannot be reduced to tangibility without losing their differences. One may say that without tangibility these differences could not exist, but that is quite different from imputing to tangibility the ability to produce those differences. This abstract way of expressing the matter has advantages, even if it is dull. It is a kind of intellectual shorthand, saying much with a few strokes. To give it the sense of living speech one must translate it back into the language that directs attention directly to the visible world, to public experience, to the manuscript expansed.

There is another advantage. Thinking in terms of visibility, and thereby recognizing that visibility is imputed by us to Nature because we can see her, puts more than the usual emphasis on the fact that our vision of Nature is not straight away equatable with her visibility. We are familiar enough with the fact, but emphasis upon it arrests our habitual naïveté of regarding the whole outdoors as immediately in our possession. We know it isn't; but, as has been said often enough, thought is quick, and when heaven and earth, the sea, and all that in them is are mentioned, we leap, as it were, to a globular picture of Nature contained and containing. That looks a little absurd when one stops to consider it seriously. Doubts arise as to whether Nature's visibility is like that. Those doubts accumulate. So the proclamation of a special sort of independence for vision, although it may accomplish some liberation of thought, requires some attention to consequent restraints upon that freedom. In seeing Nature we do not see her visibility. That has conditions and by those conditions what we see is controlled. They require attention. The chief of them are light and darkness, relative location, and optical structure. Any analysis of them is complicated by the fact that they are interwoven in Nature to begin with. Nature does not combine them as if they were originally detached. We discriminate them by directing attention now to one and now to the other, so that each of them is analyzed, not by itself, but in the context of the others. There is always need of caution in analysis if intellectual deception is to be avoided. Although nothing whatever in Nature is ever "left to itself" in such a manner that we can determine what it would look like, where it is, and what it would do if there were nothing else, analysis proceeds as if this were possible. Caution is needed when we turn from analysis to synthesis, from taking to pieces to putting together again. We are often deceived into thinking that we have found original elements which were once put together to make, by simply combining, what Nature herself is. Atomic theories of that sort have always been disputed and for the best of reasons: namely, that Nature is never so disrupted. Atoms are at least in space, and we are always at our wits' end to determine where a single atom by itself would be or what it would do. So left to itself, it has lost all determination. It ceases to be even an atom. This simple illustration indicates that visibility is not a composition of the factors which are found to control it, but the effective coöperation of those factors in determining what is visible. Space, for example, is not an independently original container in which Nature is spread out in order that she may be visibly expansed.

Light and Darkness

Later I shall give particular attention to light. At present, I take light and darkness in their obvious familiarity and in their recognized control of what we see. In the absence of light, we are in darkness. The statement is banal. What it proclaims is a matter of everyday experience. It is, however, not always true— we can be in darkness in daytime simply by closing our eyes; we can be in darkness even when light is still present. And since we can also be in darkness with our eyes open, we have ample proof that the natural difference between light and darkness is something with which opening and closing the eyes alone has nothing to do. It may have much or everything to do with observing that difference, but nothing to do with its existence or character. Neither our eyes nor the bodily optical mechanism connected with them are lanterns which light up a world originally dark. Light and darkness are natural phenomena not dependent upon our experience. They would be natural phenomena even if they were never observed. Of course we should not say so unless we did observe them, but that obvious fact is of no importance; everything we say about the visible world is relevant to our observation of it, and observers are not the creators of what is observed. Light and darkness observed and light and darkness unobserved may be allowed to be as different as one pleases. The consequences of this permission, however, are that such a difference cannot itself be observed and that no observation can carry us to its definition.

Light and darkness are natural phenomena. There seems to be no good reason for supposing that they have not always been such or that they are not co-existent in Nature. They were early regarded as great

powers struggling for supremacy. That view of them
still haunts us; we pray the Lord to lighten our darkness and to defend us from perils and danger. "Light"
and "darkness" are great words. They have evoked
great literature. All that is evidence of their power.
They control our vision, giving us the extremes of a
dark, formless, and impenetrable infinity, with nothing
distinguishable and tending itself to disappear, and
light so blinding, so overpowering that we see nothing
else and try to escape into darkness to shut out that
blinding light. Peril and danger both ways, and escape
from one to the other. They are thus, not in separate,
but in mutual or complementary control of our vision,
with extremes indicated which would divorce them,
while in between runs a scale, as it were, of shades
and shadows from black to white, from white to black,
from darkness overcome by light to light overcome by
darkness.

This view of the matter, although very primitive, is
yet a beginning of knowledge. In one way it does not
misread the facts; the control of our vision by light and
darkness has been so beaten into us, made so habitually
familiar and so much a part of our very being, that its
primitive character is forgotten, although survivals
of it remain in our elaborated theories and assist the
understanding of them. The search for more light
with which to dispel darkness goes on. The primitive

phraseology has been altered, the primitive fact remains. Calling attention to it may seem like an impertinent and irrelevant interruption of more important pursuits. Yet calling attention to it stimulates the asking of questions which can critically probe uncriticized habits of thought.

Just what do we mean, for example, by the absence of vision? We habitually speak of darkness as the absence of light, turning darkness into a negative thing although the experience of darkness is far from being a negative experience. It can be terrifying. It can also be instructive, for it gives us a sensory sample of the total lack of boundary distinctions, of something without borders separating it from something else. It is not like a black circle on a white background or a black globe with discoverable surroundings. It is, however, something visually experienced and has as much right to be named "visual" as anything else. It is a very concrete and palpable infinity. Although it cannot be touched, the adjective "palpable" is appropriate to its felt intensity. Our bodies may still retain the sense of organic integrity, and yet we can be surprised on touching them with our hands as if we touched something alien. There is no need to retail experiments—to be in the absence of light, to be in darkness, is to be most peculiarly lost, to be in a sample of infinity which knows no dimensions, to be in something which as darkness is formless and void and in which only the sense of bodily integrity remains for guidance; and so much of that can, by experiment, be made to vanish that the sense of one's bodily posture is lost and the direction of sounds disappears. Since experience of darkness as darkness, as the absence of light, is a visual experience, shall we now say that to be in darkness is equivalent to the absence of vision? I find I cannot say that.

With darkness lightened, the circumstances have changed as if a miracle had been performed. The sensible infinity has vanished, to be replaced by limiting horizons and the vault of heaven. We must now *approach* infinity by thinking of boundaries removed, pushed back to the vault of heaven, there to be sensibly stopped, but still pushed back in imagination as if we were like Lucretius's javelin thrower, going to heaven's rim and throwing a javelin still farther, and as if Nature, responsive to that effort, now let that hurled missile fly on forever with the velocity we had given it, unless some other missile throwers set up a competition in the realm of the inane. So we push on beyond the realm of competition to keep an infinity unbounded, making it impossible for the javelin thrower to reach the last station for a throw. In the light we make the stock model of the universe. We let the expanding sphere triumph over the expanding cube, although we

know that it is just as easy to construct a cube about a
sphere as to construct a cube within a sphere. It is
notable that in the light, constructions of the universe
are controlled by the curved, not by the straight. At the
last there are no tangents. At the last, if you traveled
forever—and perhaps "forever" isn't really necessary—
you would arrive home. In the absence of vision would
there ever be such constructions? Could there possibly
be such constructions in the dark?

Such questions are crucially important. Philosophies
of "experience" usually forget that they are philosophies of being in the light—daytime philosophies even
when written with a candle's aid. Philosophies based
on the theories of science usually forgot that science is
knowledge of being in the light and that its theories
tend, as they do today, to become at last theories of
light. We will have light triumph over darkness, because the latter means to be lost and the former means
to be found. We even take photographs in the dark in
order to see what things look like there. And what do
we not photograph today? Nature goes on in her ac-
customed way, letting day follow night and night day.
The old battle between light and darkness goes on.
The visible world seems, however, to be on the side
of light, for although light and darkness condition our
vision, our vision, as an experience of being in the
light, takes command of our own battle with igno-

rance. We put the sphere around the cube and are happy for a season, sure now that tangents are no longer possible at the rim of the universe. Everything that goes, eventually goes round. Some of us venture to say that even space is curved. Yet it might seem more rational to make space cubical because of its historic three dimensions.

Much of all this looks suspicious. It illustrates, however, the control of light and darkness over our vision and over the habitual analysis of the visible world. That analysis from beginning to end is a sight analysis extended and refined. We may help it out with the aid of other senses; but it is a sight analysis which is so helped out, and when it is so helped out the other senses do not bring it help in their own independent character. They are employed as senses of those who see. Theories of Nature, of the visible world, of the universe, cannot help being "visionary." That adjective has currently a disparaging accent. I use it for an emphasis before turning it into "optical." Theories of the universe are optical. If any of them are visionary, it is because there is so much in the visible world that escapes sight altogether. Since we do not see the invisible, we habitually picture it and think of it as if it might be seen. This practice helps our thinking. It makes conversation, discourse, and exposition easier. We see the spatial and the temporal, but neither space

nor time, for example. Yet every one of us is pretty
sure to have a picture of some sort of them both. It is
our pictures that deceive us. Nature's perspectives are
not deceptive; we live by them and rely on them.
Theories of those perspectives may induce us to form
pictures of perspectives which Nature never exhibits;
then, letting the pictures control our thinking, we are
often led to deny the reality of natural perspectives
and are at our wits end to find a place where these
now unreal perspectives exist. Abilities we do not see.
We cannot picture them, and because we can't, their
existence has often been denied. We are often led to
deny the existence of colors in Nature, not because we
do not see them or because we do not know that
seeing has nothing to do with the colors we see, but because we have made a picture of the universe to which
color is irrelevant, although that strange picture,
which is neither varicolored nor black and white, has
in it regions, realms, fields, atoms, corpuscles, granules,
quanta, vectors, dimensions, distances, velocities,
perspectives, curvatures, and even light. We help ourselves out by calling the picture a theory, forgetting
that "theory" means *spectacle*, means something like
what is *beheld* in a theater, only with emphasis on the
plot instead of on the actors and the scenery. The plot
cannot be seen with the eye. It is seen intellectually. It
is something which the mind grasps—as if the mind

were like a comprehending hand. The mind we do not see, but how we picture it!—something that can receive impressions like a piece of wax, a room whose furniture is ideas. Pictures, pictures, pictures—they are the life blood of many theories. I often wonder what would become of many a theory of Nature if the *mind* were not pictured as a *receiver* of *impressions* made on it by an external world or of *messages* delivered at its door.[1]

Light and darkness—they are not pictures. What they reveal and conceal is not a picture. No pictured mind makes them or what they reveal and conceal. We are in them, not in a picture of them, and they control our painting and sculpturing of the universe. *Put out the light*—nothing, not even darkness, is left to paint or sculpture.

Relative Position

Our vision is controlled by our relative position. This fact is familiar and needs no proof. The visible world looks different from different points of view. This,

---

[1] "Our sense of touch tells us quite definitely that one body is hot and another cold. But this is a purely qualitative criterion, not sufficient for a quantitative description and sometimes even ambiguous. This is shown by a well-known experiment: we have three vessels containing, respectively, cold, warm, and hot water. If we dip one hand into the cold water and the other into the hot, we receive a message from the first that it is cold and from the second that it is hot. If we then dip both hands into the same warm water we receive two contradictory messages, one from each hand." Albert Einstein and Leopold Infeld, *The Evolution of Physics*, New York, Simon and Schuster, 1938, p. 39. I have often wondered what sort of uniform Nature's messenger boy wears.

however, is not our fault *unless the visible world itself is*.
That "unless" cries for proof, and proof is impossible.
Only the fault could prove ourselves faulty and could
do so only in default of us. In other words, the visible
world not only *looks* different from different points of
view, but *is*. There is no privileged point of view in
Nature. We fail utterly in trying to establish one.
Setting down the failure to our limitations is a monstrous exhibition of stupidity. It leaves "our limitations" with no identifiable or even conjectural significance. The best we can do is to repeat in as many
ways as we can think up the helpless formula that since
every point of view implies a viewer of it there can be
no point of view without a viewer, and so without a
viewer there can be no points of view. The formula is
not helpful. At best it advises us either not to consider
points of view at all or to consider one's own exclusively, leaving "one's own" without determination.
Here again we have an example of talking about something else than what is professedly talked about.
There may be in Nature matters of greater consequence than points of view, and a little dialectical
jugglery may convince us of it and turn our attention
to those more important matters. The dialectic just for
the fun of it is nonsense and ought not to deceive anybody who is interested in points of view. One so interested will quickly discover two things; first, that

these points are relative, or that none is privileged; secondly, that they nonetheless cohere.

Absence of a privileged point of view and, consequently, of a privileged position may now be affirmed as characteristic of Nature, as an original principle of her structure or constitution. Our habits often run counter to the principle on moral rather than on intellectual grounds. Complete relativity of position in the visible world, when affirmed as a result of analysis, often seems preposterous and unbelievable because we are habitually egocentric and geocentric in practical matters. Living is an hourly vital necessity which limits the moments of reflection, making the latter like interruptions of the more important by the less. Going to school is discipline, not life, a fact which often disturbs reformers of education who would have the school otherwise and who thereby run the serious risk of destroying a rational attitude toward life. Yet we all want to lead our own lives and to be prepared for them, although we do not know what they are going to be. This moral egotism is deep-seated. As a force, it is far more potent than genuinely reflective thinking, egotistically cloaks itself with the latter, and in spite of the fact that both our bodies and our planet are always where they happen to be, gives to each of us the status and the supreme privilege of a detached and disinterested observer. The roots of dualistic philosophies go down deep into the soil of moral struggle, so deep that the food that nourishes them is often forgotten. The more, however, one reflects on the stars, the seasons, the swarm of animals, the spectacle of birth and death and cities and wars, as if one actually were such an observer, the more dualism seems wholly inappropriate, becoming more and more repellent and indecent. Then one would be a St. Francis with even death one's brother, surprised that children of one parent should engage in petty quarreling.

It has taken a long time, as historians are still not tired of pointing out as if it were for the first time current news, to free the study of the visible world from all that egoistic tendency. They speak of the Copernican Revolution, note how it has outmoded the ancients and forced upon us not only a revision of astronomy but also of our general outlook upon life. The antique is something to be collected for its museum value rather than diligently studied for its wisdom. As if he were commenting on the fact, Thomas Hobbes said long ago when speaking of the ancients: "If we consider the time, the present is the oldest; and if I consider the men that wrote, I am not sure that they were older than I who am now writing." There is the note of the Copernican Revolution—the accent *modern*. And yet we moderns are still under the shock of Relativity. It is news and sells well. Relative position is still somewhat shocking. That there is nowhere in the whole universe a fixed frame of reference, with all past, present, and future positions determined thereby forever with exactness, impresses many today as the complete denial of space instead of a clarification of what space is: a character not to be detached from the visible world. Yet we need not go to Einstein to be told. We need do no more than imitate him in attentively observing what the visible world is like.

Then we see, in spite of our egoism and our preference for our planet, that each of us is always at *the* point of view and that everything else that has location has that privilege, to be the point of view also. We have only to go somewhere else to find this out, from New York to San Francisco for example. From each city the lines start out to all the other cities there are. So far as seeing is concerned, the only difference in the matter of location is that of seeing more or seeing less. Should an astronomer fly to the moon and observe the heavens from that point of view, he would report back to earth what he observed to his fellow astronomers with the same confidence they have when reporting to one another from the many observatories scattered over the face of the earth. There is no doubt about that at all. We do not have to be told it. We live and act by it despite our egoism. And here we find,

perhaps unexpectedly, the reason for our preference for
the sphere over the cube. That is now no egoistic
preference. It is a natural necessity. Nature does not
let localities be without a sphere. The cube has corners
and corners can be always turned. Let a straight line
go on forever, it gets nowhere; it cannot turn a corner.
The circle is complete, finished, perfect. Cords can be
drawn in it, and those cords removed and placed outside as tangents; but let them then go on forever and
they get nowhere—they turn no corner. A straight
line is the shortest distance between two points, but
the points must be *compass* points. Such elementary
lessons as these require no other teacher than the
visible world. If they did, who taught the first geome-
trician? and is it not absurd to imagine that he learned
his lessons by first making axioms and definitions and
then proceeding to demonstrate supposititious propositions? Nature said to him: "Come and see." One like
Euclid saw the invisible, saw that which required
several books to expanse before the reading eye, saw
that of all those many propositions none was privileged,
but that all were mutually tied together. And one like
Spinoza would write an ethics so structured geomet-
rically that without God, the unity of that structure,
nothing could be or be conceived.

Relative position, naturally conditioning our vision,
leads on thus to condition our thought. All our theories

are in one way or another attempts to do something like that which Euclid and Spinoza attempted. The visible world is their ultimate source, setting before us in actuality the example for theoretical constructions to follow. The Copernican Revolution was in one way a release from intellectual bondage; in another way it was a new servitude. Transportation to the sun does not establish a privileged point of view. A vision of us from the sky is not superior vision of what we are. Perhaps it is not strange, when the forced revision of thinking involved is considered in its general bearings, that the Copernican Revolution should have begotten a new kind of astrology, marked by a different sort of superstition from the old. It could scarcely lead men to consult the stars in order to be forewarned of their coming fortunes or to find in the accident of their birth under a particular constellation a presage of their biographies. Such things were not to be expected. But looking too much at the stars and seeing the earth reflected there has led many a gazer to conclude that human life is very much of an astronomical career, with physics and chemistry in control of it. Fatalism was reborn to be differently clothed. Its priests did not wear peaked caps or have magic wands. They wore the clothes of civilization and used the spectroscope. They did no tricks, despising such subterfuges. They had no secrets, no occult sources of information. With them everything was open and aboveboard. Yet something happened to our fate and to our self-respect. That which had been called the "soul" and held to be very precious might still keep its name, and keep it in many ways in saner fashion than before, and yet be infected with stoic resignation, aggravated by nostalgia. Hell went completely, but heaven lingered. The intellectual consequences of that famous revolution transformed the study of man. It gave birth to a new psychology. Human nature became something quite different from Nature. How the former could entertain the latter or the latter the former became a dialectical problem, which ought to be disposed of prior to any competent approach to a valid interest not only in morals and religion but also, strangely enough, in science itself. It all looks rather tragic and rather comic that by letting the earth go round the sun, any man should lose his soul.

These words are not written to hold out the hope of recovering a kind of soul hardly worth saving. The Copernican Revolution has not yet done its work thoroughly enough. Having released us from mastery by the earth, it has not yet released us from mastery by the sky. In a way it has left the earth precisely where it was before, only now the rest of the universe looks down upon it. We are not yet free from the obsession that we have won by sheer hard thinking a privileged position, from which the whole heavenly host could be properly seen in ceaseless procession around it, or that Nature, the visible world, the universe, is actually a curious sort of globe, bulging here and there perhaps, expanding or contracting, and floating somehow in what is called "empty space." If that is the result, we might just as well get back to earth and let the sun rise and set as it used to.

Relativity, however, will not have it so, for it is relentless in its consequences. The recognition that position is relative forces us to recognize that all spatial discriminations are likewise relative. The large and small, the near and far, the up and down, the fast and slow, shapes, configurations, distances, boundaries, motion, and rest—all refuse to be defined in isolation. The fact becomes impressive when set over against our habits, although these habits attentively examined exhibit it. If a man walks four miles in one hour, he will at the same rate walk sixteen miles in four hours. We are quite convinced of that, and we habitually think that the distance, the rate, and the time are independently determinable. But we confess ourselves in error by writing the formula $d = rt$. It is one of the first formulas we write. Herodotus spoke of the distance between two places as the time it takes an unburdened man to go from the one to the other. The unburdened man has his rate of going, and it is so many miles an hour. It is now clear that we do not put time and rate and distance together as if each of them first existed separately and were later combined. Nature, the visible world, the universe, had them together before we disassociated them for our convenience. Of the three, the rate can look like the most constant, in spite of being sometimes fast and sometimes slow, because it appears to be a native possession of the goer with natural limits set to its amount between "can't go at all" and "can't go any faster"; but being "so far per unit of time" it is like the distance formula expressed in one of its terms. When we leave out the rate and start with the distance and time alone —sixteen miles and four hours—we have to import motion, to take a step further, and motion at a rate.

One needs, I think, no more complicated illustration to exhibit the inevitable road to relativity in all spatial determinations bound up with the visible world. We are dealing with no illusion unless that world itself is an illusion; if it is, that illusion is in no particular rectified by using its principles of relativity to arrive at a spatial system that is free from them. Nothing is thereby clarified. Everything is confused. Nature's title to visibility is not only found faulty, it is wholly lost. More than distances, times, and rates are lost. Light and darkness are lost also and all that is in the light. Sizes, shapes, boundaries go, for there is no

size without another, no shape without another, no
boundary without another. We only deceive ourselves
when we think there is. But if we do not so deceive
ourselves, then the conclusion stares us in the face that
all those spatial distinctions, although evident in Nature and daily familiar, are wholly irrelevant when
applied to Nature herself. She is not sometimes in the
light, sometimes in the dark. She is neither big nor
little; she is not cubical or spherical; she is not sometimes here, at others there; she is moving neither fast
nor slowly. Yet it is clear that she is of such a character
that all these discriminations are necessarily found in
their relativity when she is analyzed and subjected to
experiment.

The pervasive character of relative position infects
the visible world, but not as a disease. It is rather its
health—its beating heart, so to speak, although the
principle of relativity does not beat. When we deal
with it, we find that it is expressible and that the best
language for expressing it is that of mathematics. Equations are not *applied* to Nature. And they are instruments of discovery only in the sense that they discover
what follows from them and whether, because of what
follows from them, they need to be corrected or modi-
fied. They very genuinely express what Nature is, not
photographically, however, but in her unity and integrity. As unified and integrated as the visible world,

she is definitely seen, and a philosopher, happy when he can say much in little, may proclaim that we behold unity in multiplicity before our eyes. Clearly we do. But if we would take a further step and try to do more than simply to proclaim—try to clarify the meaning of unity in multiplicity in a way that is operatively effective—then mathematics becomes the best language that we have. Here is the seat of all mathematical enthusiasms, both the sane and the insane. Here is the reason why our credulity is at a maximum when we are confronted with statistics and why we tend to accept propositions backed up by the figures of mathematics when we would normally reject those same propositions when backed up by what appear to be figures of speech only. Here is the reason the more rigorously we think, the more what we say assumes algebraic form with constants and variables equated. Here is the reason some have said that if there is a God, he must be a mathematician. All this because mathematics is, not applied to the visible world, but discovered in it and so discovered that eclipses of the sun can be predicted to a nicety. It is no wonder that we would have all knowledge mathematical; we imagine that if we could so have it everything could then be predicted. Our intellectual habits are not original laws of thought. They are biological habits formed because our familiarity with Nature is vital association with her, not something derived from the sense of touch.

Optical Structure

Even a superficial examination of the eye reveals that our vision is very much conditioned by optical structure. We have no eyes in the back of the head, and that is why we do not normally see what is behind us. What lies behind us is out of sight, but not out of the visible world. That simple illustration is sufficient to indicate that the conditioning of vision by optical structure may go very far indeed. Imagination may play with it and hit upon many a discovery which can afterward be confirmed by experiment. Painstaking study of the eye, however, discloses astonishing things which imagination would not guess. There is so much here that could be said, and it would take so many books to say it, that some reduction in the interest of this essay is required. Pertinent illustrations are more relevant than any attempt to appear erudite.

I recall a remark of William James to the effect that we do not see out of the palms of our hands or from the middle of our backs. Such obvious remarks were characteristic of him and often more instructive than pages of forced reasoning. This one halted my own reading—the kind of moment when one reads no further. What is Nature from the middle of the back? Take her with the

palm of the hand, but without vision! One may now
meditate for hours—for days. How petty now have become all commonplace considerations of the eye! Two
winkers and blinkers one on each side of the nose, and
Nature both before them and behind the middle of the
back. Clearly it is not the distinction between light and
darkness with which one is now confronted, but the
distinction between the presence of optical structure
and its absence. In spite of their practical importance,
eyes, have, in a way, become trivial—samples of optical structure, not at all the source of it, samples only,
and, although still called organs of vision, more like its
products than its originators. I think of Bergson and
his suggestion that the eye is a consequence of the
élan vital,[2] of an impulse toward vision, not the result of
an evolution proceeding gradually by slight but trans-
mitted organic variations—more like the imagery that
comes to mind when one thinks of the configuration of
iron filings about an instrument *thrust* into them. I
think of Molyneux in his *Optics* exclaiming: "He that
made the eye shall see!" Could eyes by the wildest
stretch of imagination *be* in a world not optically structured to begin with? In the absence, not of eyes, but of
optical structure, could any creature whatever have an
experience of a spatial world? If these questions are
answered affirmatively, we then meet probably the

[2] *L'Évolution créatice*, Paris, Félix Alcan, 1909, pp. 95–96.

most stubborn of our difficulties in understanding anything. We have an *in vacuo* so bewildering that it serves
neither experimental nor theoretical purposes. "In
space" becomes an expression which needs to be defined before it is used, and such antecedent definition
free from any taint of optics is not attainable. The *inside* of hands do not help us, nor do the *middle* of backs.
And a maker of eyes will make them as a man makes a
camera.

Further consideration of optical structure would now
seem almost unnecessary, for the hint is clear enough
that Nature's space is not an *in vacuo* of any sort or
anything originally geometrical. It is rather the optical structure of the visible world, not conforming to
some geometrical configuration, however, but being
the structural unity of all possible configurations. It is
in that sense that it is the integration of the optical.
That is why it has no boundaries as if it were a place
with barriers around it progressively removable farther
away in imagination and consequently worthy of the
name of "infinite extension." One may now be bold
enough—if boldness is required—to affirm that just because space is not infinite extension boundaries are
progressively removable in imagination and that no
existing boundary can be decently termed finite in any
other sense than that it is not progressively removed.
An acre of land is not a finite piece of real estate. The

optical character of space becomes more and more
evident the more the natural refusal of spatial distinctions to part company is examined. Ceasing to think of
space as in itself a glorified empty globe, yet as having
three dimensions stretching out into infinity, although
its radii have no terminal points (or, perhaps, only one
at the center in which they all unite), and as containing, invisible to any eye, fixed positions, directions,
distances, shapes, circles, and all the conic sections
mapped already for planets, stars, and comets to follow
—ceasing to think that way about space is one of the
greatest liberations of thought a philosopher, at least,
can experience. He is saved from drowning in a sea of
troubles. Kant, from whom I have learned much of all
this, aimed, I think, to save us from such a fate; but he
obscured salvation by letting himself be haunted by the
ghost of John Locke and be influenced too much by
Euclidian geometry. These defects, if one pleases, may
be forgotten. His stubborn insistence that Nature experienced is always Nature already spatialized is the
thing that really counts. Not even the stars in heaven
escaped. And this, he insisted, is not "idealism," although a commentator might insist that it is because of
the doctrine that space, although a necessary character of Nature in experience, could not be a character of
things-in-themselves. How it could be affirmed in the
one case and denied in the other is mysterious. It is just

as difficult for phenomena to be in space as it is for noumena. Kant's penetrating analysis supplemented by the principle of relativity implicit in it leaves no other mystery than that of creation generally.

The important conclusion which now confronts us is that Nature forbids two spaces or two optical structures. Clearly but one is characteristic of her in all our attempts at acquiring knowledge of her. Another beyond her leaves the "beyond" without *spatial* significance. That may be read into Kant as the effective significance of his doctrine of phenomena and noumena, and it justifies his opposition to idealism. Having but one space to deal with, the importation of another is only confusing. When we speak of space as one or two or many, we are, I think, speaking of geometries which it is possible to construct just because there is space, not because *a* space must have *a* geometry. Perhaps, therefore we ought not to speak even of *one* space, but ought rather to affirm that so far as space is concerned pluralistic considerations as involved in counting are wholly irrelevant. We are not confronted here with *either* one *or* many.

Under this general conditioning of our vision by optical structure, special and peculiar illustrations of it take on a character different from that which is often assigned to them. Our vision of Nature ceases to be a distortion of what she is and becomes rather what she

is in consequence of her own inherent integration and
relativity. In terms of that the so-called distortions are
explained. They are not due to *us* in any other sense
than the character of a photograph is due to the camera which takes the picture. It is really amusing when
more confidence in the matter of cosmic veracity is
placed in optical instruments which we invent than in
the natural instrument used in inventing them. He that
made the camera shall see. If he distorts Nature by
looking at her, every optical instrument he invents distorts her equally. The whole science of optics becomes
the story of a great illusion and hides its mythology by
trying to use language free from psychological implications, as when we say that the sun does not *lighten* our
darkness nor *show* us the way, but that it *emits* light
and that by means of that emission *we*, by some extraordinary power of transforming that emission into a visible
world, see the glory of it and find our way about; as if
a god for some strange reason had thus arranged it in
order that we might find out that we are deceived
when we think that what we do is really what is being
done or that, in view of the struggle for existence, those
who are deluded by vision would have an advantage
over those who are not. This tendency, repeatedly exhibited both by philosophers and by scientists, to make
all things different the moment *we* or our minds or
souls or consciousness are brought in, gives to *us* a posi-

tion so privileged that a skepticism which can be only dialectically stated is its ultimate reward.

If, therefore, one wants explained why *we* should see parallel lines converge, or not see the front of a house when we are looking at the back of it, or see a straight stick bent in a pool or two moons when only one is shining in the sky or distant stars so many miles away that they would be seen by us even if they had ceased to be, or why some of us should distinguish colors which others of us do not distinguish, or who sees Nature as she really is—and all the rest—I can do no more than to send such a one to those far more competent than I am who explain all these troublesome matters by performing experiments which, when formulated, exhibit no initially privileged position whatever, assigning to our own bodily optical structure and to the world around it an identical natural status. I have never found any other sort of explanation. "Due to us" explains nothing at all. "What we do" explains much. What we do is exhibited in our lives, and what our lives are cannot be determined apart from that initial intimacy with Nature which forces us to avoid the supposition that there are independent explanations of what we do and of the world in which we do it.

The supposition that there are such independent explanations is often entertained, but not for the purposes of knowledge. The entertainment of it, if knowledge is to be the consequence, obviously makes the great problem of knowledge that of the relation between the two explanations. Rigorous attention, however, to what the discovery of that relation would involve discloses at least this important fact, that our sciences either would be no longer necessary or would remain what they are, knowledge passed on from generation to generation and bettered more or less in the passing. Could we discover that relation, what would the discovery amount to? Would it free us from going to school or stop us from going to church? That question is worth much attentive reflection. I have frequently wondered how much philosophers and scientists wonder what the consequences would be if the all-pervading unity of ourselves with Nature should be so explained that why it should be at all would be perfectly clear. When we ask for an explanation of existence—why there should be existences, why they should behave as they do, and what they exist for—for what are we asking?

Why there should be vision conditioned by optical structure I have never found explained. That there is vision and that it is conditioned by such structure are both recognized without appealing to evidence, and appealing to evidence brings not only confirmation of a natural recognition but also steadily mounting proof that Nature herself is optically structured through and through, that she is preëminently the visible world, the world wherein existences are present and operate, and that "wherein" as "space" is, not *in vacuo*, but in an integrated optical structure, the meaning being the same whether we say that Nature is in space or that space is in Nature. This optical integration is explorable, and optical science is the consequent knowledge. Yet even before it is explored we live with its conditioning and see it, the expansed integrity, before our eyes. Nature's visibility is progressively clarified by exploring its conditions—light and darkness, relative position, and optical structure—and with that clarification is found a clarification of the character of space.

Space

The conclusion now reached about space has explanatory value. With it attained, we may now ask with some relevancy: Why *should* spatial discriminations be what they are? I have already suggested that a detailed answer to that question is to be sought in the several branches of optical science. There are, however, other considerations already hinted at which are worth attention irrespective of a reference to such abundant literature. Vulgar language lisps distinctions which later on are made articulate, binding together the processes of thought, as if Nature, as we learn to speak, subtly slips in categories to control the babble of our tongues. Places, for example, have their place, and this going from plural to singular instead of from singular to plural fructifies eventually into the place of all places which is now a place in a new and extraordinary sense. The accident of our native vernacular has nothing to do with a shift like this. The place of all places is space, but space has now ceased to have the character of *a* place except in terms of grammatical usage. There is a place for everything, but no place for space; yet places are still located in other places. If apart from places, space is said to have dimensions just as places do, its dimensions are not determinable as theirs are, but are said to be infinite. Since the infinite defies measurement, we are perforce obliged to define infinity. A place greater than any definable place is seductive as a definition of infinity of space, until we rigorously consider it. Then we find that such a definition robs "greater than" of the meaning it has when applied to any actual comparison of places. Although it is as easy to think of a greater place than that just thought of as it is to think of a larger house than the one we are now living in, we know that that kind of thinking is just a progressive halting of "greater than" and implies no eventual stopping. No infinite place is reached that way, just as a series of progressively larger houses does not end in a house larger than itself. Some other definition of infinity is required if infinite space is to be a character of Nature, not an example of the comparative degree of an adjective.

The principle of integrated relations supplies such a

definition. It has now become a commonplace in philosophy and in the analyses of continuities. Irrespective of its length, every straight line has its middle point. This is one of the simplest illustrations. The admission of that middle point carries us perforce, when we go on to divide the halves of the line at their middle points, not to a number of middle points greater than any assignable number, but to an integration of middle points to which "greater or less than" is not applicable. In every straight line that integration of middle points holds, no matter what the length of the line is. The line always has its half, its quarter, its eighth, and so forth, and it is not necessary to add "forever" to the "and so forth," because the eighth is *half* of the quarter, the quarter is *half* of the half, and the half is *half* of the whole. This sort of infinity is actually in the line. It is not something which is more nearly approached as the division is continued. A line one inch long has this sort of infinity as actually as one a mile long. Furthermore this sort of infinity grows richer the more it is examined, as one can discover readily by employing other means of division than the half that are relative to the whole line.

This integrated or intensive infinite is nothing vague or abstract; it is evident and concrete. It, not the vain infinity of prolonged dimensionality, characterizes Nature's spatial distinctions and gives an intelligible meaning to the distinction between the infinite and the finite; now it is a distinction of character, not of quantity, for that which is commonly called finite in view of that vain infinity may be infinite nonetheless. An inch is as infinite as a mile. One square is as infinite as another—so is one cube or one sphere. "An infinite or finite number of apples" or "an infinite or finite number of stars" is now a meaningless expression for a number greater than any number is not a number. But in view of integrated infinity, all mathematical operations are illustrations of what that infinity is. And so the expression "in space" gives to "in" a meaning different from "*in* a place." One can walk upstairs and downstairs in one's house, but not in infinity. That new "in" becomes a very useful preposition, exhibiting its peculiar meaning in a variety of contexts—in danger, in the mind, in intention, in consciousness. In such expressions we do not have an indoor and outdoor placement, and when we let the "in" be of that sort we deceive ourselves. The affirmation that all existence is in space does not mean that there is no existence outside except in terms of a purely verbal opposition between "within" and "without." "In space" implies no *either-or* in the "in."

Illustrations could be multiplied. Enough, I think, have been given to make it clear that the natural integration of all spatial relations and distinctions visible before our eyes is what space as distinct from place is, that it is this integration which gives to the consideration of space its intelligibility, and that it explains why mathematics is the kind of language necessary to carry that consideration farther than naïve observation. In so far it can be said that spatial relativity is explained and that it has been discovered why spatial distinctions should be what they are, without implying that it has also been discovered why Nature's space, the space of the visible world, should be what it is. The first "should" is intellectual; the second, moral.

In this intellectual comprehension of space we ought not to overlook the fact that it is acquired by optical means. Without that aid it is not achieved. Our thinking is impotent when we try to conceive it otherwise. There is no *a priori* space, if we mean by that that space can first be defined and then looked for afterward. That which is *a priori* is the visible world, and that world is not a definition. Let it be given in intuition or in consciousness or in our minds—but that admission admits the peculiar "in," for there is no *let it be given outside*; there is now no outside that, as "outside of," is intelligible. The visible world is *a priori*, not because we perceive it or are conscious of it or have in intuition substitutes for it by which we are led for our purposes to believe in an external world or act as if there were one, but because without it space could

neither be nor be conceived. It is not strange that
Spinoza should make extension an attribute of divinity, that Berkeley was afraid that Newtonian science
would substitute space for God, that Jonathan Ed-
wards could affirm that space is God, and that Newton
could think that the whole visible world was immediately present in the divine sensorium without the inter-
vention of eyes to see it with. It is not strange that so
much philosophizing has covertly disguised the proposition that, after all physiological and physical processes
are over in us, vision ultimately becomes a seeing without eyes and yet the seeing of an optical world.

Nor is it strange that the visible world should be
equally the residence of the sightless and the seeing, as
we naturally take it to be. One is tempted to say that
since there are ways about and places to visit all neatly
integrated, anything that can move will seek the ways
and find the places suited to it. As a matter of fact that
is what we all say, only some of us are so sensitive to
ways of saying it that we like such expressions as "the
uniformity of Nature" better, call them presuppositions or assumptions of thought, and proceed to find
out how both sightless and seeing conform in their goings about to those presuppositions and assumptions.
I often think that a relapse into the natural poetry
that is born in us is decidedly worth while as a means
of intellectual clarification. Given ways and places,

what are they for but to be sought and found? Should
anyone be surprised when we find out how they are
sought and found even by sightless creatures?

Space is here called "optical," not because of a prejudice for the eye as over against the ear or the nose or
creeping hands and feet or a rolling stone, but because
optical instrumentation is native to it, is in control of
spatial determinations, and is actually evident only in
vision. I cannot set it down as a vagary or as something
freakish that optical instruments and optical structure
are wholly indispensable in the exploration of the spatial world. Microscopes and telescopes were doubtless
very surprising when first invented, and they still surprise children and even adults. They have been regarded as implements of magic rather than as instruments for enlarging vision and assisting accuracy. The
wonders of the spectroscope and the camera are still
with us, and the new telescopes and microscopes now
under construction stir even the hard-headed among
us with a sense of miracle. Yet, in spite of all invention,
the eye is the last resort. It is the one ultimately precious optical instrument. So we both waste it and cherish it. We abuse our eyes astonishingly—not only in
careless fashion but also in the search for more light—
content to sacrifice them in that search. We are willing
to run the risk of blindness to secure better vision. Yet
we cherish our eyes, doctor them, correct them, im-

prove them, help out our failing sight with substitutes for them. All this supremacy of optical instrumentation is fact, not prejudice. It explains why the adjective "optical" fits the noun "space." The fitting is justified by the consequent clarification it brings. Alleged contradictions and impossibilities disappear or become wholly natural consequences of optical integration, consequences which that integration would lead us to expect. The problem of the application of mathematics to Nature disappears, because there is, not application, but discovery. The visible world becomes a source of explanation, not an existence to be explained.

Light

Light is a great paradox, and we may be sure that it was so before the first chapter of Genesis was written to tell us that God created light before its sources. When we consider the subject, looking upon that chapter as poetry, not as science, we find ourselves in a similar predicament. We declare that the sources of light come first and light afterward, although we have to confess that the sources are found after the light has come. Science reverses the order of creation and discovers thereby that it has depended for its intelligibility on an unescapable paradox. There must be light before there can be a theory of it involving the sources of it. This is empirical fact. Obviously the subject matter of a theory is usually identified before the theory is constructed; but in the case of light the identification, although in some respects not different from identifications in other cases—matter or heat or electricity, for example—has the peculiarity which the paradox expresses. There must be clearly identifiable materials, such as the traditional earth, water, air, and fire, before there can be a theory of matter, and that theory may have the consequence that we find matter to be the source of those materials. Many theories follow that pattern. None of them may be wholly free from the suspicion of paradox; every theory of a source of what are commonly called phenomena must be so shaped that the phenomena are thereby accounted for, and in shaping it for that purpose the phenomena, not their source, guide us both in construction of the theory and the verification of it. That is why theories change with more adequate analysis of the phenomena. If, for example, the quantum theory of matter displaces the atomic, it is not because we have attained first a better knowledge of matter, but because we have acquired a better knowledge of its products.

Now, among the admitted products of light is Nature in her visibility, and light may accordingly be, at least tentatively, defined as the condition of visibility. The definition is apt, because we do not hesitate to affirm that without light Nature would be invisible and

we should have no vision of her. We confidently appeal
to experience in the matter. Busied with theories of
light, we are often annoyed when the obvious is mentioned. In this case the annoyance is natural enough,
because stopping to attend to *this* obvious fact may very
easily halt the theory in its development. It's a nuisance. We seem forced to be content with the pronouncement that light is "the condition of visibility,"
and to say no more. We may, of course, proceed to
examine conditions of visibility when Nature is visible,
but we do not thereby get rid of the nuisance. We
examine *these* conditions in the *light* of *the* condition,
and what we affirm of *these* conditions appears to be
quite nonsensical when affirmed of *the* condition. One
example: *a* condition of visibility is light moving with
the velocity of approximately 186,000 miles per second; but *the* condition of visibility does not move with
any such velocity. Although we may admit that *the*
condition moves, we must also admit that we are then
thinking of the sources of light. As long ago as Empedocles and doubtless long before him we were offered
as illustration a man carrying a lantern. Light goes out
from the lantern and lights up a visible region for the
man. When the man moves, that region moves; when
he stands still, it stands still. *The* condition of visibility
moves in that sense, and it may have any velocity be-
ween zero and the man's speediest motion. This, how-

ever, is only a cumbersome way of saying that considerations of movement are irrelevant to *the* condition. There is always that condition no matter how the source of light moves. And now, to import into the region of visibility a velocity of light at 186,000 miles per second looks, at first blush, simply monstrous.

It looks now as if the going out of light from the lantern was *a* condition of visibility, but not *the* condition; since *the* condition has now become like a constant, always in force when there is out-going light, our attention may be directed to the latter only, letting *the* condition be now irrelevant. This seems to be quite unavoidable if the theory of light is to make progress. There is justification for setting *the* condition aside when theory is concerned. If we are justified in appealing to experience to validate the outgoing of light from its sources, we are equally justified in making the same appeal to justify its incoming to its recipients. The simple and readily understood illustration of Empedocles may serve again. The lantern carrier may put out his carried light. His illuminated region may then disappear. It is easy to imagine it disappearing altogether and yet leaving the man seeing stars in the sky, which he did not see before because of the brightness of his lantern's light. The light from those stars must have come to him, and if he is allowed to give that fact the kind of attention that astronomers give it, he will find that it is not wholly nonsense to suppose that if he were to journey to one of those stars and be there, having left his lantern lit on the earth, he could see the light from his lantern like a distant star in the sky, although from the star to which he had journeyed he could see nothing else. That distant lantern star would not supply him with an illuminated region about himself such as he had had on earth. He might not see any illuminated region at all, just as he did not when he put out his earthly lantern. Indeed, one need not give him much astronomical attentiveness in all this matter. He must have had, even if he paid little attention to it, the experience of walking along a road at night and seeing lights in the distance behaving like those of his imagination. He knows very well the distinction between lights to see by and lights to be guided by. On a stormless starry night the sailor is not afraid of being lost at sea; what he fears is a ship that carries no lights.

Obviously, now, outgoing and incoming light should have the same velocity under similar conditions of outgoing and incoming. Although the light going out from the lantern seems to be limited to the illuminated region about it, disappearing into darkness, it must pass beyond that region if it is to be seen from afar; its velocity must now be independent of the circumstance that the lantern light may or may not move or be carried. It must be far greater than that of the man—great enough to make it possible for a man to see the spangled heavens at a glance no matter how far away the separate stars may be. It must be the greatest velocity there is, so far as vision is concerned, if different things are to be seen at a glance even if they are at different distances from the observer. *The* condition of visibility has now returned to haunt us in terms of the velocity of light. There is the paradox. It has been a nuisance ever since optics began to be a science and especially since Galileo attempted to measure experimentally the velocity of light.

My interest is in the paradox, not in the hope of removing it or of inventing a new theory of light to astonish the world. In these matters I must plead the privilege that a supposed philosopher is supposed to have—that of academic freedom of speech, even if the speech turns out to be offensive. Thus far in this essay I have had considerable confidence. Now I have little, and I must confess that I am often amazed at the confidence of others who accept theories of light credulously without understanding them. That remark is a sample of the offensive things I am liable to say—not that I have not said such things before, only then I felt justified. I would avoid showing disrespect for theories of light. It is difficult for me to do, for here is a subject concerning which, up to date, we ought to be allowed to call one another fools freely and with impunity. If, considering the paradox, I maltreat the theory, I cannot help it. Let it be said that I do not understand it.

There is a habit into which we repeatedly fall in the use of language of which I have already given several examples. It is both useful and abused. The abuse of it is often of no serious consequence. In my reading I have repeatedly come upon the statement that "science teaches us so and so." Of course "science" does no such thing. It is trivial to point that out unless such an expression is the symbol of recognizing in those who work in those branches of knowledge commonly called "science" a supreme and final authority. As shorthand the expression is useful in avoiding a multiplication of words. As a symbol it is pernicious. I am tempted here to digress and to comment on the extraordinary credulity the advancement of science has been allowed to bring about and on the extraordinary circumstance that one who relentlessly points this out is usually regarded as an enemy instead of a friend of science. In intellectual society science ought to have no enemies, and it needs no friends—except generous people who will pay its bills, for it is among the costliest pursuits of knowledge. When friends and enemies become a moral or religious matter, then Heaven help us in the great enterprise of educating the young not to deceive themselves.

When we say that "light does" this or that, it is

highly important to know whether the word "light" is shorthand or symbol. The word is mischievous. It is noun, verb, and adjective, and consequently it permits the formation of properly constructed sentences which read intelligibly enough, but become bewildering when their meaning is analyzed. We may not go so far as to affirm that "light lights light," but often we approach that mystifying utterance. The English use of Latin and Greek derivatives helps us manfully in verbal jugglery. We ought to admit it instead of covering it up. We ought to wear an ironic, if not sardonic, smile on our lips when we name a *granule* or *quantum* of light a "photon." I admit, of course, the convenience and propriety of a discriminating nomenclature; but I have suffered so much from grammatical intelligibility and fall so frequently into it myself as a means of escape from difficulties that I know how easy it is to fall a victim to the magic power of neatly turned sentences and to deceive oneself into believing that one has said something profound when one has said, perhaps, nothing of consequence. When used as a noun, qualified by adjectives, and made the subject and object of verbs, is "light" shorthand or symbol? Is it shorthand which relieves us of the burden of repeated enumeration of particulars which are easily identifiable by using their names like sun(light), moon(light), star(light), fire (light), spectrum(light), and many others? Is it short-

hand for particulars like shades and shadows, reflections, refractions, opaquenesses, transparencies, and
the like? Or is it symbol of an authority, a power, a
material, a substance, an energy? The answer, when
one considers either common or technical usage, is that
it is sometimes one and sometimes the other, but usually both combined. There is the paradox again, and
again it looks like a peculiar sort of paradox.

The peculiarity may be suggested by considering
something like a parallel. We all know well enough
that motion "moves" nothing; it does not itself move.
Yet we constantly speak as if it did, and with great
advantage, for thereby the motions of moving things
are clarified. Only the careless are tricked into thinking
of motion as an authority, a power, or an energy. Only
the stupid would assign to motion a velocity all its own.
The language which the wise use may sound gram-
matically as if they did, but they are not deceived by
the sound. The language may be paradoxical; the
thinking is not. For in thinking "motion" is shorthand,
and a most effective language is constructed as a consequence. This is all clear enough. Only the stupid are
deceived.

Now we use the language of motion as the language
of light also, and out of that use arises the peculiar
paradox of light. It has been admirably and impres-
sively stated by Sir William Bragg.

Light brings us the news of the universe. . . . Light, . . . using the full meaning of the word, transmits energy which is the mainstay of life, and gives to living beings the power of observation: and it is akin to the matter of which all things animate and inanimate are made. The universe is its sphere of action.[3]

The last sentence transposed is: "Light's sphere of action is the universe." There is the paradox. The quoted words may sound poetic or like the expression of an enthusiasm. Yet when one considers "the full meaning of the word," attentive to its many uses that grow out of the distinction between light and darkness familiarly experienced in the alternation of day and night and in opening and closing the eyes, it becomes increasingly difficult not to repeat in one form or another those quoted words. Something like them seems to be wholly inescapable. Yet they look like the greatest paradox a man can utter. How can the universe be light's sphere of action when light, "in the full meaning of the word," is as responsible as those words make it? The transmission of energy, the mainstaying of life, giving the power of observation, being akin to all that is animate and inanimate—what is there to be added to the universe? What is there left that Nature does not contain? It looks very much as if heaven and earth, the sea, and all that in them is *are* because there *is* light. The full meaning of a word.

It is, I think, unnecessary to go into minor para-

[3] *The Universe of Light*, New York, Macmillan, 1933, pp. 1–2.

doxes growing out of this conspicuously major one. A philosopher is tempted to do it. It is good sport, but hardly clean, to point out inconsistency after inconsistency, confusion after confusion, nonsense after nonsense, to convict the best sellers in popularized science of the abuse of language, of tricky illustrations, of patently false statements, of unnecessarily infecting words with ambiguity, of talking down to the intelligent as if they were stupid, of inventing fairy tales and a new mythology which uses for its gods Greek words which the Greeks did not use for their gods—all that is very easy to do, but it is rather indecent, even if much of it is merited in defense of sanity. Sinning against the light may be forgiven for even that sinning acknowledges its authority.

As I have said, my concern in this essay is with the paradox, not with the theory of light. The latter interests me profoundly, not because it explains light, but because the consequences to which it leads in the exploration of Nature are so magnificent. I have almost a childish awe of optical instruments, although I have lost all awe of big as over against little things and of little as over against big. And optics has convinced me that if primacy is to be given to any vision, it must be given to that of the human eye, and when so given this turns out to be relative primacy after all. And I must envy the extraordinary acumen required in building

up the theory. Apart from all this the theory leaves me
a little cold, as if it were little more than a mathematical enthusiasm. That enthusiasm is natural. One
cannot go far in the subject of mathematics and escape
it. We usually begin the study with its branches, as if
they were independent, and find as we proceed that
they cohere. We apply, as we say, mathematics to Nature and in doing so begin to suspect that even where
we have failed there is *a* mathematics, could we but
conceive it, which would fit. And time and again where
there has been failure the requisite mathematics has
been found later and has welded together apparently
different and exclusive patterns of Nature's behavior so
closely that they then appear as if stamped from a common matrix. Nature's matrix—that would be mathematical; that, expressed in equations, formulas, functions, would yield predictability at the maximum. The
enthusiasm is warranted, for combinations already
wrought through the extension of mathematics have
broken down barrier after barrier. Sir William Bragg's
words illustrate this. They themselves—in my reading
of them—are not the expression of mathematical enthusiasm, but an indication of a unity in Nature toward which the unifying extension of mathematics in
different fields of inquiry leads. The unity is clearly
fact; the theory is an accommodation of the facts by
finding in them coherences and interrelations which

can be mathematically expressed. When these coherences and interrelations are regarded as operating beings, I cannot help suspecting mythology.

The scientist may neglect the paradox—may set it aside as of no consequence in his labors. This the philosopher cannot do. He is not concerned with scientific problems, nor is his reliance a matter of their solution. His interest is humanistic first of all. I have come to dislike that adjective, for "humanism" today often suggests a polite superiority of character or a pleasant medicine for that spiritual nostalgia which sickens the soul when faith has apparently lost its foundations. "Art still has strength, take refuge there." Let there be a "Testament of Beauty" when the Old and the New no longer bequeath a marketable inheritance. That seems too much like a surrender of human dignity. Furthermore the antithesis between science and philosophy is conventional—a convenient academic division of scholarly labor, not a subtle serpent to divide our allegiance. Each of us is scientist and philosopher combined. Each of us wants weights and measures standardized, and each of us wants to live a good life. If those who are named philosophers insist that the latter is more important in the sense that without it the former is insignificant, they do no more than emphasize a truth of which each of us is naturally convinced. I say "naturally" because it is a truth which haunts us from the cradle to the grave, is present acutely at birth, at marriage, and at death, and is not the result of priestly or scholastic instruction. That is why I have said that the philosopher's interest is humanistic first of all. And now when I mention "philosophers" I mean, not men who, like me, are distinguished by being listed in a university catalogue or by membership in certain learned societies or by degrees after their names, but all sorts and conditions of men. We all speak of *our* world, *our* lives, *our* God. None of these is ours. But this turn of speech is forced by Nature from our lips. We are all philosophers when that is recognized, and that recognition is a recurrent stimulus to examine our intimacy with Nature and to keep it free from distortion.

So, pitting the paradox of light against the theory is not finding fault with the theory, unless the latter is offered either as an explanation of the paradox or allowed to generate unbearable confusion. The Astronomer Royal has printed on the title page of a book[4] the following question from the poet Longfellow:

> Were a star quenched on high,
>   For ages would its light,
> Still travelling downwards from the sky,
>   Shine on our mortal sight?

As if in answer from our nearest star we read on page

[4] H. Spencer Jones, *Worlds without End*, New York, Macmillan, 1935.

174: "We see this particular star where it was about four years previously; it is actually somewhere about 200 million miles away from the position in which we see it." Strictly, this is not an answer to the poet's question. I am not sure that the Astronomer Royal intends it to be. He may be only inducing the reader to ask the poet's question by citing a circumstance connected with the theory of light. But such astronomical circumstances are often accepted as answers.[5] Were our nearest star quenched today, we should still see it for four years where it was about four years previously. This paradox is much too much. It is quite useless to debate now whether we see our nearest star where it is or where it was. That question has become, if not irrelevant, quite meaningless. For in a situation such as this we should not allow ourselves to be deceived by large numbers—200 million miles away. They are impressive, but not more instructive than little ones. With the velocity of light at 186,000 miles per second or at a mile a minute and considering the house across the way, or our hands and feet, or any visible part of our bodies instead of our nearest star, the argument in answer to the poet's question is the same. The house across the way, our hands and feet, any visible part of our bodies—we see them all where they were previ-

[5] A. O. Lovejoy, *The Revolt against Dualism*, Chicago, Open Court; New York, W. W. Norton, 1930, pp. 18–20.

ously; and, however short that "previously," they are all actually some distance, however short, from the position in which we see them. Does it help us to understand anything at all, if the paradox of light is made as paradoxical as this?

The question I repeat expanded a little is now, not whether we see things where they are or where they were or observe events when they happen or after they have happened; it is a quite different question. Now the question is: *What do* we see? Nothing in heaven or earth or sea or in all that in them is, nothing in philosophy, nothing in science answers that question if the vision of our eyes is excluded or made a derivative of what we discover by its means. Such *is* the paradox of light, and attempts to resolve the paradox do no more than generate other paradoxes more complicated and without end. Then there are worlds without end in a sense never dreamed of in anybody's philosophy. If there is any explanation of the final paradoxes, it is the initial paradox that explains them. In the full meaning of the word, light from beginning to end is *the* condition of visibility. That condition explored as best we can is found to be a compulsion to utter such words as those of Sir William Bragg. Only I would transpose the last of the quoted sentences: Light's sphere of action *is* the universe.

The Visible World Again

For the purposes of this essay I have let the paradox of light speak for itself, so to speak, after vainly having tried to do something else. That something else seemed increasingly unimportant the more I worked at it, so I will not mention what it was. But I feel that the preceding section is very inadequate and confess that only the desire to get this essay finished, if possible, keeps me from rewriting and enlarging it. Brief as it is, I hope it has made its point. I leave it, however, more impressed than ever by the power of a word. That word is "light." When I try to bring before me what the use of that word unequivocally identifies, I begin, as everybody else does, with lights. If I want an example of what lights are, a candle flame is good enough. How often I have seen it pictured in the books, sending its rays through a pinhole to find itself inverted on a screen—the beginning of optical wisdom. Like many another, I performed the experiment when a child. The candle flame *was* upside down on the screen; more properly its *picture* was, but somehow the candle flame got through that pinhole and painted that picture of itself inverted. The book explained how. It all seemed very, very simple. The simplicity has vanished with the years. Today my grandchildren perform the experiment with cameras bought in a store. They may not yet have gone to books for explanations, for the camera is a toy for taking pictures. By and by they may do so, and I pray God to give them brains enough to be surprised. That simple experiment with candle, pinhole, and screen, the first I ever consciously performed in optics, has become for me one of the most remarkable experiments ever made—my own eyes made it while I was reading the book which led me to make it with a box—and no final explanation of it has yet been made. Probably, however, I should rather say that all explanations are still in terms of candle power, in terms of what a candle flame can do.

What remarkable things it does! We are so used to being told of them and to reading about them that we seldom stop to turn what we are told into questions and try to embarrass the candle flame with them.

"Why do you send out your rays in all directions at once?"

"Because otherwise I might miss the pinhole and photographers would then have to take pictures by statistics instead of by appointment or when they pleased."

"What becomes of the rays that don't go through the pinhole?"

"Various things happen to them, but in general I may say that they are dispersed; some of them, for example, fall on the surface around the pinhole and show its color, unless all of them are absorbed by the surface."

"But they make no picture of you on that surface?"

"No, at least not under the conditions of your simple experiment."

"If only some of your rays go through the pinhole, how can they make a picture of you on the screen?"

"I refuse to answer; I do the trick and it is up to you to find out how."

"But it is a difficulty?"

"It is."

"And you won't explain it?"

"No; but some of you questioners explain it by waves."

"Then your rays are also waves?"

"That's what *you* say; let it go at that for the present."

"Why if you go through the pinhole both as rays and as waves isn't your picture right side up? That is what one would expect from waves; they spread out after going through an opening and don't turn over."

"That's amusing; how does anybody know they don't turn over? At any rate my turnover is an experimental fact."

"Why then do we see you right side up?"

"That's a child's question which you ought not to ask. Seeing, you see, is your reversal of what I do and so you *must* see me right side up although my picture is upside down on your retina."

"But I've heard of a psychologist who succeeded in having your picture on his retina right side up. It made him sick at first because you now looked upside down and disorganized his movements. In less than a hundred hours, however, although you still seemed to be upside down, he had little trouble in moving orderly about and conjectured that if he had been born that way, you and your picture would always have been the same side up. Now what do you make of that?"

"First, that he wasn't born that way, and secondly, it is all a matter of lenses."

"Well, then, what is a lens?"

"Don't ask me; all I know is that without lenses you and I would not be having this dialogue. I wouldn't be a candle flame. Neither your picture nor mine would be taken."

"Would nothing be left?"

"Nothing visible; but yet there'd be light."

I have risked such persiflage because although childish in a way its childishness is of a very penetrating sort. That imaginary dialogue hints at nearly all the basic problems of light and ends with "light" as the last word to be uttered, and to find a meaning for that last word one has to retrace the steps by which that last word was reached. It is a marvelous journey from the pinhole experiment to the word and then from the word back to the pinhole; from lenses to without them and from without them back to them again.

What I wish that I had the gift to do is to exhibit the power of that word "light" as a name for the conductor of that journey as that power is exhibited in the literature of those peoples whose languages have been articulate in the expression of it. This would not be a theory of light. It would exhibit the paradox, but be quite unconcerned about it. Whatever vocal sounds these peoples used—φῶς, *lumen*—or whatever visual characters they imprinted on wood, stone, or paper would be of no consequence. The word in its power would be the same, and the gamut of its use would stretch from candle flames to gods. The story of "light" as a word employed would not be a theory, would not be a paradox. It would be the story of the dreams and visions of mankind, of the rising and the setting sun, the one we see day after day, the many others that imitate his service. Were that story written, philosophers and scientists would be far outnumbered by other contributors, and they might have a claim to the most conspicuous place if they did not so frequently put out the light and rob Nature of her visibility.

So the visible world remains preëminent in control of the enterprise of learning. It has lost all semblance of a psychical addition to a material body equipped with sense organs and a nervous system. It has every title to be Nature's own being in Nature's own right, independent of us, seen as we see it because our own constitution is enmeshed in it—all this when there is light. When there is not light, then there is no description and no depiction of what remains. Let there be no light—we can frame the order in words and conjecture answers, but when we rigorously examine those answers and probe relentlessly the words we use, we do not approach an identifiable world or an intelligible world. We approach darkness; then that goes, and "formless" and "void" become last words, and totally without light those two words are meaningless. "Formless" is a *sight* word, and "void" is a *space* word; and the space word without the sight word—who can guess at its meaning?

Again the optical character of space confronts us. Bring back the light—*there* is the visible world. Brought back, it has found a new title. It is a world *now*, a world generating a *then*. *Now* there *was* yesterday and *will be* tomorrow. Past and future have, as it were, come into being. They are not *now* divided by a vanishing point futilely sought and named "the present." They are divided by a present world; not a world presented to an observer in moments that flit from a vanished past through a vanishing present into a future impossible to overtake, but a world presented in a steadied glance, alive not only with a marvelous display but also with change, with movement, with action and reaction, stimulus and response, cause and effect, a productive world wherein there are histories of things that change and grow, a metabolic world wherein everything feeds and is fed by everything else. Such is the visible world expansed as Nature's being. It is now no longer like a colorless model waiting to be colored or sculptured by a magic called "us" or "the human mind," but like earth's soil waiting to be tilled. Nature is preëminently the visible world.

Perhaps this chapter is needlessly long. My temptation is to make it longer, because the more I contemplate the visible world before my eyes, observe what it contains even as I look at it from my window, and then go on to think what I might see of it if I went traveling with the tourists, the merchants, and the explorers who risk their lives in climbing Mt. Everest and flying in the stratosphere, the more I realize how it contains our lives all the way from creeping babies on the floor to speculators about the sky. I write freely about Nature as a whole, about "The Universe," and I am haunted all the time by a picture of something like an enormous globe before eyes that look upon it from without as if that picture would be a vision of what it really is—an enormous globe with emptiness around it which is space. I turn to the writings of philosophers and find a like picture haunting them. But I must admit defeat and find them defeated too. They and I were not born outside the world which we see. They and I have to admit it. They and I never went to a school beyond the utmost limits of the sky to learn how the earth goes around the sun. And so, to keep myself from being deceived I must set aside that vain picturing, return to my relative position in the midst of what I see, and refuse to let Nature be in space and admit that space is in Nature.

Then space becomes something quite different from an emptiness which the universe never completely fills and which in spite of that has some sort of geometry. It becomes that shifting yet integrated interplay of the geometrical distinctions I observe, of all the heres and theres, the rights and lefts, the ups and downs, the nears and fars, the shapes, the sizes, the bulks, the configurations, the places, and of all that for which I use the adjective "spatial." For them all together there is no separate place. And when this looks astonishing, I find the cause of the astonishment in the "look." All that I can learn about light and optics becomes increasingly clear and positive evidence that it all *must* look that way and that I cannot possibly conceive it as looking any other way. This is not making my inability to conceive it otherwise the test of truth. It is rather the recognition that my inability is a consequence of

primary. With an event—be it ripening and rotting or any other—there are before and after, from ten to nine and from ten to eleven, from nine to eight and from nine to ten, from eleven to twelve and from eleven to ten, and so forth, not forward only or backward only, but backward and forward or forward and backward for every hour that the clock strikes.

Events are primary. They are the generators of present, past, and future, the only reliable indexes of what time and history are. It is a mistake to begin with past, present, and future as if these were initial divisions of time with the present a point moving continuously forward and thereby successively dividing time into two equal parts. A scheme of time like that is not identifiable. It belies the facts. Events do not occur after that pattern. To suppose that they do is to make of time a monster devouring itself or being devoured by the duration of events without either repletion or exhaustion. Or it is to make of it a preparation for the entertainment of events, as if time kept open house for transient visitors and kept a guestbook wherein arrivals, departures, and length of stay were noted, with varied comments made by the departing, sometimes expressing a vain wish that they might come again and sometimes acknowledging a hospitality which kept permanent quarters for them to which they would surely return at a fixed date: an endless procession of events, some never to return, others recurrent but always older, others expected but held back, having met with accidents on the way for which, strangely, time had also kept a room. Evident facts are not clarified by unintelligible monstrosities.

Past, present, and future are adjectives before they are nouns. They qualify events before they qualify time, and only after they have been allowed to qualify time are they turned into nouns, *the* past, *the* present, and *the* future, as if they were original divisors or divisions. In qualifying events, those adjectives indicate a classification into kinds of event rather than a sequence of events all of the same kind. The classification is in terms of "presence in" and "absence from" Nature, and events absent from are either past or future. Such is time's scheme as Nature declares it, and none of us, until heaven has sent him misfortune, has the slightest doubt of it. An event not present in Nature is either a past or a future event. Present events are; past and future ones are not. In a way, past and future events are events by courtesy only; eventfulness is not in them. A past or future hoeing does not hoe a garden; past or future writing does not write a book; the past or future shining of the sun does not shine; the past or future transits of Venus do not transit. That a present event should leave or emerge from the class of past events and find a place in the class of future events is obviously absurd. It finds a place in the class of past events only by ceasing to be *an* event. When attention is directed to the class of future events, that class tends to break up into subclasses calling for further qualifications, such as "necessary," "possible," "probable," and the like. Attention to the grammar of time language discloses the natural syntax of time.

Events are observable, and most conspicuously so in the visible world, for there they can be watched in associated unity. I look out of my window and see black smoke belching from a chimney and disappearing into the air while pigeons fly hither and thither in flock formation or stop to rest and a white cloud floats almost imperceptibly above; my window, the buildings, and the sky alone seem stationary. There, before my eyes, are events in their natural relation and framed by my window. My imagination playing with the scene does no more than enlarge the framing; it does not change the pattern of the scene—changes bracketed by other changes and all bracketed by the apparently changeless. The pigeons are not flying from the past to the future, but from resting place to resting place and *while* the smoke belches from the chimney; the smoke does not belch from the past to the future, but *while* the cloud floats; and the cloud floats *while* my window frame stays still. All these "whiles" bracketed in a unity is Nature's scheme of events, her identified time structure. And so far forth *the* present is just that scheme, and in such a present every event is whiled and no event is whiled in *time* if time is supposed to be anything like a preparation for entertaining the whiling.

Such is the elementary fact, and from it is to be derived whatever else is said about time. It is the leader, not the follower, in matters of understanding—the basis for the intelligibility of all the more that is said. *The* present, being the bracketed unity of all existing whiles, has not an independent while of its own; it is not itself an event. It does not come out of the past and go into the future or out of a chimney into the air or from one place to another or from nothing to nothing. Events in their relative duration diversify it, but no event of the kind it displays either starts it or stops it. That fact and that alone gives meaning to "eternity," to "forever," to the "infinity" of time. We have the kind of infinity which is not *more than any* duration, but which is *in all* durations.

Starting with events observed in their bracketed relation and relative duration, one is led progressively to clocks and calendars and ultimately to something comparable with Newton's definition of *tempus absolutum, verum, et mathematicum*,[1] but one must reject the imagery

---

[1] "Tempus Absolutum, verum, & mathematicum, in se & naturâ suâ sine relatione ad externum quodvis, aequabiliter fluit, alioque nomine dicitur Duratio." *Philosophiae naturalis principia mathematica*, Definitio VIII, Scholium I, Editio MDCCLX.

of its last word *fluit*. The three adjectives, "absolute,"
"true," and "mathematical," ought to be read together as three emphases on the same character—an
integrity kept in all the relativity of events. This is most
clearly exhibited in the equations of mathematics by
the symbol t. It is a symbol for variations that keep
their own character no matter what happens to the
symbol in the equations. The "time" in the equations
is something very curious when viewed in the light of
what is done with the symbol. It is, for example,
squared. A squared time, t^2, is incomprehensible in ordinary language. Indeed nearly all the operations performed with t are equally incomprehensible in that
language. They are not at all incomprehensible in
mathematics, for that science is full of similar symbols
which are allowed to behave outrageously, if their behavior is construed in terms of the language of conversation. If we were told that it would take "25 minutes
squared" or "625 square minutes" to get to the station, we would not be thankful for the information.
But in mathematics $(25t)^2 = 625t^2$, and no mathematician is confused; that symbol t, although it points to
a clock, enables him to use all the resources of mathematics—powers, roots, dividends, divisors, quotients,
exponents, coefficients, sines, cosines, vectors, and the
like—without disturbing that pointing. As I have indicated, symbols other than t are mathematically used

in the same way. Noting such use here is relevant because I am writing about time and indicating how that
symbol in its use represents something about time
which is *absolutum, verum, et mathematicum*. It is not a
symbol for something that *flows*. It is a symbol for
something to which flowing or not flowing are quite
irrelevant, something which is in Nature, for otherwise mathematics would be powerless to formulate or
to predict. If that symbol is thought of as one for a
flowing, if it is thought of as a symbol for something in
its own right divisible, squarable, and the like, confusion is the inevitable consequence. In its *operational effect* that t is eternity, is *always* a constant and an infinity, not in the sense of a number of minutes or seconds or fractions of a second greater than any assignable
number, but an infinity in every operation involving
any number of minutes—time's integrity in events.
Nature's events are subject to it and *never* escape it, for
it is what "never" and "forever" mean. And so time
as five minutes and time as forever must be distinguished. The former is not five minutes of eternity; the
latter is not minutes without end.

Our attempts to conceive an eventless system are defeated. Naturally the cessation of the pigeon's flight
can be generalized, for we observe it starting and stopping in the present world, and each flight with its own
while integrated with all other concurrent whiles is

unique and not repeatable. The second flight is not the first flight again. Considering the flights alone, the pauses between are not entitled to be named events. There is nothing doing. Those pauses may be generalized and unified into a single pause with nothing doing. Since the scene observed contained only so many flights, it might have contained none. Since it contained, by the same reasoning, only so many events, it might have contained none. The scene I observe from my window may be as still as the picture that hangs on my wall, a picture of men toiling with the sun shining on a cornfield. There are no events in the picture. It's a forever scene, a little eternity, paused like the Grecian urn of which Keats wrote. There's a little of Keats in each of us. Forever will those men toil without toiling. Forever will that picture be expectancy unfulfilled— forever the pause of toiling men who have homes waiting for them all through that endless pause. An eventless world—but not wholly so, after all, for the beholder cannot be left out of the account. There is much of Keats in each of us, and that is why none but the most stupid escape the beauty and power of his ode. Pauses have their beauty, their expectancy, their terror. Hours of waiting are hours of high intensity and strain. None of us needs proof of that. Hours with Nature's pauses are among the most sublime. A visitor to the Grand Canyon, absorbed by the scene, feels Nature ready for an astounding display of power. A group of chatty tourists is hushed into silence. Any speech is like a profanation. If that vast chasm should suddenly burst into action, that sleeping power awake—what then? "I will lift up mine eyes unto the hills, from whence cometh my help." Why?

Of course there is an obvious answer: we are made that way. Of course we are. One doesn't have to argue about it. Leave Nature out, however, and then ask whether we are made that way. Is there any sense in turning what Nature does to us into what we do to her when we are so fatally her children? But let there be sense in it for the sake of having a "discussion." Then, take us out, and what is left for Nature to be or do? Or let *us* make Nature, contrive her as an instrument for our purposes or as a toy to play with. Where do we get the materials and the plan? Let us, preferably, turn our attention to time and history, try out those potent words, find them carrying us back to events. Then we find that we are sharing a joint eventfulness. A world without events has become unthinkable, not because we are so made that no matter what Nature is we must, even in great pauses, remember and expect, but because we live in a system of events, in a dynamic world, not in one waiting for something to happen before anything happens. Eternity was not before Nature began. It is in the present world observable in the

bracketing of events and in Nature's pauses, and carried in mathematics by the symbol *t*.

Nature's time-scheme or structure, so obviously displayed in the visible world as the unified or integrated
bracketing of events in their relative duration or whiling, is the source of our knowledge of time and history.
That it is an ultimate source of explanation is proved
by our inability to explain it itself. Every such attempt
is caught in the network of events. The language used
expresses the entanglement. All the instruments used
exemplify it. The imagery employed is the imagery of
events—the flowing river, the march of time, the course
of nature, progress, evolution, growth, development,
the seasons, birth and death, cities and wars, ripening
and rotting, everlasting waiting for something to happen, eternal expectancy. We are inescapably caught.
Nature expansed unto all eyes is expansed as *the* while,
as while events are. Nature expansed, whether we mention eyes or not, is none the less while events are. Nothing whatever is gained by trying to conceive Nature
to be whiled in another sort of while from which events
are absent, until Nature becomes present to be the
great event which interrupts a pauseless pause. Nothing is thereby gained; we are defeated.

Time, then, is not a calendar with dates antecedently
fixed with which events are subsequently correlated.
Nor is it a clock antecedently dividing a dial of its own

into seconds. Nature falsifies all such views of time by
letting the bracketing of events be exhibited wherever
we turn to look at them in their actual and effective
occurring; and that occurring is also a concurring,
making up the only present world there is. It is in that
world that events come to be and from it that they
pass away. It is in that world that they succeed one
another. They do not come to be out of the past and
pass away into the future. Their concurrence is not a
competitive race along a track to see which can first
reach a goal, leaving the others behind impotent on a
wholly vanished track. Nature presents no such time-
scheme as that. She presents actual and effective concurrence and, by presenting it unified, coherent, integrated, makes it possible to express loosely in ordinary
language and rigorously in mathematical language
that which is constant in the whole concurrence. Then
we say "forever" or use the symbol t. Then we have
knowledge of time; then we have found the natural
principle in consequence of which we, vitally partici-
pant in Nature's scheme of time, are retrospective and
prospective beings, bracketed in her bracket of time,
whiling away our lives while she whiles away her
events, finding the integration of that whiling capable
of such expression that, weak as we are, our power to
deal with events grows with our knowledge. We are
less and less at their mercy. Subtract ourselves wholly,

as we often futilely try to do in imagination—then Nature's events are relentless, without mercy or accommodation to our welfare. It is as if Nature were interested only in having events happen no matter what they are like or what their consequences may be, caring only, and with a caring which is not care, that their integration is kept intact—a being jealous of nothing but its own integrity, and that integrity mathematical; a state so jealous of its own government that there is no court in which to plead, no justice to dispense, no excuses to be admitted, no goods that are rewards, and no evils that are punishments; a being so alien to what we find ourselves to be that there is no common ground of fellowship at all.

Such a picture is instructive, although it is not a picture of what Nature is. It is instructive because it can make vivid what time is like. It enhances the sense of eternity, of order, of connection, of coherence, of a changelessness in all concurring. But it falsifies Nature by leaving us out. While we are in Nature, we are just as much her residents as the heavenly host. Our presence is just as much of an event as any other event that comes and goes. Restored to where we belong and with our idiosyncrasies acknowledged fully as much as those of hydrogen, then—although we may still claim, if we are pleased to, that Nature is no respecter of events, that she cares no more for us than she does for hydro-

gen, is no more anxious about what we do than about
what it does—we must admit that, with us as natural
as any other of Nature's beings, her time-scheme of
events is effectively found to be profitable. It is a
scheme spelling "possibility" all the while. That word
we do not read into Nature by some arbitrary act of
our own. What that word means is a discovery as genuine as any other. Its meaning is verified again and
again by experiment, and every experiment is itself an
event. The only objective picture of eventful Nature
we can tolerate, if we are thorough, is a picture of
possibilities realized and in realization. This does not
mean that we must be in the picture. It means that our
being in the picture makes any other sort of picture—
even the picture of Nature in our absence—intolerable.
That is why we are forever saying that Nature "does"
this and that; or, fearful lest the word "Nature" should
convict us of poetry, we use "matter" or "energy" or
both together and say that they "do" this and that;
or, again fearful of a *doer*, we change from the active to
the passive voice of the verb and say that this and that
"are done" and, in the doing, Nature or matter or
energy "is transformed." But all the while we are dealing with events in their natural concurrence, finding
them to be integrated, no matter what they are, and
finding that they can be profitable, finding that just
because events are let and hindered in their whiling
they are indexes of the possible.

Nature as the world in which events are present is thus discovered to be the index of a world of possible events. In observing the pigeons' flight, their pausing, their flight again, their pausing again, flight is the index of a possible pause and each pause the index of a possible flight. Each is also the index of impossible events. Flying and pausing are vibratory, so to speak. The second flight is index of a possible third in the present world and also of an impossible first. The first is not returnable except as a third. Observing the third is not observing the first, just as observing the third is not observing the fourth. Here before one's eyes the sequential character of events is disclosed. And the important point here for knowledge of time is that this sequential character is derived, not from a single event, but from the bracketed scheme of events whiled. To make this emphatic I could almost risk saying that *our* memory and imagination have nothing to do with the matter, for it is quite impossible for me to think of remembering or imagining anything except through vital participation in a scheme of events which is whiled. Over and over again it has been said that we *live* time rather than think it and that when we try to think it, we fail and become confused. Then, why try to think it? Why not ask: What is it that we think about when we try? The answer to the latter question is easy and within the compass of a child's understanding. We think about flying pigeons, for example, and that sort of thinking makes past and future intelligible. Flights are finished in the present world. The adjective "finished," however, means that they are over and so have ceased to be events strictly—pigeons not in flight are not flying pigeons. Having observed a finished flight, we name it "past." It is out of the present world and out of it for good and all. It has become a wholly impossible event. *The* past is dead, impotent, only the present is vital, dynamic, eventful. But a second flight and a third observed there in the bracketing of events affords a sequence and the object of sequential thinking. So there are possible flights and those we name "future," flights that may occur in the present world, but are not occurring. All visibly before us is what we think about when we think about time as something we live. We live it in events, but not independent of them. Our memory and imagination are consequences of Nature's time-scheme, not the strands out of which that scheme is woven.

Yes, Nature, in being eventful, sets the pattern which our memory and imagination follow. Living her time-scheme is the vital realization of what it is. One may say it is the best example of it. Yet, having allowed ourselves this privilege, we soon find that we must limit it to that of recognizing what the past and future are—names for vanished and not-vanished possibilities, for a flight finished and for one possibly to begin—so that our interests turn to the discovery of what is possible, to reliable anticipations. This is indeed our major concern, and Nature makes it perilously clear that it is something to be concerned about. The illustration of bracketed events seen from my window is good enough for a sample, but not very impressive in spite of my attempt to make it so. The farmer planting a hoped-for harvest, sowing his hoped-for cotton and linen cloth, breeding his hoped-for animals to furnish clothing and food, caring for his wood plots in order that there may be fire and lumber —all his labor for hoped-for results on which depend both his security and ours—all that is a far better example. Nature, although needing nothing of his labor for her own security, nevertheless responds. She furnishes him with the seeds that eventuate in a harvest; she provides the possibility of the realization of his hopes through the sweat of his brow. If she fails him, he is helpless. That she may not fail him is first his prayer and afterward his agriculture. Relying on her, he turns artist and engineer. He watches the weather and would control it if he could. She gives him dry land, and he waters it; barren soil, and he fertilizes it; storms, floods, pests, and plagues, and he guards against them. She makes war upon him, and he fights her with her own weapons as best he can. In all his toil it is her natural implementation that he uses. He knows no other kind. He began with praying for help when in trouble, he ends giving thanks that the help comes with his labor, not for the asking, for he has learned that if it came just for the asking, Nature's natural providence would be turned into a tumult of response to the whimsical prayers of men. She could not be relied upon equally by all.

The point is, of course, that Nature, showing no respect for the farmer's toil, shows him what that toil must respect if it is to be profitable. She, after all, grows all the vegetables, grows all the trees with their fruits, breeds all the cattle, in her own bracketed scheme of events; or, better, perhaps, they are all grown and bred in it. It is no wonder that we personify her as if she knew what she is doing, planned it, prepared for it. She is like a remembering and imagining being, dropping acorns on the ground and expecting them to grow into oaks because she remembered them doing it; like a farmer buying radish seeds to plant in early spring. The seasons, the swarm of animals—all a remembering and an imagining. Nature's time-scheme and Nature's productivity are not initially different. So Nature is historical, letting finished events go in the production of present events and letting present events get finished in the forever present. We discover the history and write it down, and we talk of past events and future events as a consequence. Nature as "historical" provides the reckoning. A ripening and rotting, a tale, a clock, a calendar—they hang together.

Verbs

It is worth noting how like a mirror of Nature's scheme of time is the use of verbs with their modifiers. There are the tenses, with a major division into imperfect and perfect, or into simple present, past, and future, and perfect present, past and future. Grammarians are often blind leaders of the blind, but they often carry lanterns which do give light. I often think that "adjective" is a neat word suggesting a missile thrown at a noun to make the noun take notice; and the "accusative case" also—as if the accused object had to bear up under some guilty charge. Grammarians in the matter of the tenses of the verb usually begin with the simple present, go to the simple past, and then to the simple future, just as Touchstone did. It is the natural way of going. First Tom must run, then one can say he ran; one must say he ran before one can say he will run. If Tom did not run at all, who can say that he will? So we go from present to past and from past to future, leaping over the present, as it were. I am thinking of Tom, the Piper's son, and the tale of him. We jingle it in the past tense to our children: he stole a pig, he ran away, the pig got eat, Tom got beat, and went bellowing down the street—a progress, as it were, from crime to punishment. It is a finished history. It may be told in more lively fashion in what grammarians call the historical present: Tom steals, he runs, the pig is being eaten, Tom is being beaten, and he runs bellowing. Here is time lived, and we see at a glance the difference between a tale in the making and a tale made, a sequence of living events and a sequence of dead ones. Both are from crime to punishment; but we must have the sequence dead if we would use it for future reference, put a stop to it, mark down a period, and where we put the period makes much difference. Of course, in the historical present we stop with Tom's bellowed running, but is that over? Is the tale ended? Yes, from a literary point of view, but from the point of living time, no. Finished events, finished sequences of events, the past—there is the source of understanding events and of instruction for the future. An unfinished event, an unfinished sequence of events, leaves us helpless. We must have the past as a period ended in some way or other if we are to have events in changeless character with their interdependence fixed. Not until a man is dead can the tale of his life be written.

All this is intensified when we regard the tenses of the verb as imperfect and perfect. Then the need of the perfect is conspicuous and consequences flow from it. Tom runs is quite different from Tom has run. The perfect isolates his running as a completed and self-inclosed event to be examined by itself or as pivotal in a sequence. Here events are before or after the completed event. It is a divider. It is closed in by antecedents and consequences. It changes the course of events, giving them, with its completion, a different swing. "Running" becomes the name of an event, no matter who or what runs—Tom, a river, the sun, a machine. "Running" suggests legs, as we use "motion" to free our thinking from bondage to specific means of getting about. Motion becomes the great and indispensable event all the way from the least of the inanimate to the greatest of the animate. Nature is turned into a world of motion. Theories of motion are born. They all follow a pattern, from motion as qualitative, of different kinds, to motion as quantitative, of the same kind, to motion measurable and calculable and expressible finally in mathematics, the only competent language for this progress in knowledge from motion exhibited in Nature, as of many kinds, to motion expressed as the integration of those kinds. God or something else is thought of as a Prime Mover. From Tom's theft to the ultimate source of motion—that is the sort of road theories of motion travel, and they cannot help it if they look to Nature for support. The theory of motion is motion expressed in a mathematical equation or with finished or perfected motion in control—Nature in the present perfect tense of the verb "to move." Crime and punishment have either gone or been, for theory's sake, transformed into motion.

The pluperfect is the "more-than-perfect" tense, and that sounds like a contradiction. The "more than" is dynamic even in the perfect scheme. Tom had run. There is expectancy in the pronouncement: what next, what will follow that perfected tale of crime and punishment? If he had not run, if he had not stolen, if it had not been for the past, if the past had been different, what then? The deadest of dead tenses seems to be alive. The dead past has us in its grip. "Let the dead bury their dead!" They never do; the living do that, and they bury them with the pluperfect tense, with "had been" and "if it had not been." The pluperfect is more than perfect because it is like a resurrection of possibility even in the dead past. It is the time of agony, a vanished agony, to be sure, but none-the-less potent. How different the course of events would have been if it had been otherwise. How different history would have been if the Great War had not been fought. We live the agony of the pluperfect in the present; we call life a struggle, a game, a sport, a play, an agony of laughter and tears, a drama played out, but played out as if it might have been played out differently.

It seems unnecessary to carry on from the comedy

and tragedy—the more-than-perfect—of Tom's history into the theory of motion. The point is the return
of possibility through the perfected past with its suggestions of a different perfection. I cite a standard example, one that is found in all the textbooks. For the
theory of heavenly motions the sun had moved around
the earth for ages. What if the sun had not so moved?
It was a revolutionary question. Obviously an ingenious student of cosmic motions might have risked the
supposition—so evidently contrary to observation—
that the earth moved around the sun, just to see what
could be made of it, without being immediately influenced by the pluperfect tense. He would, however,
be exhibiting that influence; it would confront him
with a resistance to be overcome. He would have to
dispose of it. He could not escape the history of the
heavens as Nature displays it and as men write it. The
ingenious man, the rebel, the reformer, is a pluperfect
man. He is sure to meet resistance and to have a hard
experience. Reformers are always talking of the inertia
of the past, its dead hand on the present. They want
to free us from it in spite of the fact that there is no
escape from Nature's inertial past. We call upon them
to show us that we have not known, or do not know
correctly, what that is. We tell them that the past cannot be changed; they ask us if we really know what the
past was and if we really think it could not have been

different. So we are in agony again—agony in knowledge, in morals, in religion—because of a tense that hints at more than the perfect.

I leave playing with the future perfect to the reader. Tom will have run. Yet I may suggest that here we have the pluperfect projected, the future outlined as if it were already perfected, but with its perfection possibly avoidable; for Tom can't complete his history before it is completed, and since it is not yet completed he may escape it. Each of us is more or less troubled by the thought of his completed future. Some of us resort to fortune tellers in order to be told about it, in order to prepare for it, in order to change it if we don't like it. This wanting to know one's fate or fortune in advance in order to know what to do about it is a little amusing and very tragic. The old Greeks wrote their greatest dramas about it, to show men caught in the tangle of their fate because knowing it in advance they tried to avoid it. Provision for or against what will be pluperfect—the future perfect—is not wisely made that way. All prediction is of that which will be pluperfect, and all purposeful action is guidance by the pluperfect projected.

One could go on at great length, letting verbs perform as great, possibly the best, expounders of time. I have commented on their tenses, but in doing so have been forced to use their moods and voices. There are the mays, mights, cans, coulds, woulds, shoulds, oughts, let there be's, participles, and the infinitive. The infinitive is worth many pages. Its effectiveness is in isolating actions and performances, in marking them out for consideration by themselves as if they were active ingredients in compounds, infused, as it were, into inert substances to make them move or live or perceive or think, and so turning what a thing or a man does into a force that makes him do it. We are carried into a realm of forces, powers, energies, of many sorts, and soon we begin trying to correlate them or reduce the many to one. And here we are introduced into one of the great enterprises of learning, which has attracted explorers of Nature for ages. We want to command the infinitive. And the thing that impresses one more and more as the search for that command is followed through history is that the road leads straight to mathematics, or, better, it leads more and more to the exclusion from consideration of what cannot be or is not mathematically expressible. The realm of the infinitive impresses us as the realm wherein truth can at last be attained, the realm of what it is *to be*—and that in present, past, and future, and in perfect, pluperfect, and future perfect, in actuality, in necessity, in possibility, and in probability. Something like a pair of scales, a balance, an equation is approached. If there is a little of Keats in all of us, there is also much of Pythagoras.

All we need to know—is it that Beauty is Truth and Truth, Beauty or that the tale is of Numbers? The infinitive in its participial form is in all of us—living, dying, loving, hating, hoping, fearing, laughing, crying, blessing, cursing, praising, praying, walking, breathing, thinking, moving, being; but, as both Aristotle and Hegel insisted, just being is a pretty poor thing to be, poorer and poorer the further we move away from living, dying, thinking. Nature's tale of being, reckoned in terms of an hour ago and after one hour more, may drive us to mathematics and give us power to control and predict the course of events, but it does not give us Nature. Yet it does make time impressive. It does arouse in us the sense of infinity and eternity. It shows that our thinking is time-bound by Nature, along with being space-bound.

Verbs give language its vital, dynamic, energetic character and make it a reproduction—one might say an imitation—of Nature's time character. Nouns we look upon as names for substantive things, things that we ought to be able to take in the hand, put in a box or a bottle, store in a warehouse, a container, a retort, weigh in a pair of scales, do something to or with, and all this even when the nouns are names for actions and events. We find that a substance like rubber stretches, call the substance elastic, and find ourselves talking about elasticity as if it were a substance and could itself be stretched. We talk about heat as if it, too, were a substance that made things hot. The history of knowledge is full of performances of this kind. The performance is easily rendered into a logic of language in which "is" is the only permissible verb, and then hardly a verb at all. "John strikes James"—there is life and action. "John is a striker of James"—there is death and nothing doing. Such logic has its uses, but it is clearly not an index either of time or of eternity, even if it has the appearance of being the latter. It is an invitation to be as algebraic as possible and thereby discipline the conjunction of variables. But this disciplined language has to be translated back into the living language of time to amount to anything more than just the discipline it is. That living language is necessary if the dead language is to be intelligible. So when one writes a logic—a logic of any sort—one has to fall back on the living language in order to make the logic understandable. So, too, when one writes about time one is caught inevitably in a vibrant network of the tenses, moods, and voices of the verb. In my own writing here I have tried to use words that conceal temporal force, and I have, of course, not succeeded. It is that fact that impresses me. Is time a noun? What is it a name for? When I try to answer, verbs have me by the throat and I need their tenses, their moods, their voices, their imperfect-perfect vibration, their transitive and intransitive character. My speech is a life in words, a kind of metabolism, as if I fed on Nature expansed before my eyes to find that vision transmuted into historical speech. "Once upon a time" is the beginning of every tale, even the tale of time.

The Clock

With the bracketing of Nature's events patently observed in the visible world and vibrantly expressed in the language of verbs, we can speak of time as quantitative without meaning that time itself is something of which portions may be consumed, used, or wasted, or that it is itself a duration of which fractional durations are longer or shorter. An hour is, not an hour of time, but an hour by the clock, and that hour is an event, the perfected revolution of the minute hand around the dial. Nothing has been used up except something of the clock's machinery and nothing has endured except that eventful revolution and what is bracketed during it. But we have a selected duration which may serve as the measure of other durations; we can neglect the specific character of all durations—smoke, pigeons, cloud, window frame, and minute hand—and pay attention to duration only; we have the time that answers the question: How long? In no other sense does a clock keep or measure time. In no other sense is time taken as a period in which something or other is done.

Yet the advance from events to clock has brought with it remarkable advances in human knowledge. From-hour-to-hour becomes a standard bracketing of events and the measure of the length of every tale that is told in Nature. Time-how-long is thus the tale of time as a reckoning, but not as a story. The story is for the time being forgotten. In other words, it may be as one pleases—natural, like the history of animals or stars, or quite fictitious, like tales made up to entertain or to instruct. By losing life and excitement the stories reveal a quantitative unity of time-how-long residing in them. We are in the world of the clock, wherein we think of the clock, not as an ingenious piece of machinery which is wound up and runs down, but as a dispenser of t or of eternity, to those who look at it to see what time it is and to events generally that they may have their measured duration. Time-how-long is, however, a question. Clocks are among the answerers. Without an answerer, however, time-how-long is a meaningless ex-pression. Then there is nothing to be measured; noth-ing ripens or rots. There is no ticking. There is no time at all. The advantage gained by forgetting the clock is not the advantage of finding a time when nothing com-parable with a clock existed. There *was* no time before time *is* as found in the present world from hour to hour. Forgetting the clock and the specific character of events is a provisional act on our part. We must remember the clock and events again to get back to Nature and to keep our provisional flight to measured time true to what it is a provision for. We do not fly into an eternity alone with itself.

It is the clock that defines one of the great problems of time. Nature's scheme of events is not itself a problem. We are vitally familiar with it—actually behold it, as I have indicated—as her own character which we study and use. For both study and use we need the clock, and that need is ours only in the sense that we find it needed. One might say that it is born of a necessity in the scheme of things, just as are our hunger and our thirst. And as a problem of hunger and thirst is that of getting competent food and drink, so a problem of time is that of getting a competent clock. In neither case are we left solely to our wits, for Nature supplies without our asking food and drink and measured time. For the latter it ought to be sufficient simply to name the sun, the moon, and the stars and the seasons. It is trite to say that they were the first keepers and measurers of time of all mankind. They are Nature's clocks, and they set the problem of being transformed into a dial in the poke, into the many kinds of chronometers men have invented in the hope of having at last a standard time to which all natural clocks conform and which is kept by a device one can carry in the pocket or set up in a laboratory and so know when one is on time, when in season and when not, or how long it takes to do this or that or to go from here to there. This measured time belongs to Nature; she does not belong to it. It is a way in which her events are fitted together.

This natural way of fitting is not, I repeat, itself a problem. The problem is the discovery of the best clock. Nature's clocks are synchronized without any industry of our own, but the choice from among them of the best clock has required ages of industry and is not yet wholly satisfactory. The history of that industry is exciting reading. Although it is available in any good library, I find a pretty general—I might say natural—belief today that Touchstone took something like a Waltham watch out of his pocket. The error is not very serious, except for some loss of magnificent poetry and imagination which many of our common words no longer suggest. What is a "watch"? Try the verb instead of the noun. What is a "clock"? Hear the chimes ring instead of looking at a device on the wall. What is an "hour"? If one will forget "sixty-minutes," a long and fascinating journey is in prospect back to hours lived and not ticked out—from sixty minutes back to *my hour*. With these hints of history, let the problem of the clock be this—to be in season though the seasons change; to have sixty minutes instead of the longer and shorter hours. For Nature's seasons, her days and nights, her hours, her moons, her years, although they synchronize, are longer and shorter as events. The clock would standardize them.

In other words, we invent instruments to measure the synchronizing of events. So there are clocks. Such as we now have, have thousands of inventive years behind them, and the familiar watch we carry about is a very recent arrival.[2] The best of clocks have to be checked every day in order to keep the time that Nature keeps. Although the method of arriving at the checking has involved very complicated calculations, the operation of checking has been reduced to a very simple performance. The result is announced to the world every day. The radio now sends it abroad in the twinkling of an eye. Yet the industry of keeping time goes on painstakingly from day to day in order that clocks may be set to the proper time. On the keepers of time our lives have become dependent.

But do they keep it? Many of the scientists to whom we look for answer are now telling us "it all depends." The answer is perplexing. Many of us wish they would answer by either yes or no. The reason why they hesitate is the important matter, and that reason, as I

[2] The earliest known sundial, believed to have been made about 1500 B.C., is of Egyptian origin. Fifth-century Greece had also the water clock. Possibly Gerbert, a monk and later Pope Sylvester II, toward the end of the tenth century invented the weight clock, but it is not until the close of the thirteenth century that we find authentic information about such timepieces. Portable clocks or watches, powered by a spring, were developed about 1500, and in the eighteenth century the essential mechanism of the modern watch was achieved.

understand it, is that quantitative time, as anything to
be discriminated from longer and shorter events or
Nature's own synchronizing of events, requires that the
accuracy and locality of a clock cannot be independently determined. I confess that the way the reason is
often stated and illustrated confuses me. Clocks seem to
behave outrageously and incredibly and disappear altogether in a complexity of vectors. I have nothing to
look at and see what time it is. "At the same time"
seems to lose every shred of intelligible meaning. The
difficulty lies, as I see it, in overlooking the difference
between the synchronizing of Nature's events and the
determining by a clock *a* time at which they are synchronized. I look at my clock, and it tells me that the
time now is ten o'clock. At that time by my clock Nature's events are synchronized whether my clock is correct or not. They are, for that matter, synchronized
while the pigeons fly. It makes perfectly good sense to
say that all Nature's events in their actual occurring
occur at the same time. But that does not mean that
they are occurring at a universal ten o'clock, so to
speak, which some particular clock declares. There is
no such clock, because no such clock can be constructed to keep time irrespective of the local conditions governing its construction, just as the pigeons
cannot fly independent of the locality in which they do
fly. In other words, timekeeping by a clock is a natural

event synchronizing with all other concurring natural events and is never free from the incidence of its own concurring. How could it be? Or again, simultaneity is not determined by a clock, because the clock itself is involved in what simultaneity is.

I do not know what those who tell us fairytales about the way clocks do or may behave when transported will say to all this, but it is the sense I find in the mythology. And it strikes me as good sense, for it warns us that there is no such thing as *time kept* independent of the optical structure of Nature. In that sense there is the insistence that in thinking of Nature it is an error to think of space and time independently. One must think of them together as space-time. And that is precisely what we ordinarily do and what we actually observe. One has only to look out of the window and see that the bracketing of events is a bracketing of their whiling *when* they are *whiled*. A whiling device like the clock is a refined epitome of it all. But the device needs constant regulation and checking. And the best means found of doing this is to enlarge the competence of mathematics, for in that science we learn how to deal with increasing competence with equations of variables. It is a science that makes increasingly clear what integration is, and Nature is found responsive to that increasing clarity. The response is in the perfectly obvious and in the less so, for we are mathematicians

when we walk four miles in one hour, just as we are
when we measure the velocity of light. But it is pitiful
if the mathematician in us makes us forget the walk or
the lighted glory of Nature. Although invented by us,
the clock is a natural object. It belongs to heaven and
earth, the sea, and all that in them is. It is not a privileged sovereign doling out the seconds to perishing
events to let them live for a brief span of eternity. It is a
humble and competent servant who answers the question: How long was the tale and how long is it likely to
be? But only perfected tales have their measured time.
There is no evidence that Nature's tale is ended. Her
tense is still imperfect, although her tale as told today
contains many a perfect and pluperfect. Her story is
still haunted by that more-than-perfect tense.

The Calendar

Since every tale begins with "once upon a time," a
determination of "time when" is desirable. It is essential to the writing of history. Calendars are invented to
meet this need. They are not wholly artificial, for a
pattern to follow is supplied by Nature, yet they are
arbitrary because Nature does not supply only one
crucial event, so privileged that all her events are
thereby divided into before and after; she supplies
many. Any one of them would serve the purpose, pro-
vided it were generally accepted and the consequent

calendar afforded a clearing house for all the calendars men have been pleased to invent. I am writing now in the 72nd year of my life, in the 163d year of our independence, and in A.D. 1938. But in which of Nature's years am I writing? That question alone is sufficient evidence that Nature herself has no calendar. It may also suggest how the vast amount of labor of chronologists and historians has combined with the comings and goings of earth's peoples to establish a calendar which can be generally used. Touchstone's wisdom may again be recalled. It is a little unfortunate, perhaps, that he hit upon ten o'clock as his crucial point in the calendar of his tale. Heaven's fortune had not sent him twelve. With twelve the sun would have appeared dividing the day into the hours before and the hours after, and the natural pattern of the calendar might have been a little more clearly in evidence. From noon to noon, inclosing the sun's completed circle of the day, the day is divided into its halves. There, one may say, is a pattern for the perfect calendar, but one is forced immediately to add that it is good for a day only. The day will not serve the purpose of a crucial point, even if it is true enough to affirm that all its yesterdays were before it and that all its tomorrows will be after. This sort of stretching backward and forward completes no circle. The year will not do, for the like reason, although it is naturally divided by the solstices. The principle involved in these illustrations can be generalized. Any cycle can afford the pattern of a calendar, but the generalization of that fact affords no calendar at all. The cycle may be Nature's favorite pattern in all her historical processes. History may be, as is sometimes said, only a repetition of itself, but the repetitions would follow the examples cited, yielding no privileged repetition which of itself divided all the others into before and after.

The problem of the calendar is, therefore, a practical one. The requirements for its solution are, first, the selection of a crucial event and, secondly, the dating of other events before and after according to stated periods. Because the crucial event cannot be the present world, it is of necessity some past event quite arbitrarily selected, but memorable to those who select it. The selecting, when made, must itself be a present event. Strictly speaking, it has no date in its own calendar although it may have one in another. The illustration given above of what might be called my personal calendar makes it unnecessary to give further examples. One calendar can be included in another, but no one calendar can include all others. The crucial event is, consequently, an appearance both of a beginning and an end, the beginning of all that follows after and the end of all that came before. So we speak of the continuity of history, and, since there are many histories and many calendars, we sum them all up in the continuity of time. The continuity is falsified when represented by the image of a line or a one-dimensional continuum extended in one direction. Past and future are not localities, the one waiting to receive immigrants from the other. Bergson has sufficiently exposed the confusion arising from any such geometrizing of time. A better image is suggested by a child piling blocks on top of one another—a new block on an old one, but never an old one first. The first block is not old until the second is laid down and its age is its conservation in the building process. As an event its laying down has ceased to be, and as just that event it will never return; but that vanished event has left the block as a foundation for the others to come and has given it its connection with the mounting series. The pile built, but not in the building, affords an opportunity for a calendar. The illustration is, of course, an artifice to aid in clarifying time processes in Nature. An acorn falls to the ground, and the event leaves the acorn subject to the play of its surroundings upon it, conserving it and also altering it, making of it an oak. Then the life history of a tree has been accomplished and can be written calendarwise, with the acorn as the beginning of the oak.

The dates in a calendar are not events, but periods of the measured time of the clock. In other words, the

successive arrangement of "times when" is an arrangement which employs "times how long"—so many
seconds, minutes, hours, days, months, years, centuries. I emphasize this obvious construction of a
calendar—a crucial point which is an event, but not a
date, and all other points dates, but not events—because when it is overlooked the illusion is apt to arise
that the calendar expresses what Nature's time is like
much better than the tenses of the verb. In other words,
preoccupation with the calendar fosters the habit of
thinking of time as an original sequence of periods divisible in terms of the divisions of a clock. An originally
empty time becomes then strangely filled with concurrent events. Freedom from the control of such a
wholly unintelligible conception is essential to any
understanding of historical processes. These processes
neither fill nor consume time. They are adequate evidence that a "beginning of Nature" is a wholly meaningless expression. They are also evidence that there is
no date in any calendar which is so privileged that Nature is more really what she is at that date than at any
other. She is just as much today what she is as she has
ever been. The beginning of things is always "once
upon a time," and that means where the historian begins; he always ends in a present world which is the
only intelligible division of time. It is appropriate to
speak of the crucial event in a calendar as a point in

time, if one does not forget that it is an event, not a date, and if one recognizes the futility of trying to find the present by dividing the calendar.

I do not know whether Tyndall's once famous address before the British Association for the Advancement of Science in 1874 is much read today. It was a great document when I began the study of philosophy, and the passage most frequently quoted from it still vibrates in my memory.

Abandoning all disguise, the confession that I feel bound to make before you is that I prolong the vision backward across the boundary of the experimental evidence, and discern in that matter, which we in our ignorance, and notwithstanding our professed reverence for its Creator, have hitherto covered with opprobrium, the promise and potency of every form and quality of life.

This is more than an acknowledgment of matter as weighed in a balance or computed in terms of resistance to acceleration. It is also an acknowledgment of promise and potency. But what are they? They, not matter, are what the backward vision prolongs. Matter weighed or computed is not the exhibition of them. They are read into matter, and read backward into it and not forward from it. Matter may be weighed or computed today without any hint of any form or quality of life. One may confidently affirm that what it is today is precisely what it has always been and will be, and, consequently, that it has no privilege in a calendar, that it fixes no date when power and potency began to be exercised. They are ever in exercise, but only in the present tense, never in the past or future. The sun does not shine or exhibit its power and potency yesterday or tomorrow. There is no privileged date for what Nature originally is. As in the illustration of the child building with blocks, the top block affords the opportunity to "prolong the vision backward," so that the whole building now has the character of a forward march of time from the first block to the last—the first block becomes the origin of the pile, the promise and potency of its form and quality. That is the way Nature works with her time. We are daily familiar with it, since we daily live with it and are enmeshed in her joint conservation and alteration ourselves. We are taught by Nature that all her events in their occurring are jointly conservative and alterative, jointly retrospective and prospective, and our memory and imagination are the consequence. Historical inquiry is also a consequence. By the aid of what is conserved in the present world we prolong the backward vision calendarwise without, however, arriving either at a first or a crucial date which has a privilege. The reason is that the crucial date is now. We prolong the backward vision only to see that Nature *was* always doing the sort of thing she *is* doing now—conserving and altering. Her age is not measured by a calculation of birthdays. Her duration is not a matter of the passing years, for those years are among her performances. We say that her duration is infinite, but we need to remember that its infinity is intensive, not like that of a supposed pigeon's flight, which never begins and never ends, but like that of the divisibility of a line, however short. Spatial images of time can be innocent enough if Nature's eventfulness, with its effect of conserving and altering, is not forgotten. They can assist the recognition that time and space should not be divorced in thought, since they are not divorced in Nature. Then, prolonging the vision backward, time may be allowed for historical purposes to march forward with the years dated in any calendar one likes. The present is left without a date. Origins of the present have found their dates among the vanished events of the past, and products of the present will find theirs in the calendar's projected years.

Matter

The preceding sections have, I hope, indicated how natural it is to extract from Nature's eventful character a time-scheme, as if it were the prescribed framework of activity. But if time is emptied of events, there is nothing left to do but conjugate verbs, measure seconds, and calculate years. The result may be a straining of vision to see eternity at a glance with Nature held in its embrace and expansed as a vast stage on which the ordered drama of history is played out to fit the jointure of space and time. The stage is attractive imagery. None of us escapes it wholly, for the visible world is much like a play beheld. We witness the performances that there go on, and seek favorable seats from which to watch them. On the stage the actors appear and disappear, have their entrances and their exits, speak their pieces, and when off-stage have either finished their parts or are waiting to appear again before the curtain is finally rung down. The career of anything, no matter what, is like a dramatic episode set in embracing scenery, which an audience might behold could they find admission to the theater of time. Yet through it all runs a stubborn persistence which is not the plot, which is not the story told, which is not a tale of crime and punishment. The story which, first and last, claims our surpassing interest is the history of Nature, her whence and whither. Yet when we try to write it, we are haunted by a persistence to which whence and whither cannot be assigned. To this stubborn persistence we give the name "matter."

Matter has its performances, but they are not dramatic unless clothed with pomp and circumstance. For matter is ageless, never young or old. Its performances are transformances, and in its own terms, conceivably repeatable at any time if we could find the key to its transformations. Moved as Tyndall was by history, pro-

longing the backward vision, reflecting on stars, the
seasons, minerals, plants, animals, men, birth and
death, cities and wars, the pursuit of happiness, art,
poetry, religion, science, we may confess a kind of reverence for matter and discern in it the promise and potency of every form and quality of life. History seems to
force that reverence on a candid mind. The substance
of what is must be fruitful. That which is something
behind or underneath, supporting and maintaining the
passing show in its historical continuity, must have resources as unlimited as the spectacle beheld, making us
mount ever higher—almost to God, but not quite.

And the permanence of matter can escape historical
considerations by arresting time. Then matter becomes
the material world, the physical world, an external
world set over against ourselves, leaving us in an
equivocal status very difficult to define or clarify. Our
familiar status, which I have called our natural one,
our status as recognized companions with heaven and
earth and sea, is clear enough and does not cry for
justification by appeal to any agency which can be
styled external to that companionship. We may style
that companionship our given status, but are forced to
admit that we cannot identify a giver other than itself.
We try in vain to set up within it a contrast between
giver and receiver in forms other than the terms of give
and take of daily life, as one takes the pills and precepts

from one's doctor and along with them the consequences that follow. Such gifts are intelligible as gifts,
but who writes the prescriptions and what apothecary
fills them for Nature? The external, the physical world?
Are we not then using only alternative words for
matter? Substance, inertia, resistance, solidity, the
dead weight of the hard-to-move, the horror of sheer
emptiness, always the something that is there filling the
present world with its presence during every period of
the calendar and at every second that the clock ticks,
something as unescapable as space and time themselves, lasting and keeping its own constitution while
events come and go telling the tales of history—that is
what we usually name "matter." Because in its own
constitution it is so different from the visible world
and because it is indestructible, we try to picture it as
an externality—pure, extended, self-sufficient, and
self-contained, while history with all its vibrant life appears to be a curious and wholly unaccountable supplement. From life to death becomes "from dust to dust,"
but there would be "from dust to dust" even if there
were not "from life to death." So we incline to think
of matter as the perpetual off-stage of all that is dramatic, whether that be present, past, or future, whether
it be the march of the heavenly host or the cities and
wars of men, or Nature expansed unto the eyes of all.
From it and to it are all entrances and exits, while it

itself remains, unaltered in character and with promise and potency read into it in order that Nature may appear with dramatic effect.

One may vary the simile a little and say that Nature appears now as matter clothed and it is our cognitive necessity to strip that clothing off in order to find the real skeletal structure it conceals. Something like theoretical physics in the agelong search for the constitution of matter becomes a last philosophy, a "metaphysics" in the literal meaning of the word, a dogmatic ontology, needing revision from time to time, teachable rather than livable, like the geometry of Euclid. The situation in which we now find ourselves is perplexing. There seems to be no sound reason why we should not assign to theoretical physics the status of knowledge of Nature; but if we assign to it the status of knowledge of an independent external world, that status is not only repugnant to our vital experience from hour to hour and to the obvious world which we observe, but it also robs "externality" of intelligible meaning. There is no difficulty with externality when we consider Nature as identified in this essay, beyond the difficulty of finding a reason why Nature should be at all. The difference between inside and outside a house or inside and outside our bodies is intelligible, but inside and outside Nature is not. That statement is not a willful expression of personal opinion. "Matter" and "the unknowable" have been linked together for ages, and trying to *see* "matter" by looking through a microscope is trying to see matter with the human eye. Refining the aids to vision leaves vision still in control of whatever is seen.

The search for matter began long ago and was prompted by the same sort of obvious circumstances which prompt it today. Nature's materials are abundant, and many nouns are required to name them. A house of stone is not a house of wood. One does not need illustrations of a different kind to bring to recognition what is basically meant by "stuff," "material," "substance"; and "matter" as a name for any sort of stuff is but a synonym. So far, we may have very little knowledge of matter, but clearly we have no difficulty in identifying it. Knowledge begins by discovering such simple truths as that a stone house is more durable than a wooden one. It is spurred on and begins to accelerate by discovering other simple truths: chiefly that materials change. Nature's materials are abundant, but their changes readily suggest a reduction of their multitude. The wooden house burns down, leaving in its stead a heap of ashes. They are the ashes of what once was wood, but are now wood no longer. Other materials besides wood can also be reduced to ashes. Seeds are materials which may be grasped by the hand and sown broadcast over a field, resulting in a harvest of seeds multiplying many times the number sown, while in between there has been the display of first the blade, then the ear, and then the full corn. It is needless to multiply illustrations of what all of us are perfectly familiar with. The point is that they illustrate simply and intelligibly the initiative of the search for matter. Materials are reducible. They are transformable. Eventful Nature is also material, with the consequence that her space and time seem like emptinesses filled by something that persists in spite of changes and has a native constitution or structure of its own.

The search for that persistence has been marked by two apparently conflicting aims, which have been indicated in the illustrations by the words "reduction" and "transformation." How many materials are there in Nature? How is one material transformed into another? That the two aims apparently conflict is, perhaps, more instructive for an understanding of them than the answers given to the specific questions just asked. The questions are in a way independent and interdependent. If, for example, we knew how one material is transformed into another, the number of materials in Nature might be of no consequence. Each might be transformed into any other, whether the number was large or small. In this case no material would have the exclusive right to be called "matter." If, however, there are materials which cannot be transformed into others, the number becomes initially important in the effort to discover the method of transformation, and the untransformable materials would have first claim to the title of "matter." In stating the conflict in this way, I am not trying to exhaust the logical possibilities involved, but am indicating, rather, the motivations that have characterized the pursuit of matter from the beginning. The alternatives suggested have not been arbitary. They have arisen naturally in the pursuit.

It is clear, however, from the record of that pursuit that the search for a "first material" has been conspicuous. The multitude of materials suggested a ready classification of them into the solid, the liquid, the airy, and the burning, giving us the four "elements" or "natures" of antiquity—earth, water, air, and fire—which are not yet lost in current speech and still linger hidden in the terminology of science. I suspect that even today when the most erudite ask what is the nature of anything, they are haunted by the answer "of earth," "of water," "of air," or "of fire"—the solid, the flowing, the gaseous, the caloric. It is difficult to rid ourselves wholly of such suggestions; of some one of these natures or compound of them every material must be; they exclusively occupy space, and the current definition of Nature's matter in our dictionaries is "whatever occupies space" or the "substance of physical things." We should allow ourselves to be a little amused now and then that matter should be the matter of material things or the substance of what is substantial. But let the moment of amusement be a relaxation from a too serious slavery to words; and let space occupied be the presence in Nature of earth, water, air, and fire, for we were familiar with that before we went to the dictionary. But those four lend themselves to analysis.

One consequence is the definition of *a* material in analytic terms, or the restriction for analytic purposes of the precise use of the word to those materials which apparently admit of no further analysis. The number of such materials cannot be fixed in advance, for it depends on the experimental possibility of further analysis. But the analytic procedure involved forces the distinction between simple and compound materials. The simple are changeless in character although that character may take on different forms. Gold, for example, is always gold although under different circumstances it may be liquid or solid. Compound materials are made up of simple ones and may also exhibit differences under different circumstances. Such a view of Nature's material character was generally orthodox within the memory of living men. Any suggestion that the simple materials were themselves transformable was regarded as a heterodox return to the days of alchemy. That, however, is not very important. What is important is a revision in attitude toward what "matter" is. That potent word could still be a name for all simple materials, but it directed attention to what was called the "properties of matter," so that "matter" came to mean anything that had those properties. The "structure" or "constitution" of matter became more important than the irreducible character of first materials. This was both an intellectual liberation and a defeat. It was a liberation because it brought out clearly that Nature's material transformations were not clarified simply by performing experiments in analysis and synthesis. Or, it may be said, these experiments revealed the necessity of a consideration of structural and combining principles for a better understanding of what actually occurs in Nature. It was a defeat in that the words "matter" and "material" tended to diverge more and more in meaning. In other words, the qualitative differences between first materials, by which they were identified, became exhibitions of an underlying structure which supported them, and this structure *as a material* was past man's understanding. Matter became unknowable except in terms of its manifestations. Experimentally there were many materials; theoretically there was one matter, and attempts to make this one matter one of the recognized elementary materials left all thinking about matter in a confused state.

I hesitate to prolong this analysis of the career of a

word. And I dislike the word "materialism" because of its controversial suggestions. Let it be, however, a name for no more than an attempt to understand Nature's evident material character; then the history of materialism shows clearly enough that the attempt to understand material persistence in Nature leads to a transformation of materials into matter and leaves matter as *a* material in a highly equivocal status. Materials are readily identifiable as materials. We can, as is frequently done, speak of them figuratively as the building blocks of the universe. Matter, however, is not one of those blocks, for it is now what they all are, not as a convenience in nomenclature, but as the structure and inherent constitution which they all possess. But can matter be both the structure of all materials and also the structure of one material in particular which has thereby the privilege over all others of being *the* material of Nature?

That question has recurred many times in the history of materialism. It has been acute whenever the factor of structure has been under intensive critical examination. Then atomic theories which superficially appear clear and understandable are subjected to vigorous assault. Their simplicity becomes suspicious. No one, I think, would accept them were it not for the fact that their mathematical rendering appears to be so convincing. But that rendering is convincing only when we allow atoms as atoms to be all in the last analysis alike, not atoms of this and that, but atoms simply with no "of this or that" attached. One can now hardly refrain from asking what is the structure of *the* atom, the unit of matter? It is needless to point out that this is one of the exciting problems of present-day physics. It is apparently making us akin to the alchemists who, much less than a century ago, were so condemned. It is now almost orthodox to hold that the atom can be broken down and the secret of the transformability of materials discovered! Would we then discover *a* material which is matter?

Answering "no" to that question is not, I think, an expression of personal opinion or prejudice. It is, rather, the frank recognition that any transformation is a historical process, that the time factor is unescapable, and that all that can intelligibly be said to escape that factor is the principle of transformation itself. To believe that that principle is discoverable is natural, for the fact of transformation is evident enough in Nature. The changing seasons exhibit it; so do the history of the solar system, the history of the earth's crust, and all the metabolisms of living creatures. When we speak of Nature's "history," we are speaking of something totally different from any conceivable rearrangement within the limits of any conceivable original material. When we try to think of such a material and name it "matter," we are compelled as by an irresistible force to impute to that material promise and potency and let them on their own initiative do the work of transforming it not only into all forms and qualities of life but also into gold, silver, oxygen, and hydrogen. I cannot deny promise and potency, but I cannot admit, in the face of the evidence, that they are active factors in the production of Nature's varied scene. I do not drive a nail into a piece of wood with promise and potency, but with a very material hammer. I never transform materials without the use of other materials. A "first material" named "matter" is, for me, an utterly meaningless expression. Energetic words, words redolent of promise and potency, I cannot avoid, because Nature's processes are historical. They are continuously making the present world different from what it was, but are doing it through material agencies. Work is actually done; it is done by material things; it is productive work; it takes time; when it is done, but not before, its history can be written, the factors coöperating in the result can be discriminated; and the only intelligible explanation of the process is the discovery of the way they have coöperated in the production of the result. Those factors were the promise and potency of the result only because it shows that they are. That which persists throughout the historical process is not some original material which never changes in character, always remaining just what it is and nothing else, but it is, if I may use an expression less current than it used to be, "the laws of Nature." It is our part of our cognitive business to discover the laws to which the transformation of materials conforms. Our progress in doing so seems to depend on dealing with as elementary materials as possible. It seems likely that in the discovery of their structure the "secret" is approached. It looks, however, like going out of bounds to impute to that structure promise and potency as if it were a material. Let "matter" be a name for the structure, or let it be a name for promise and potency, the baptism is not the sanctification of a material or of "the substance of physical things."

In dealing with matter as I have, the aim has been to emphasize the importance of a historical approach to it. I do not mean especially an approach through the history of materialism itself, although that is highly instructive. It can reveal how the search for matter has varied and shifted as efforts have been made to make that search more and more understandable and to make it meet successfully the open declarations of Nature. These are basically important. They declare that a dynamic and productive world of materials is clearly identifiable. And these materials are clarified for our understanding of their coöperative working only by the aid of the results attained by that coöperation. Thereby a historical process is defined. A present requiring a prolongation backward into the past and also a present continuation in eventful character is precisely what a historical process is and also what material Nature is. The view that "matter" is a name for some hidden, inherently changeless, everlastingly permanent, and only apparently alterable material or substance or cause of the present visible world is a view I would avoid—not because I dislike it, but because I find it meaningless. Like anybody else, I can say in words that "matter" is a name for the unknown cause of Nature and our association with her which we name "our experience," but then I know not what I mean. When, however, I let "matter" be a name for material Nature whose materials, like hydrogen and a roast of beef, are identifiable, or let it be a name for the structural principles involved in laws of transformation, I find the search for matter understandable. Materials and metabolisms impress me as evident facts which are never altered by speculative excursions into the unknowable. In short, although our ignorance of Nature is vast, material Nature is not unknowable; the "Unknowable" is, in effect, only a name for the desire to create Nature out of nothing in order to discover how she was created.

For an understanding of Nature's material character, then, the distinction between what is historical and what not is of basic importance. Change is obviously not changelessness. Nature's material structure does not change, but that structure is not the structure of a privileged material as over against all others. What Nature once was, is, therefore, no more what Nature really is than what she presently is. In this way only is intelligibility found in her time-scheme. We discover what that scheme is, but not why it should be. Mental sanity requires that these two questions be kept distinct. I do not and would not overlook the latter of them. It is, perhaps, the ultimate question which claims our interest as human beings vitally involved in the pursuit of happiness. To that pursuit Nature seems to be wholly indifferent, as if she knows not what it means and yet bears children whose lot in life is laughter and tears. That paradox makes us what we are, and it is her paradox, forced upon us by her events and forcing upon us the obligation to distinguish between what we know and what we aspire to be. Let us, prolonging the vision backward, play with the past like an evolutionist or, going into our laboratories, break up the atom to discover the original source of energy, banishing from Nature every form and quality of life; then words like "promise" and "potency" fall from our lips, if heaven and earth, the sea, and all that in them is, are ever to be what they are. Matter does not materialistically dress itself up without presenting a story to be told—the tale of time.

Teleology

In contemplating any history, whether of the animate or the inanimate, none of us escapes the sense of issues and rarely the sense of drama. Nature stirs in us the suspicion of plot or design, of purposes first conceived and then executed. Many historians are fond of telling us that what we now name "science" had its origin in a primitive dramatic rendering of Nature in terms of willful forces which conspired or contended for the control of natural events, and whose favor man courted. In this I think they are mistaken, for it is clearly written in history that science grew out of the use of tools and the practical needs of counting, calculating, and measuring. The progressive reliance for effective action more on the machinery of Nature, her tools and instruments, than on prayers and sacrifices, making of these latter a last resort when all else fails, grew out of a development of those tools and instruments, not out of a reduction of religion to knowledge. The last resort has always been and still is to the maker or makers of heaven and earth. Primitive man and modern man are alike in being at bottom animistic, blessing and cursing as a last resort, thanking and not thanking, hoping and fearing. Both insure themselves against "acts of God," and both by the payment of some premium. It is not wise to be supercilious in the writing of history. If the eyebrows are to be lifted, let it be done with irony. The value and significance of science and knowledge lie, as they have always lain, in its benefits, not in a contrast with the sense of drama or the bowed head. Nature is teleological in fact. Her time-scheme declares it, and our knowledge is dependent on it.

There is, however, a radical difference between recognizing teleology and trying to account for it. "Nature does nothing in vain" is a sound enough maxim to follow if we mean thereby that her ends justify and clarify her means. Indeed one cannot help following it. Virgil's farmer, happy in having found the causes of things, was happy in the discovery of definite factors combining in the production of specific events which declared the competence of those factors to produce them. It is always what happens that leads to the discovery of what has happened. Were no results attained in Nature, were there no composition of forces determining one direction rather than another, it is difficult to see how we could have any interest in causes or in the conservation of the past in some manner in the effected and effecting present. The search for origins always runs back from specific products which define the lines which the search must follow to be successful. The questions are always: What did produce this specific product? What can produce it? What product may be expected or will eventuate when specific factors are artificially combined? Teleology in this sense is both unescapable and the source of intelligibility in historical processes. Indeed, it may be maintained that it affords the definition of what intelligibility is—the discovery of an order or orders in Nature which are not only followed but which can also be expressed in formulas that in their turn can guide practice. Teleology and intelligibility go hand in hand. The laws of Nature are the laws which production illustrates. They make the production understandable.

It should be clear, then, that teleology and mechanism are correlative rather than opposed. They are contrasted in that without the teleology the mechanism would not be discovered and that the mechanism alone does not reveal what the teleology is. But we are under no obligation whatever to assign to either a rival's privilege. It may sound extravagant to affirm that nothing happens in Nature without machinery. The evidence clearly points that way, unless one hates to be called a machine because of associating that word with factory-made products exclusively or with the elementary lessons one learned in mechanics about levers, pulleys, screws, and inclined planes. The science of mechanics began with the study of those simple tools, but it has vastly increased its scope, guided by the prolific

suggestions of that humble word "tool," so that the
hand is a tool for grasping and the eye for seeing. This
expansion of the tool makes anything that runs a
machine when in order; when out of order, it ceases to
be that particular machine. Thus nothing in Nature
that runs escapes being a machine except in the opinion of those who think that the fructifying use of that
word debases the things to which it is applied. If Nature can rejoice, I must believe that she rejoices more
over the machine which makes an automobile than
over the automobile made. In order to be impressed by
her attitude one need not, however, believe that Nature rejoices. One needs only to consider how levers,
pulleys, screws, inclined planes, gases, liquids, solids,
and the like are found in Nature so variously unified in
operation and working so effectively in the productive
enterprise that, without the aid of anything like a
factory managed by a human corporation with a board
of directors, there are the stars, the seasons, the riot of
vegetation, the swarm of animals—mechanism and
teleology supplementary and complementary.

I have been reciting the obvious in the interest of intellectual clarity, to indicate that Nature puts us under
no obligation, when addressing her, to choose between
the language of teleology and that of mechanism in
order to be either polite or sane. There are enough
wars in the world without inviting mechanists and

teleologists to engage in one, recruiting innocent students for the battle. There are, however, obligations which such wars suggest. Words should be used with discrimination and not allowed to provoke misunderstanding. "Teleology" is at least relatively harmless. It calls attention to such facts as that origins cannot be discovered or histories portrayed unless there are specific and identifiable products or ends. An egg does not become a chick unless it is a chicken's egg; one does not go halfway home unless there is a home to go to. Such simple examples identify Nature's teleology clearly enough. But "final cause" and "purpose" point to a multitude of controversial essays. No purpose is thwarted when a chicken's egg becomes a breakfast or when one goes halfway home without intending to do so. For intelligent understanding of any history or any process involving time, the end justifies the means, but it clearly does not produce them. Only in works of art is there the semblance of an end controlling the selection of means for its production. Such works are natural in the sense that we as natural beings produce them in consequence of our own natural organization. We discover Nature's teleology and then use it, but it is fundamental for what we are and what use we make of it.

I refer again to Molyneux's exclamation: "He that made the eye shall see!" If that maker could see with-

out eyes, it was clearly superfluous labor to make them.
When we speak of a desire to see, we are imagining
ourselves blind and having been told that there is a
visible world which might be seen if we had the appropriate organ; but how foolish it would be for a sightless creature in its ignorance to equip itself with that
organ if there were nothing to be seen after working
that miracle. Let Nature herself be wholly miraculous.
One may be driven to that at last. Once explained as a
miracle, the discovery and use of natural teleology remains precisely what it is, irrespective of that explanation. Knowledge has in no respect been changed. We
have still to discover and write the natural history of
the eye and to study optics and physiology if we want
to learn about eyes, correct their deformities, aid our
failing vision, and invent optical instruments to enlarge and extend it. In doing all this _we_ may be artists,
but we are doing no more than employing Nature's
teleology and illustrating it in our own way, just as a
plant or an atom does in its. An artist for the whole of
Nature, without one jot or tittle left out—we may find
ourselves compelled at last to believe in that with all
our heart and soul and mind and strength; but that
artist, we must admit, has made the whole of Nature
precisely what it is. If we ask why he did so, there is
but one conceivable answer in Nature's terms—that is,
that teleology might be exemplified in fact and that it

should be acknowledged and lived, with all its far-reaching consequences, by every creature. That there are creatures in Nature who make that answer is, perhaps, the most significant illustration of her teleology. Teleology does not explain why there is teleology, but it does explain the human belief that it has a significance not expressed in its existence. It does explain the religious attitude.

It explains also why our knowledge waits on eventualities, both in its retrospective and in its prospective character: it is from first to last historical, not the result of a collision between "thought" and "things," "mind" and "matter." It is a collision only in the sense that a fish swimming in a pond is, an animal doing what its natural constitution permits in its natural element. We persistently use such words as "mind," "consciousness," "soul," "power," "energy" to indicate the cause or reason why behavior in Nature is what it is; but we have to admit that such words identify nothing observable in the way we observe the actual occurrence of events. Of course we recognize—are conscious, if one will—that we observe, suffer, act, and think, and that we actually change the course of events, being in this matter true causes. I cannot understand either skeptics who doubt it or ardent affirmers of it who think that thereby they are explaining why we do what we do. A living man may dig his own grave, but a dead one does not; but I do not see how invoking life or consciousness explains the difference or adds to the situation anything which clarifies it, even if the invocation does identify the difference between life and death or between body and soul. Agents acting characteristically in historical processes we do identify, and also the consequences of their so acting. That is precisely what we mean by "cause" and "effect." A builder does build. A spider does spin. A radish seed does grow. Oxygen does rust iron. A man does see the world about him with himself in it. Such examples clearly indicate the facts with which we deal, declare our knowledge to be historical, and explain our use of potent words.

In saying so, I do not mean that such words are merely nominal, as if they indicated something having being in name only. If they did, why buy radish seeds for planting or send a child to school? Power and potency are real enough. They are the source of all values. They are, however, not detachable from their possessors in a manner which allows us to bottle them up by themselves and put them in storage. One cannot put a mind into a refrigerator and thereby cool off a heated brain. Nor can one put a mind into a head and thereby transform a brain into a message-receiving station. Nature clearly does not work in such ways, nor do we. She may be a material lady, but she paints and powders and is astonishingly whimsical. That is why she is interesting and courted. Personification of her, with a little poetry added and comedy and tragedy allowed, is often a better introduction to what she is than all our mathematics and our discoveries of her mechanism. Without her promises and potencies she is not worth looking at. Nor is she an object of knowledge in any other sense than that it is her teleology we try to understand. Her time-scheme is cognitively exciting. From it arises the incentive to learn lessons in her school, entering it at birth to be nourished and taught from hour to hour while our tale is reckoned and written into her history. Happy is he who knows the causes of things, because with that knowledge retrospect and prospect jointly become the guides to such happiness as is attainable.

Here I must recall the tenses of the verb, recall the fact that every event in its occurring is a present event. Past events are historically but not causally related to it. I do not mean that they have had no influence or no effect on the course of events or the march of time. The effect, however, *has been had*. It would be foolish to say that past events have wrought nothing. It would be equally foolish to say that they are working after they have ceased to work. The house I live in was built prior to my living in it. I complain about it and might change it more to my liking. But I can do nothing about its original building. I must repair or build again. I cannot change the past, nor can it change me; and that sort of truth prevailed when the house was built, when its building was a present building. Clocks and calendars help one little in expressing the relation between past and present. The tenses of the verb make the relation and the consequent sequence clear. What I work with or what any agent works with has been worked with before. That is the clear and inevitable rule, no matter what time it is by the clock or what date it is in the calendar. Nature grows older only in terms of her events. Her age is not an antiquity. Obviously one is older at the end of one's life than at the beginning. Increasing age is almost an alternative expression for teleology, for increasing age is the present undergoing transformation and laying, as it were, the foundation for the next step. It is like a man walking. He takes a first step and then a second. The first step does not cause the second to be second, but the second causes the first to be first. Had it no follower, there would be no reason for calling it first; nor would there be any reason for calling the second "second" if it did not push back, as it were, the first into the past. The discovery of causes is the discovery of agents which act in that fashion. A seed is a cause of its own growth in age because it acts characteristically in response to the characteristic action of other causal agents upon it.

Such, without exception, is the causality we find in Nature. A dead sequence running back into the past is not what causality is; it is an exhibition of what the present *has been* and an exhibition derived from the present—a recovery of infancy, not an advance in age. Teleology makes that recovery possible by revealing what causation is.

The past recovered, no matter what it is the past of, is all on the same level, although sequentially arranged in a calendar and timed by a clock, giving us dates and periods. It is, as far as it goes, a *sub specie aeternitatis* and yet waiting, as it were, to have something happen to it—something that will resurrect it, give it movement and life, or enlarge the understanding of it by making what caused it more evident. Apart from this imputed waiting, which is imputed promise and potency of events to come, the past has no natural time character at all. There is nothing imperfect about it to lead to a future or to that perfecting which adds another item to its list of dead events. This character of the past is, I suppose, the reason why we so often confuse history made with history in the making, as if the former produced the latter, although the natural fact is the reverse. We discover history backward, but write it forward, and properly so, because Nature's teleology is thereby illuminated and the causes of past events are better understood; but to transform the prolonged backward vision into the discovery of an original cause, destined of itself to produce the teleology in events, is to make that original cause the cause of time and to make us wonder, if we rigorously examine that result, why time was necessary. Why should that original cause change at all, or why was it not already all that was going to happen? Granted for argument's sake that it once was, we learn from time that it was then a present world. But to learn what a present world is, one in which causes operate and coöperate actually and effectively, we do not have to search the past. Nature's teleology establishes that fact. We do not make it so.

History

I have coupled time and history in this chapter because it seems clear to me that all our knowledge of Nature is bound up with her scheme of time, and that we as living beings are also bound up with it. The view that knowledge is mediated by anything else than our bodily organization seems to me unsound. In plainer speech, the view that it is mediated by "messages" received by us at the door of "the mind," informing us that there is a world external to them and enabling us to adapt ourselves to it seems to me to be intolerable. It transforms the consideration of knowledge into a hopeless dialectic, which is abundantly illustrated in the literature involved. Personally I am less interested in that fact than in another. The dialectical game is easy to play. It is easy to show that "realism" forces one to "idealism" and that "idealism" forces one to "realism." I could even take this inevitable dialectic as proof that Nature is dialectical through and through, piling paradox upon paradox, making us, for example, see her in intuition, without eyes, after all the antecedent conditions of visibility have been fulfilled and, having done so, enabling us to discover those antecedent conditions. I am not at all averse to such strangenesses. Like most human beings I find Nature strange. The sense of being a stranger in a strange world is, I think, as acute in me as in any other man. To pursue happiness in a world where it is so easily wrecked in one's despite—who does not feel the strangeness of that? Yes, Nature is strange, but not a stranger. It is with her as not a stranger that our knowledge is concerned. And that is why the reduction of knowing to an ultimate dialectic seems to me to be so unprofitable.

Let that reduction be knowledge of what knowledge is. But I have never discovered that thereby one knows anything about the stars or about the life of man. That sort of knowledge remains to be acquired, and that sort is the sort that counts. Thereby the captain steers his ship and the physician wages his humane war against disease. As over against such knowledge or as supplemental to it I do not understand what "knowledge of what knowledge is" amounts to. Nature as the world of sailing ships and ailing men I cannot look upon as cognitive of anything. I cannot take it as a means of knowing a world more real or more fundamental, which can be regarded as the cause of what we observe and reflect upon. Observing and reflecting are all of a piece with Nature, just as sailing and curing are. They are directly, not indirectly, engaged with events and intimately bound up with Nature's teleology. All our learning is a learning about this direct union. Bodies collide, but a collision theory of knowledge throws no light at all on the collision of bodies. It only makes the messages collide, to our bewilderment.

Knowledge of importance has always been regarded as the formulation of discovered causes and effects, as when it is discovered that nitrates fertilize the soil. In such cases the meaning of "cause and effect" is clear and the fertilizing of the soil by nitrates is an event, historical and teleological in character. In a world where such events happen it ought not to surprise anybody that there are beings that can utilize them, since there are beings that do. In other words our "consciousness" is an example of Nature's teleology, an example of a high order due to the high order of our own constitution as it fits in with Nature's so that we observe and reflect on her and have her principle of cause and effect at our command within the limits of our own effectiveness. I can find coöperation, not conflict, between Nature as we observe her to be and Nature as we discover her to be unless I permit myself the astonishing privilege of excluding myself from her cause and effect, from her teleology, from her exhibition of history, from her scheme of time. We know her in terms of her actually observed processes reduced to formulas, but not in terms of messages to be decoded.

History, therefore, should be a primary category in a first philosophy. It sums up so much of what Nature is, brings out her vibrant character as the present, eventful utilization of what she has been. With her there has ever been the building on what has been built, and only in the building is that progressive operation in effect. That is why we can write histories of rolling stones and intellectual vagabonds. Nature's motherly care provides for both, when there is any talk of provision—provides for the stars, the seasons, the swarm of animals, the spectacle of birth and death, of cities and wars. When there is no talk of provision, she yet remains the domain of histories and of histories so knit together that any one of them is never actually performed or adequately written in isolation from the rest. We call her fertile, for histories are like the fruits of her constant labor.

Chapter Four ✳ THE UNIVERSE OF DISCOURSE

Coöperation

THERE IS coöperation in the pursuit of knowledge, an interchange of discoveries, opinions, and results, a communication which would put agreement in the place of disagreement. We are not left each to his own devices, but employ the aid of others. We may ask how such coöperation is possible and by what means effected, but such questions cannot be answered unless coöperation is recognized as something natural and original. Indeed, Nature herself is a system of coöperation and interchange of one sort or another. We live in such a system and find coöperation in evidence wherever we turn. Action and reaction, stimulus and response, motions varying with the circumstances under which bodies move, events never without a field in which they occur, growths which in their life histories coöperate to advantage or disadvantage with their environments—nothing that happens in Nature is free from a context in which some sort of action and reaction is present. Give and take is the rule, even when the destruction of giver or taker is involved. If we now ask how all this coöperation is possible, the bare fact of it is the answer. We cannot begin without coöperation, without giving and taking, and find then how giving and taking are possible. We have only to try, to become convinced of failure. We may make assumptions of factors to explain coöperation, but they are assumptions of factors that give and take, act and react, interplay with one another. If, however, we ask how the coöperation and interplay are effected, we can turn to Nature with some hope of finding an answer.

In this chapter I am concerned principally with human coöperation in the pursuit of knowledge. I am not worried about its possibility. Like everybody else, I take it for granted and so assume no arbitrary or personal privilege. I only follow the rule. I would affirm, however, that the rule is followed, not as a presupposition assumed deliberately or after reflection, but as an unavoidable natural circumstance. We assume it no more than we assume that we live. If I am told that we may not be alive, that after all life may be an illusion, I can be only amused or irritated; for I do find that our knowing is an engagement with "after all." And life as an illusion makes me wonder what it is an illusion of. Of "real" life? Then I must wonder what "real life" can possibly be like. Let Nature be, after all, an illusion; heaven and earth and sea in their intimate familiarity are still the objects of human knowledge, and give and take is the rule followed in their eminent domain. Nature may be full of unrealized possibilities. There is evidence enough of that. But there is no evidence that the rule of give and take was ever one of them. All the evidence confirms its ever-presence. Time and history are unperjured witnesses. So I cannot admit that human coöperation in the pursuit of knowledge forms an exception to her general rule. We take it for granted, but do not assume it as an hypothesis in need of verification.

Giving and taking are thus mutually involved in a natural event which is in no need of justification for being what it is or having the effect it has. This is true all the way from the simplest givings and takings which form the subject matter of the natural sciences to the elaborate giving and taking which characterize all learned discourse, with its arguments, debates, and controversies. The attempt to promote knowledge by means of discussion differs from the attempt to promote it by means of test tubes only in the means used; both means can be analyzed as methods of coöperating with Nature. In this sense Nature may be called a universe of discourse with as much right as she may be called a universe of chemical elements or a universe of motion. The structures of chemical elements may be transformed into the structure of the atom, and that, along with the structure of the starry heavens, may be transformed into the structure of a discourse printed in a book. It would seem to be senseless to try to make sense out of Nature, were not discursive speech as much coöperation with her as is digestion. The latter is an assimilation of her materials so that they become blood, bone, and tissue and so that we grow in stature. The former is an assimilation of her character so that it becomes articulated speech and we grow in knowledge. Both might appropriately be called "metabolisms," the kind of change which is also an exchange and can involve both a building up and a breaking down. In the use of clearly articulated language we profess to say in words what Nature is. We find ourselves misunderstood or accused of unintelligibility, so we try again, seeking to find a common universe of discourse wherein disputes may be settled. It seems as if we lived in such a universe, as if all our questions were already answered there, and as if we failed to find the answers or failed to make ourselves understood because the various uses to which words are put divert us from the right way.

Is heat a substance? The question seems intelligible, for it has the grammatical form of intelligible questions. The attempt to answer it, however, forces us to discriminate between hot things and heat and also to make clear what a substance is. The question and answers to it have involved much controversy in the effort to make them intelligible. Yet it is difficult not to believe that the controversy may be obviated. The difference between hot and cold is familiar, and so are the facts that hot bodies make cold bodies hotter, becoming thereby colder themselves, and that cold bodies make hot bodies colder, becoming thereby hotter themselves. So we begin to consider temperature. That word may lead to many problems, but we can now deal with equal temperatures and discover that unequal temperatures tend to become equal. We call the discovery a law of Nature—the way hot and cold coöperate. In a manner, hot and cold have vanished, and only degrees of temperature remain. It looks now a little absurd to ask whether temperature itself is hot or cold. The suspicion is aroused that it is just as intelligible to speak of cold as substance as it is to speak of heat after that manner. Temperature may be troublesome, but we can measure its degrees and thereby remove a controversy, even if another arises. Who can doubt that this is progress in knowledge or that "temperature" names something natural although we are unable to put it into a bottle all by itself to be poured out in degrees on demand? The measurement of temperatures is an excellent example of progress and has had far-reaching consequences in physical science. What temperature is apart from hot and cold may remain a matter of controversy, but degrees of it have become a commonplace in discourse about hot and cold. The difference between them has become like that between plants and animals when we regard both as living beings. Hot and cold have not been abolished from Nature by reducing them to degrees of temperature any more than plants and animals have been abolished by reducing them to degrees of life. The examples cited are examples of the way our knowledge of Nature grows in unity. In discursive language that way finds expression, making such language like a mirror of Nature.

It is objectionable, therefore, to affirm that "the articulation of language can never be the articulation of things."[1] The "never" overdoes the matter, even when qualified by the following "the." Language is clearly an articulation of words which purports at least to express what the articulation of things is and uses things in the expressing—sounds in what otherwise might be all pantomime, itself vividly expressive. We read faces as well as books. A book on physics, although part of the physical world, is not that world, nor can that world be put on a library shelf and catalogued for pur-

---

[1] George Santayana, "Some Meanings of the Word 'Is,'" *Journal of Philosophy*, XXI (No. 14), 365, or *Obiter scripta*, New York, Scribner's, 1936, p. 189.

poses of reference. The book is, however, a reference to the physical world which would expose that world's articulation. That the book is a reference and that the articulation of its language can never be the articulation referred to are the reasons why the book is valuable. They prove that the story of the stars can be written as well as the story of a man's life, although the written story is neither the stars nor that life. What language is, is more important than what it is not, even if language is required to express what language is.

The affirmation quoted above impresses me more as a piece of moral advice than as a clarification of speech. Bacon's "words are wise men's counters" is cited in connection with it. Hobbes was more explicit: "Words are wise men's counters, they do but reckon by them; but they are the money of fools."[2] The folly of taking words as other than counters to reckon with is abundantly illustrated in human discourse. We try to avoid it by inventing new counters which tend to make the reckoning more effective and to keep it from degenerating into a dialectical play of words which the articulation of language permits—as if one were entitled to say that the nonexistent must exist in some way if its existence in any way is to be denied. To make nonexistence somehow exist or to divide existence into two

[2] *Leviathan*, Part i, chap. iv, *The English Works of Thomas Hobbes*, collected and edited by Sir William Molesworth, London, 1839, III, 25.

sorts, the existent and the nonexistent, is either to use a word ambiguously or to disintegrate discourse instead of integrating it. So in language we have the word "being," often using the word "thing" as its equivalent, and we now affirm that some beings exist and others do not, although they may be of consequence. That which has not being is now eliminated from discourse. Here words are used as counters for reckoning, as the alternative use of "being" and "thing" indicates, warning us that when the two words are so used they are not money, for nothing is purchased by saying either that a thing is a being or a being a thing. Since language has being, we may discriminate in it "realms of being" and proceed to explore them. We are reckoning with counters. Shall we admit a realm of things and now say that the articulation of language can never be the articulation of things without running the risk of falling into a dialectic which destroys any reference of language to anything but itself?

But I find little satisfaction in dialectic, although I use it now and then to reinforce an emphasis or to indicate traps into which it is easy to fall. The articulation of things, or, as I prefer to say, articulation in Nature, is precisely what we try to discover in the pursuit of knowledge and to express in language, and it seems jejune to doubt that we measurably succeed—as if we ought to fast from knowledge in order that our perceptions might be more acute and penetrating. We do not try to discover that heaven, earth, and sea are, but how they coöperate, they and all that in them is. Hot and cold coöperate in temperature, and all things coöperate in being what they are. The articulation here involved is in Nature. It is not imposed on her by language, but in language it is expressed, communicated, and taught; that which is so expressed is not an articulation of language, although language is used to express it. An articulation in Nature has been transmuted into an articulation in language, and that transmutation is itself a coöperation. Without hot and cold there would be no degrees of temperature; without coöperation with that fact there would be no expression of it in speech, no transmutation of it into human language. That is why we persist in trying to say in words what things are and why we never worry about it until we are asked to consider how remarkable it is and how it is possible. Then we argue, debate, speculate, and do so still attempting to say in words what Nature is, still living in a universe of discourse which can yield intelligibility and mutual understanding if only we persist long enough in doing precisely what we are doing. All this indicates the importance of an examination of language.

Language Not Applied

Language is not applied to Nature. Since when used it is used with reference to Nature, it may appropriately be called symbolic, for its words and even its grammatical forms are conventional; these, in their use, are effective because in a way they stand for or represent that to which they refer. The word "bread" is not bread, even if the word is repeated in saying so. We have a natural prejudice for our own vernacular, but rarely great enough to lead us to conclude that God used it when he created the world by speaking. And Nature, as indicated in the first chapter, may appropriately be said to be symbolic because her clouds are signs of rain. We try to formulate her suggestions of this sort of symbolism in coherent discourse; we call the result knowledge, refine it by observing it attentively, by reflecting on it and experimenting with it, so that our formulations may be regarded as symbols of what Nature is. But this does not entitle us to affirm that language is applied, as if we began with it and then tried to discover how aptly it fitted the circumstance. We do not create worlds by speaking and then discover which of them is Nature. We are familiar with her before we give her a name.

In saying this I would not be misunderstood. That words are ambiguous is one of the plagues of language. One has only to try to write an essay like this to become painfully aware of the fact. If one could only write sure of not being misunderstood, if one could only find the proper words which, free from ambiguity, would

either carry conviction or make clear to the better in-
structed just where the source of failure lay! All this
indicates an application of language calling for criticism. Often we invent words whose application is
doubtful even if their meaning is clearly enough defined to indicate what successful application would
amount to. In recent years "the ether" has been a shining example in physical science, causing a great up-
heaval. Last words, like "the atom," are generally of
the same character. Systems of logic, of geometry, and
even of the universe, each claiming inherent integrity,
are invented, raising problems of their application.
There is no doubt that language is used in anticipatory
ways which make it like a prying tool trying to find
leverage in Nature to make it effective. It is natural to
make hypotheses, and there is value in making them.
I am not denying this. I am affirming something else,
which impresses me as more fundamental.

It is foolish to deny speculation its rights, but it seems
equally foolish to find in it the norm of what language
naturally is. The use of language as a tool is never free
from its use in the context of Nature. We speak and
write in the same world as that in which we walk and
breathe. No one, I imagine, would regard walking as
an application of motion to Nature or breathing as an
application of respiration. Why then regard vocalization as such? Are sounds applied to Nature, or are they

made in Nature, with their attendant circumstances? Perhaps "vocalization" leads us astray, because language and voice have become so intimately associated. A written book does not speak, but it can be read aloud. Professors often lecture instead of sending their students to the library; students often tolerate a poor lecture in preference to reading a rich book. The silent movies fail in general competition with the talkies. Each of us knows well the difference between going to the "legitimate" theater to "see" a play and trying to see it by reading the text. The dumb show and the symbolic ballet are always a little exotic and charm us more by being occasional than they would as a constant performance. We want the commentary of the spoken word. So it is not unnatural to regard language as a commentary, to use "language" and "speech" as equivalent words, and to look upon the written or printed page as a symbol of what a man would say if he spoke. What the ear hears has been translated into something for the eye to see. The consequence is that language wears an artificial look, as if it were a clever device invented in the interest of communication. It is said by anthropologists that primitive man often mistakes writing for magic, civilized and sophisticated man often makes a similar mistake by regarding speech as a kind of wand waved over Nature in order to make her intelligible and to promote mutual understanding in the pursuit of knowledge. We are often asked to define our "terms" before we use them, although as a matter of fact definitions do not come first, but last, and great pains are required in arriving at them.

Speech

The basic factors involved in the genesis of language are discernible without undertaking a long historical research. They are exhibited in the generations of men as they come and go. It may be taken for granted that the development is from speech to writing through the invention of alphabets. The evidence for such a development is good. Yet one should not forget that other factors than sounds, such as facial expression, gestures, and postures of the body, are potent accompaniments of speech. And primitive men use visible signs and markers for guidance and to memorialize their experience, as when they set up a stone to indicate that here is the place. They are expert in reading many of Nature's signs. They often make crude pictures, shape their utensils with some show of symbolism, adorn their bodies expressively, and dance, as well as beat a drum. Their language is not just sounds. Speech in its development has an accompanying scenery. This is admirably illustrated in the words in primitive languages which students of linguistics call "holophrastic" because one word has the effect of a whole phrase or even a sentence and creates the impression of using many different words for the same object and thus suggests the absence of general terms. Holophrastic words are, however, generally different words for the same object in different sceneries or occupations, just as we speak of a man as a doctor, lawyer, merchant, chief, being in this respect as holophrastic as any savage. Yet for the moment and for the purposes of analysis, the scenery of sounds may be disregarded. We may consider, then, the natural effect of sounds on those that hear them. At once it becomes clear that we cannot restrict the analysis to human beings. In Nature there is an abundance of heard sounds, in the wild as well as in the city. I think of Tennyson's lines:

> I do but sing because I must
> And chant but as the linnets sing.

The linnet's song and the poet's chanting are expressions of their states of being. It would be a little extravagant to say that the linnet sings in order to proclaim its happiness to a listening world, for the song, on the best of evidence, belongs to the bird's state of being and has a "must" about it which forbids our concluding that, finding itself happy, the linnet sang on purpose. It would, however, be equally extravagant to say that the song is not expressive or that it serves no purpose. It can arrest the attention of animals other than man. Even if we refuse to admit that the arrested attention is a recognition of a bird's happiness, we must admit that it is a recognition of a bird singing and an aid in locating the bird. The hen may cluck because she must, but her chicks respond as if bidden to a feast. Only a perverted human egotism can deny that here is speech. The evidence must be flouted. There is no difference in the character of that evidence between such cases and the talk of men. No doubt linnets and hens do what they do because of the way they are made, but so also does a man. The sounds of the wild go out and meet with varied responses by the wild. A breaking twig will make a deer prick up its ears and stand all trembling. Even in the night there are voices filling the dark with mysterious conversation to which few of us are insensible. The woods are full of vernaculars which convict us of stupidity if the prejudice for our own leads us to deny them the dignity of speech. Must a linnet sing in Italian or a hen coax in German in order to assure an Englishman that they speak?

Furthermore, sounds which are not vocalizations have effects similar to those that are. They are signals of possible adventures, warning and beckoning signals with which to play hide and seek. Examples are unnecessary. It is worth remarking, however, that when we turn from speech to consider the directive and expressive sounds generally, we approach one of the basic factors in the development of language. Here is, as it were, a prime universe of discourse bound up with Nature's operations; the carrying power of sounds joins near and far in a coöperation from which many consequences flow. It now seems natural that speech should precede writing as a method of communication. We have to learn to write, but we do not have to learn to speak, except when we learn some particular vernacular. Nature's own vernacular of sound we live with, and we speak—those who have voice—because we must.

In what way does the poet differ from the linnet except in the matter of the vernacular used? He affirms that he chants because he must in expressing his sorrow and meditations on his times, all "In Memoriam" as it were—the New Year's bells bidden to ring out the old, ring in the new. Let the dying die, but in compensation ring in the Christ that is to be! The dead had their hope or fear of resurrection; what have the living who will soon be dead? The poet writes his "In Memoriam" on paper and turns it over to a printer who publishes it for others to read. This the linnet does not do. Yet all that the poet does is bound up with his state of being and is expressive of it. His state of being in his study is more complex than that of his relative in the woods. There is a wide difference in context, and yet there is continuity in spite of it. The linnet sings, one may say, for all hearers; the poet for a selected few. No matter what one's own vernacular may be, one does not need to translate the bird's song into it. A Frenchman cannot read "In Memoriam" intelligently unless he has learned the English language. And yet—this is an important consideration—were that poem read aloud to all nations, all of them would get the melody of sound; and now we are in the linnet's world, the world of expressive voice. A song in German may be expressive of a state of being although we are ignorant of the words. The difference between singers now looks like the difference between songs without words and songs with them; the former need no translation, the latter do, and the former are the common ancestors of the latter. The former are like a language without a history; the latter like a language with a long one. So the poet publishes because he must, because his song is the expression of a social and historical fellowship.

This may all sound a little fanciful. It would be wholly so if one were to conclude that I am trying to find the origin of language in the songs of birds. I am not. I have been impressed by what a poet said, finding in it a hint of the primary significance of speech—that it is expressive first of all. It is, then, the use of the expressive character of sounds in accord with the effects they can produce. If I have been singing too much, it is because I have been trying to sing without words, although using them to bring out the fact that, despite the great variety of vernaculars which are socially acquired and are translated into one another, the original expressive character of sounds is basically motivative in the development of speech. Sounds are as physical as anything else in Nature which is named "physical." We can have a science of them called "acoustics," but they have original effects, not acoustical, which lead eventually to the expression of that science by their use. These effects are not artificial, although art is required in their development in language. The original effect is used in the development, not created by it. One may, therefore, affirm with confidence that insofar as language is a speech development it is the development of natural responses to sounds, of a give and take in Nature which explains much, but which requires no other sort of explanation itself than that employed in the explanation of any other give and take. We speak, not because we need to or because we want to, but because we must. If one will talk of needs, the need of speech is like the need of food—not a desire which comes first and then creates organs and manipulates circumstances in order to realize the desire, but a consequence of having those organs and of their cooperation with the circumstances in which they are exercised. A creature without a digestive system would have no need of food; one without voice organs would have no need of speech. Furthermore, a creature with a digestive system would starve in a world where there was no food; one with vocal cords would have nothing to say in a world where sounds had no expressive effect. One has only to contemplate for a moment these supposed extraordinary conditions to realize what a world of nonsense they presuppose. We chant but as the linnets sing.

Although, as we currently use the word "expression," some intent to express and a receptive audience are suggested, we can distinguish for analytic purposes between these suggestions and characteristic vocalizations. We may recognize in a baby's cry an expression of its discomfort, as if it were trying to make that discomfort evident, and yet deny to the baby any such recognition or any intent to make it known. The baby's original cry is not for the purpose of telling itself or others that something's the matter. Yet the cry is expressive, or without instruction the baby would not learn to use it for a purpose. Crying operates to bring relief, and it does not take the baby long to find this out. The cry passes from a physiological reaction to a directive agency. Communication has begun. It would be extravagant to regard it as a communication of knowledge or information, although that may easily be read into it. Practical consequences are to the front.

Crying brings assistance but is not the information of distress. Speech does not wholly lose this directive force, no matter how highly language is developed. A door may be closed when I ask to have it closed. My asking involves my wishes, but a communication of my wishes may not occur. Responses to requests and commands often involve no reflection or deliberation at all. When an order, polite or otherwise, is not obeyed, then consideration of the reasons why comes into play and information is desired. That desire is an awakened desire, and basic to it and motivating it in the development of speech are the expressive and directive forces of sound. From what I have read about speech[3] and from my own attempts at analysis I cannot escape the conclusion that expression, direction, and communication are characteristic of speech throughout its development. One need not insist that they are naturally so severed that there is a gap to be bridged in passing from one to the other. The passage is, rather, continuous, gliding from one to the other; this gliding is itself a consequence of the effective character of sounds. To be startled by a noise behind one, to turn around or run away, can hardly be called having knowledge or having received information, but it is on the way thither. Much polite conversation is sheer entertain-

[3] Especially books like J. O. H. Jespersen's *Language* (New York, Holt, 1923) which impress me as marked by unusual penetration and insight into a subject so often distorted by fanciful speculation.

ment and loses its character when it becomes didactic. Most of us are sensitive to the change and resent it. Talking about the weather in order to get started has become a byword. "It's a fine day" and "Yes, it is a fine day" are not the posing and the accepting of an ontological proposition. It has been frequently noted that the chatter of children at play together is often not conversation at all, although having the semblance of it. In general, speech may be compared with an obbligato, having its own theme, yet playing with other themes, receiving and giving special emphases thereby. Whether the emphasis falls on expression, direction, or communication depends on the circumstances involved.

From the threefold character of the natural effect of sounds it is possible to indicate with some success how "the parts of speech" develop in a spoken language. It is, however, far beyond the scope of this essay to attempt an exhibition of this development. The important consideration here is that the development is largely in the interest of communication. That is, parts of speech facilitate discourse, articulate and order it. They make more and more effective in sentence structure the coherence of expression and direction, and by doing so they have now in that structure the effect of affirmations and denials. These are like answered questions. "It's a fine day." "Well, is it?" One needs only to compare this with the weathered introduction to conversation to sense the difference involved. We are now in the situation of saying what is so or what is not so. We are in a universe of discourse in which correctness of speech has become a controlling principle. That universe has not been entered by a miraculous leap nor has it miraculously come into being to order a disordered chaos of sounds. What has occurred is a development of their natural effects. In the universe in which that development has occurred are found the criteria of correctness. They are found by reversing the process which led to the demand for them, by returning closer and closer to expression and direction. In the whole process speech has been developed rather than applied. The parts of speech have grown out of that to which they ultimately return; the whole problem of correctness is whether in discourse that growing out of and returning to has been distorted. That it should not be distorted is essential to successful communication and instruction. The particular sounds used have no privileged sanctity. That which is required of them is that they so combine to produce the question-answer effect that intelligibility is the result.

Pantomime

There is, however, a tendency to overemphasize speech when considering the bases of language. Its historical precedence to writing as a carrier of informa-

tion and a means of instruction has given it a kind of
initial preëminence, so that we often unwittingly assume that, strictly speaking, when there is no speech
there is no language. Deaf-mutes, of course, refute us
without any necessity for argument. They can converse
without the aid of speakers; with that aid they can be
taught to become erudite, to read the lips of speakers,
the words on a printed page, and even, at times, to
speak. It may look like a miracle, but it is only the
miracle of language generally, proving that, in spite of
certain organic defects which impede it, a specific organic metabolism can yet be developed. A deaf-mute
can study logic and get as mixed up about "p implies
q" and about "involve" and "entail" as the rest of us.
Swamped in our own difficulties, we rarely stop to
wonder how far his and ours are alike. Emphasizing
speech is an aid in clarifying expression, direction, and
communication, and also in finding clues for the development of the parts of speech and the migration of
words; it ought not, however, to involve neglect of that
natural context of pantomime in which speech is itself
an emphasis, like the punctuation of a silent show with
admonitory sounds.

Again, the visible world comes into prominence as
that present world which embraces both the seen and
the unseen. A pantomime tells a story without the interruption of sound. Such an interruption is an in-

advertence or a distraction which spoils the effect of the uttered silence. One slips readily from "outering" to "uttering," for the story is played out before our eyes without the need of words. A child may see a dog gnawing at a bone and ask what the dog is doing. The child is asking, not for information about a performance, but for words to express it in the vernacular the child is learning. Then what has been seen can be told. In a similar fashion we all learn to speak our own speech. To be where it is spoken is to be intellectually at home. An alien speech until mastered is like a Tower of Babel, introducing confusion and driving us back on a pantomime which everybody can understand with a minimum of trouble. There would be little power in speech if pantomime did not support it, for Nature is very far from being all sounds and very near to being all sights, views, and points of view with a shifting scenery, like a moving picture telling the story of what is going on. With this scenery we live in daily familiarity. We take it in. That vital experience is like breathing the air which refreshes our souls. It is what being a soul or a mind is. And just as in breathing with our lungs there is intake and outgo in a continuous context which is polarized as organ and atmosphere, so here in the scenery of language organs and pantomime are polarized. It is quite as impossible to dissever that polarization from its field of operation as it is to dissever the polarization of a magnet. One simply cannot take the situation from which all language springs as an imposition upon Nature or upon anything without disintegrating all discourse into unintelligibility. When we try, we end by surrendering all hope of being able to say in words or looks or gestures or in any imaginable way what things are. Things end by becoming never what they seem, and no appeal to seeming can get them back. Nature herself is very genuinely a universe of discourse. Because we live in and with her, her discourse is translated or transmuted into ours without severing the polarization involved.

We ought not to let language itself deceive us in this matter. Here we are dealing with something quite different from the conventional vernaculars of mankind. We are dealing with what all of them, as they are developed more and more in the interest of communication and the pursuit of knowledge, try to express. Some vernacular has to be used for purposes of exposition. It would be absurd to try to invent a new one and then teach it to mankind in order to have communication and mutual understanding. How would one go about the teaching of it? How would the taught learn it? The experiment is performed every time we learn a foreign language. The fact that it is performed is the fact I am emphasizing by using my native speech. No conventional vernacular means another conventional vernacular, nor is one the translation of another even if each can be translated into any other. The reason is that Nature's language is translated into all of them. Shall we stumble over the word "language" when we are considering what it is that is basically translated? Why not stumble over the word "translation"? A student once told me that οὐσία was the Greek word for substance. I asked him: "Is not 'substance' the English word for οὐσία?" Is one word the word for another word? What is it that acts like a clearing house for the conventional vernaculars of mankind if it is not a character of Nature responsible for all of them? That character she has in her own right. We live with it rather than discover it. We never invented it. We do not impose it upon her or impute it to her.

If we do not let our vernaculars deceive us, all this seems to me to be abundantly clear. Perhaps the nearest we come to a universal vernacular is in the language of mathematics, although there has been much variation in the words or terms it uses. If we ask why it is like a universal vernacular, we are again driven back upon Nature's characteristics. When we consider what that language would express within its limitations, it can readily appear to be a distillation of Nature's pantomimic effect. It is the language of a vibratory silence reduced to equations in which there are constants and variables kept in balance by the equation.

It is all like a story of events in the grip of fate. The variables vary, but are not allowed to vary in any way that destroys the balance. That is why I have likened mathematics to a distillation of Nature's pantomimic effect. It is like a universal language triumphing over all specific vernaculars. The truth it expresses is like absolute truth, and that makes the impressive supremacy given to mathematics intelligible. It explains why the development of mathematics and that of logic tend to coincide and why the ideal of science is to become mathematical. Could we express all the variations in Nature in terms of an integrated system of equations, there would be nothing further to learn! The pursuit of knowledge would have ended, and art would then be freed to work its will. We would have understood Nature and could mold her nearer to the heart's desire without first having to shatter her to bits.

It is clear, however, that mathematics by itself does not have this effect. Detach it from Nature, and it loses its masterful effect. A schoolboy may learn his algebra, proceed from simple to quadratic equations, and so forth, and learn no more than the rules of mathematical procedure, remaining very ignorant of what is going on in the world. In a way, he is learning nothing about anything. The equation, $x^2 + y^2 = 1$, of itself may set him the problem of finding out what the numerical values of x and y are if the equation is kept balanced with unity. When $x = 1, y = 0$. He has not discovered a circle. Starting with the circle, he may discover that equation in it in such a way that his knowledge of what it is to be a circle grows rapidly. The power of mathematics, therefore, does not reside in itself, but is derived from that out of which it is distilled. The science may be developed in its own way because of its own terms and operations, but the results must fit something else to be of any value beyond that of playing a game according to rule. It is interesting, however, to note that we incline to believe that they ought to fit and so to seek for significances in our terms which will make them fit. The $\sqrt{-1}$ is a bastard, for example, but since we arrive at it repeatedly, we search for a significance for it which will legitimatize it. Such technicalities of a science are here hinted at in order to indicate that the "symbolism" of mathematics is a symbol of a structure of pantomime—variables so kept in balance that a story is told, a plot unfolded, and all in such a way that the natural scenery seems to have disappeared and the effect is produced of living in the story of all stories. Mathematics tends to make Pythagoreans of us all. "If there is a God he must be a mathematician," is as much a dogma today as it ever was.

One thing, however, seems clear. Nature's pantomimic display, providing the scenery for the spoken word, is more fundamental than speech itself. The visible world makes this conspicuously evident, for in that world the speaker is like an orator on a platform, using his voice as if summoning the audience to attention and using the resources of facial expression, bodily posture, and gestures to help his vocalization. He, like Adam, is ordered to name the animals, and then, having done so, he finds none of them adequate as helpmeet for him. The story tells us nearly everything that searchers for the origin of language need to know to guide them in tracing the development of speech. Many vernaculars seem inevitable, for many Adams will do the naming. Is it likely that each Adam will name a lion "lion"? Does it make any difference what sound he uses, if the use becomes conventionally current? Or does it make any difference what sounds he uses to denote his postures and gestures and pointings? But what a task is his to translate his scenery and his own feelings into words that will express them, serve as directive agencies, and establish communication! Nouns and adjectives, verbs and adverbs, prepositions, conjunctions, and the rest begin to germinate. It is all a vital process, this transmutation of scenery and the accompaniments of vocalization into sounds which transmute those who hear them into speakers in their turn, as if they too orated on a stage. The development goes on through the invention of alphabets to the printed book, which is often illustrated with pictures, diagrams, charts, and graphs to enhance the scenic effect. We have been in a universe of discourse from start to finish, a universe in which stories are told whether we are acquainted with them or not. Just what it is to be a story is perhaps best illustrated by mathematics—variables which in spite of varying keep a balance and are in that sense in the grip of fate.

Translating

Translating one vernacular into another may now be regarded as an effective enlargement of one's own vocabulary, freeing one from verbal idolatry of one's native speech. A wag in my college days used to ask: "Voulez-vous some peanuts haben?" An Englishman may affirm that "work wearies," "labor fatigues," or "toil tires" and still be credited with speaking his own language. Such trivial examples indicate clearly that a group of people, able to use a number of different languages equally well and having thereby lost vernacular prejudice, could converse together intelligibly without keeping those different languages in separate compartments. The sense of translation would be lost and would become the sense of commanding a great variety of modes of expression. The attempt to pick out from that polyglot the exclusive vernaculars out of which it had been composed would be like our attempts to pick from the language we currently use in

conversation and exposition what may strictly be called
English. Try turning "the indestructibility of matter"
or "the conservation of energy" into pure English. The
first example recalls again my college days, when I
began to study language as language, not as vernaculars. The story was told of a champion of English who
when challenged to express the "indestructibility of
matter" in English, promptly replied, "the unthor-
oughfarableness of stuff." But where did that "able"
come from? A synthesis of vernaculars is still a vernacular, a domestication of foreign words, and present-
day English is a great example of it and full of verbal
gymnastics. Here is a definition of "matter" from the
Concise Oxford Dictionary: "the substance of which a
physical thing is made." I turn to the adjective "physical" and find: "of matter, material." So matter is the
substance of which a material thing is made! And what
is "substance"? "The essential nature underlying phenomena." I am driven to "essential," "nature," and
"phenomena" and round about in circles. What is the
matter with matter? Is all this juggling with words, this
translating of them into one another, like the Latin
"material" into the Greek "physical," mere verbal
nonsense?

It is very instructive and very effective nonsense.
Who dares to deny its power? Translating is not simply
a matter—and here is "matter" again—of from a for-

eign vernacular into a native one but also a matter within each vernacular. New words are constantly formed, and native words are supplemented by others from abroad, which become domesticated. The result may be confusing and may produce the illusion of progress in knowledge where there is none. It may also be clarifying and may assist the pursuit of knowledge. Looking up words in dictionaries may easily be the equivalent of a liberal education. The service which such books render extends far beyond that of aiding spelling and pronunciation. They show that the meaning of words lies in their being metaphors. Literal meanings are hardly meanings at all, but names assisting identifications. It is that which words carry after or with them that sends one hunting through a dictionary, having lost all interest in spelling or pronunciation. Then words are found which as metaphors have written chapters in the history of civilization. The aftercarrying, the metaphor, is a translating, a carrying across or over, for which "the passing from sense to intellect" is as adequate an expression as any other. It is as if the metaphorical character of language delivered to the intellect that which, without it, could not be found in sense, but which, with it, illuminated sense with penetrating light. So we speak of "the light of the mind," a light which never was on sea or land, a candle set up within us shining bright enough for all our purposes, a new kind of vision which pierced the veil of sense and glimpsed the real presence beyond. The world of sense is translated into the sources of its being, and the intellect has transcended sense limitations. As after translating French into English we understand French, so after translating sense into intellect we understand sense. That which was at first done in English can now be done in French. An expert linguist can speak either language indifferently, find himself at home in either tongue, and be the best of them that speak either speech were he only where 'tis spoken. Since each vernacular is a translation of sense into intellect, all vernaculars are translatable. They are all metaphorical ultimately in the same manner. The intellect perceives in sense that which is carried over to it.

I would revise the foregoing by adding a caution already noted in the preceding sections of this chapter. Sense and intellect may be divorced for purposes of exposition, and some increment of clearness may be gained thereby. But sense and intellect are not naturally divorced. They are complementary, like the poles in a field which is polarized to begin with. Intellect is not like a hostess waiting for her guests to come and entertaining them after they have arrived, dressed up for the purpose. It is more like a child born in its parents' world and growing up to learn their habits and language. Its increasing familiarity with them is a growth analogous to its growth in stature. It never *learns* the metaphorical principle. Nor does it, strictly speaking, apply it any more than it applies the principle of motion to its legs. "Obeys" is here a better word than "applies." The child is obedient to the polarizations of its existence. Its whole living is bound up with them. Even if it has the problem of getting its experience in order, we have still to ask: With what order? and find the answer to be: Nature's. The order of its hopes and wishes are subservient to that order, not it to theirs. In this we are all children. We often wish it were otherwise and sigh for Aladdin's lamp or the touch of Midas, only to become convinced on sincere reflection that such gifts would be our ruin. The only magic worth having is that born of a happy marriage of sense and intellect, the touch, not of Midas, but of metaphor, which so transmutes existence into speech that what things are and what they are said to be become increasingly a profounder intimacy with Nature. She is metaphor, pantomime punctuated with sounds, and is not out-of-doors waiting to be admitted to conversation. She is jointly translating and translated.

Ideas

Language, like light, presents a kind of paradox. We speak of "communication," but when we ask precisely what is communicated there is trouble in answering. We accept with confidence the competence of language to express what things are. The intelligibility of discourse is rooted in that acceptance, and that acceptance, as I have tried to indicate, is not at all like an assumed hypothesis. It is something native to our being what we are. If we try to prove the competence of language, we find ourselves in Hume's skeptical attitude which defeats itself. His skeptical solution of the difficulty by appealing to traits of "human nature" was indeed skeptical, for it robbed the adjective "human" of all intelligible meaning. The question: What is not human nature? became unanswerable. His "impressions and ideas" were as much "human nature" as anything else; the latter were derived from the former, and the former arose in the soul, we know not how. The disintegration of discourse was complete, and one had to begin all over again as if the disintegration had not occurred, admitting that it was of no consequence so far as moral and practical affairs were concerned. The disintegration of discourse was, in effect, its restoration to integrity. It is this sort of paradox which language presents. If language cannot express what things are, it cannot express what they are not; but the expression of this sublime circumstance requires the distinction it annuls if it is to be intelligible. It is a sublime paradox to affirm that language communicates, in the last resort, only the lack of communication. The sublimity is but little, if at all, reduced by affirming that language, professedly communicating what things are and are not *said* to be, is symbolic of what they are and are not.

It is manifestly unprofitable to discuss a paradox of this kind or to try to resolve it by inventing psychological devices which involve it. Hume, taken seriously, may be said to have demonstrated the fact sufficiently. An appeal to "ideas" or "thoughts" as symbolic of things, the turning of these into words and then communicating the words in order that they may be turned back into "ideas" or "thoughts," may obscure the paradox, but it certainly does not remove or solve it. Yet it does put an emphasis on ideas. Whether there can be thought without language was a question much discussed in the days of Max Müller, and our logical positivists seem, in a way, to have revived it and challenged attention. "Idea" seems to be the name for the major difficulties involved. It seems absurd to most of us to affirm that language communicates language or that an analysis of grammar and syntax can of itself reveal whether sentences have meaning or not. Discourse on such matters seems to degenerate. "Idea" or some equivalent of it, seems to be the word of saving grace, and the reduction of ideas to the directive, experimental, or pragmatic force of words impresses many of us as a kind of sacrilege. Vague as the meaning of certain terms in discourse may be—terms like "substance," "power," "energy," "idea"—when disassociated from the varying contexts in which they are used, nonetheless, those terms, in those contexts have an undeniably integrating effect. They are like periods at the end of sentences, closing them and rounding them out. Examples abound. The question whether heat is a substance is one to which the answer "yes" or "no" is clearly expected. To set it down as a wholly improper question to begin with, because we cannot define "substance" irrespective of such questions, results, when pushed to the limit, in rendering discourse as a whole useless. Men would not ask whether God exists, if an antecedent definition of either "God" or "existence," independent of a context in which such questions are asked, were first necessary. Nor would one ask whether *a* man is a *man* if a like demand were made. Discourse is quite different from a collection of names conventionally applied to objects, like labels pasted on bottles. Even that sentence contains an error, for one may say that discourse is like a pasting of labels on bottles to declare along with the act of pasting something else. Ideas are declared, and ideas are not pasted labels or comparable with them. We may learn from the label the conventional name for the contents of the bottle and yet affirm that we have no idea what the bottle contains. Names of many sorts are the conveyers of discourse, but not its freight. "Idea" is a name for the freight and is as conventional as any other name. Its linguistic association with vision, although lending it a sensory appropriateness, ought not to be allowed to deceive us. "Conception" is equally appropriate, suggesting something taken along with something else and something like pregnancy also.

"Idea," therefore, may be said to be a conventional name for that in Nature without which discourse would be neither intelligible nor communicative. That it is a sight word is in a way accidental and in another way very appropriate. It is accidental, since we use words other than sight words for it and also because there are languages which do not use such words—oriental languages uninfluenced by the western. "Way" would do just as well were we used to it; and so would "grasp." Santayana has Democritus "smell" a philosophy from afar, as if it were communicated by its odor. Colloquially, what one "gets over" when speaking is one's idea. Consequently, when dealing with ideas it is crucial to remember all such conventionalities. Yet a sight word may justly claim appropriateness, because it is in the visible world that the carrying-over effect of what is seen is most prominent. There things have their own individual "look," which may be said to be theirs exclusively and not transferable, and they have also a carrying-over look which they share with other things.

That carrying-over look expands and tends toward a maximum, exhausting itself finally in a word such as "being." What it is to "be" anything is precisely what we want to know, and when we try to find this out the universe of discourse both expands and contracts, the look of things carrying over more and more to the embrace of other things, but in doing so, eliminating former looks because they restrain the expansion. Haltings on the way are denoted by the most appropriate words we can employ to assist the understanding of why the halt was made. Nature loses more and more of her variety, but her integrity is heightened, her wholeness more evident; we seem to have arrived at the last word or words that can be uttered. Possessing them, we climb down the ladder, so to speak, and see Nature in a new light. Her vanished looks now return and are like illustrations or exhibitions of her story's plot.

All that is old, very old. I can't imagine any student of Nature unfamiliar with it, no matter how wildly he may speculate. Old Thales, reputed first philosopher in the western tradition, seems to have made "water" the last word, finding in that element the generative source of all things—water, something akin to what we drink, but more ambient, whose vital rarefactions and condensations are productive, making this old earth now look like an island floating in an eternal sea all islanded in one way or another, with water rare or dense washing every shore. Does a modern philosopher with his "energy" do anything different in principle? We all want to attain the most inclusive look, the look of something which, even if it cannot be seen as water in a pool, is seen as oxygen and hydrogen are seen in water. Their look, in turn, may be the look of them in something else. We bring to bear the aid of all our senses to get hold somehow of these ultimates, never wholly content to let them be simply incidental to the procedure which drives us to them. The names we give them may be influenced by names in that procedure, but in the end we find ourselves trying to sing in words a song without words. All this, as I have said, is very old as the method of saying in words what things are. The pattern of it persists. When I now say that it is all a search for ideas, I hope I may have freed the fact from bondage to the conventionality of words. One must sing the song in many words, sing it in the varied vernaculars of serious students of Nature, if one is to realize the harmony of Nature and the discords of our singing. The great philosophers and the great scientists are far more alike than the discords of their words would indicate. That is why they debate and wrangle. They are trying to get their instruments in tune for the great symphony.

So it is not our languages which make a concerted

universe of discourse. They are consequences of living in such a universe, and vary as instruments vary. We do not expect the linnet to sing "In Memoriam," but we do expect poets to note the linnet's song. Like the lark, we all, even mathematicians, sing at Heaven's Gate. If with Santayana we add, "but not in Heaven," it is because we allow Heaven to be a non-natural idea which Nature does not exhibit in her integrity. Heaven can make all our languages inadequate when we turn to Nature, but when we turn to her we find that it is her ideas we try to grasp and then to carry in the vehicle of speech.

One may be excused, I hope, for approaching poetry in this matter of ideas, for it is somewhat irresistible. Ideas elate us, and when we have found one we are likely to forget our clothes and run through the streets shouting "Eureka!" as is fabled of Archimedes. We rush to publication. We must tell it to somebody and, having lost heat through that impulsion, we may become prosaic. Let prose be written.

It has long been held that ideas are acquired by us or that we receive them or that they are imparted to us. Whence and how do we come by them? There are controversial answers to that question. It is generally admitted that some ideas we manufacture and that we manufacture them out of other ideas. This drives us back upon ideas we do not manufacture, to original ideas, and these, if not acquired, must be native. But "native or innate ideas" are very troublesome. The expression indicates something "immediate," something originally "given," a kind of "seek no further," and yet it carries with it an impulsion to further seeking. If the immediate is Nature, the derivation of ideas is open to analysis and experimentation. Our ideas of space and time, for example, are the ideas which we uncover by studying Nature's space and time, and they belong to her as well as to us. Those ideas may become more precise and clear as the study continues, but they do so without departing from the field or context in which they are studied. Nature remains the immediate from start to finish and becomes clearer in her immediacy. Her space and time continue to be distinguishable; but an absolute disassociation of them becomes increasingly impossible, and the dynamic and productive character of natural processes involving the juncture of time and space becomes increasingly impressive. And so far, in this direction, there is no further seeking. If we now insist that our ideas of what time and space are, are not what time and space are, we have gone beyond the immediate and are left without a clue to that from which ideas of time and space are derived. If we refrain from doing this, then the distinction between space and time on the one hand and ideas of them on the other has not been abolished, and it is indifferent whether we assign the distinction to Nature or to ourselves. The only point to placing emphasis on ourselves is to draw attention to the fact that we have discovered the ideas with increasing clearness and in that sense have derived them. In Nature they are native.

When I consult the literature and make my own analysis, all this seems to me abundantly confirmed so far as the procedures involved in the development of knowledge are concerned. Without an immediate, there is no development; and whatever the immediate is taken to be, *that* is the subject matter of analysis; and the analysis would discover in the immediate the ideas which clarify it. What does one ever discover by starting with no immediate at all or by trying to make hypotheses free from any taint of an immediate in the hope of delivering it afterward in all its variety? All attempts at that impress me as complete failures. They all assign to the supposed factors the ability to produce what they do not possess. In other words, they assign to them the ability to produce ideas of them which upon their disclosure are clues to a knowledge of their sources. In this they confess that their procedure does not differ after all from that of others. They speak with a different accent; that is all. The competence of the knowledge procedure is accepted as a natural fact. Knowledge is still, not the things known, but a possession of the ideas of what they are, and these ideas are native to the things. To refer to Tyndall again: if we discern in matter the promise and potency of every form and quality of life, in saying so, we do not communicate matter, but the idea of what matter is; and if that idea does not belong to matter, matter clearly is not what it is said to be.

Freed from bondage to vernaculars with their conventionalities, one can now make sense out of the claim of Spinoza that the "substance" of knowledge and the "substance" of Nature are the same substance. *Ordo et connectio idearum idem est ac ordo et connectio rerum.* And *idea vera cum suo ideato convenire debet,* not in the sense that ideas in our heads agree with objects outside them, but in the sense that ideas and their objects go along together and make the purging of this jointure from confusion and absurdity imperative. We should observe the expressive, directive, and communicative effect of language rather than the grammatical dialectic of words. Playing the parts of speech off against one another does not advance knowledge. It has the advantage of revealing absurdities and inconsistencies and forcing a revised approach in the study of subject matter which may better serve the seeking for ideas. It may also emancipate one from slavery to cherished modes of verbal expression. "Nature and us," "the world and the individual," "object and subject," and like expressions may now be recognized as variants of that polarization in a field on which the integrity of discourse depends. Nature may then be said to be a universe of discourse with as much right as she can be said to be a universe of matter moving in space and time. As a universe of discourse she is recognized as the ultimate ground of intelligibility, the reason why she can be addressed in many languages whose propositions communicate what she is and is not discovered to be. The universe of discourse is not like an independent picture of her hung in the gallery of the mind.

Sense and Intellect

Long ago sense and intellect were distinguished and yet recognized as joint factors in cognition. The distinction is not the result of an initial analysis of "mind" or "consciousness." It arises from familiar circumstances such as that we do not observe or reflect upon the visible world unless we see or have seen it. Sense is cognitive only in that respect. Given our sense organs in operation, the sense world to which they belong is available for reflective consideration. The consequences are the discovery of the intelligible world and the formulation of it in communicable speech. Then the sense world is said to be known. Such, in outline, is the natural *de anima* of mankind. It gives point to the old maxim that there is nothing in the intellect which is not first in sense and makes needless the addition "except the intellect itself." The needlessness is apparent when its correlative is noted; there is nothing in sense which is not afterward in the intellect except sense itself. "Perceptions without conceptions are blind, and conceptions without perceptions are empty." That was said by Kant in order to keep the integrity of "experience" intact.

This distinction between sense and intellect helps to illuminate Nature as a universe of discourse. The language of exposition and communication has its sense terms and its intellectual terms. When the latter are considered, there are so few of them that do not betray their origin in sense that there is slight risk of error in generalizing the principle. I would say that there is no risk, because when we fail to recognize the sense origin of a term our failure is due to lack of etymological information. When we are asked to define our terms, what, pray, is a "definition" and what a "term"? When asked what a term "means," what is "a meaning"? Let one run over what may be called the vocabulary of the mind, consider its terms as words, and pursue those words to their source; the result is an arrival in the sense world. Idea, perceive, conceive, understand, intuition, observe, reflect, see, grasp, infer, involve, conclude, logical, coherent, method, identity, diversity, contradiction, clear, obscure, adequate, mind,

think, existence, remember, imagine, demonstrate—
there's a list of words worth several hours of study.
Closer and closer we come to the sense world, and we
are soon wondering where literal meanings end and the
metaphorical begins. It all looks like metaphor, a
"carrying-over," from start to finish—from heaven,
earth, and sea to a rattle of sounds from the mouth;
when the *sounds* make *sense*, something is understood,
supported, held up to be kept from falling down. There
are no terms in the vocabulary of the intellect which
are not, first, terms in the vocabulary of sense. Learned
discourse is supported by the strength of metaphor.[4]

The distinction between sense and intellect is also
illustrated in the difference between terms and propositions. I, myself, illustrate the strength of metaphor
when I say that terms look toward sense, propositions
toward intellect. Euclid affirmed that a point is that
which has no parts. The point is in the sense world,
and the having no parts in the intellectual or intelligible; but having no parts is found in the point. One
can express the matter in other ways. Simply having
no parts does not identify a point. What is it that has

---

[4] This topic deserves an elaboration which I am unable to give it here. It
should be clear, I think, that both the logical and the aesthetic study of
language find their source in the metaphorical character of words. It should
also be clear that that character is the source of the vain demand that terms
should be defined before they are used and also of the illusion that so-called
literal meanings are the only *real* meanings. Meanings are names metaphor-
ically operating. That, however, is quite different from "nominal positivisms."

no parts? Is the answer restricted to a point? A favorite proposition in elementary logic is "Socrates is a man." The student is immediately warned that the proposition does not mean, "a man is Socrates," even if a man is what Socrates is. "A man is mortal," does not mean "a mortal is a man." Yet Socrates, being a man, is also a mortal. Mortals, as well as men, are in the sense world, and if we are justified in affirming that Socrates is a mortal because he is a man, the justification is the proposition, "all men are mortal." The syllogism is born. Mortality is now in the sense world, having a grip on men and consequently a grip on Socrates. It will never kill him. It will take something like hemlock to do that; but were there no mortality, neither hemlock nor anything else could kill him. If there is anything to him which can't be killed, it is matter. Socrates is matter, and therefore indestructible, for all matter is that; but the indestructibility of matter, although in the sense world, is neither a mortal nor a man.

That is all very elementary and as old as Aristotle, who was among the first to develop it into something like a coherent system. The principle involved should by this time be familiar to every student of Nature. It has given rise to much controversy and debate about "universals," but I have never found it annulled. I have found it present in all debate and controversy, and it is the thing that keeps them from degenerating into complete unintelligibility. Whether it is named "logic" or not is unimportant. It is, however, an analysis of intelligibility, exhibiting what happens when we ask, "What is this?" "This" points to the world of sense, "what," to the world of intellect, and the answer points back to the world of sense. *That* is important.

I would continue this analysis of verbal discourse by commenting on one of its most troublesome terms, "existence." It is one of those terms which often involve us in a vicious circle which it seems impossible to break. "To be" and "to exist" are rarely taken to be equivalent. It is more usual to regard "an existence" as "a being that exists," with the implication that there are beings which do not exist. This would certainly be far more sensible were there undisputed criteria of existence and did not the denial of existence so often lead to the affirmation of "unreality." Undoubtedly there are shadows, but do shadows exist? Yes, because we see them. Does everything that we see exist? The answer seems to be no. We see illusions, but they are not real. But now we need criteria of reality. Is the criterion existence, and have we gone in a circle? There is little use in proceeding in this fashion, or, rather, the only use it has is to bring the discrimination of sense and intellect into operation. Then one finds that the term "existence" is as metaphorical as any other. Its literal meaning is largely arbitrary, but there is one meaning for which verbal discourse exhibits a preference. An existence is a material, bodily agent to which the *habeas corpus* principle applies. A man's shadow cannot be put in jail as his body can. I am writing on paper, but not on the indestructibility of matter. A hen sits on eggs, not on the promise and potency of chickens. *Habeas corpus*—you may have the body, and having the body you may have also something else which no picking of that body to pieces will deliver as one of the pieces. Existence of this sort gives that primary meaning to existences which has controlled all atomic theories of the universe. It is a meaning which helps to avoid much confusion, but which promotes nothing but confusion when allowed to eliminate from Nature all that does not fit that meaning. That Nature contains both that which exists and that which does not exist may sound queer. It is true, however, if the *habeas corpus* principle is allowed to define existence.[5]

I am not suggesting that existence should be defined otherwise. It is obvious to everybody that dollars can be exchanged for merchandise, but the ideas of dollars cannot. And I recall a remark of John Stuart Mill to the effect that a man does not put the idea of a spade

[5] I deliberately avoid consideration of such terms as "subsistence" because they impress me as needlessly complicating matters.

into the idea of the ground. Yet modern "empiricism" has often been led astray by just such examples and has denied "reality" in the world of sense to ideas and similar items of discourse. The consequence has been, not a clarification of discourse, but the disintegration of it. The two illustrations that follow will, I hope, indicate how, with due respect for empiricism, discourse may disintegrate and how it may not.

The final chapter of Locke's *Essay concerning Human Understanding* concludes with an astonishing paragraph. He has been writing about "the division of the sciences" and notes three basic divisions: (1) Physica, or knowledge of things as they are in their own proper beings; (2) Practica, or the skill of right applying our own powers and actions; and (3) Σημειωτική, "or *the doctrine of signs*; the most usual whereof being words, it is aptly enough termed also Λογική, *logic.*" His *Essay* falls into the last division, "for since the things the mind contemplates are, none of them besides itself, present to the understanding, it is necessary that something else, as a sign or representation of the thing it considers, should be present to it; and these are *ideas.*" And "to communicate our thoughts to one another . . . signs of our ideas are also necessary: those which men have found most convenient, and therefore generally make use of, are *articulate sounds.*" The final paragraph concludes:

All which three, viz., *things*, as they are in themselves knowable; *actions* as they depend on us, in order to happiness; and the right use of *signs* in order to knowledge, being *toto coelo* different, they seemed to me to be the three great provinces of the intellectual world, wholly separate and distinct one from another.

Three "realms of being" *toto coelo* different and separate—could intellectual disintegration go farther?

Compare these remarks of Sir J. J. Thomson in his *Recollections and Reflections.*[6]

Stewart in his lectures paid special attention to the principle of the Conservation of Energy, and gave a course of lectures entirely on this subject, and naturally I puzzled my head a great deal about it, especially about the transformation of one kind of energy into another—kinetic energy into potential energy, for example. I found the idea of kinetic energy transformed into something of quite a different nature very perplexing, and it seemed to me simpler to suppose that all energy was of the same kind, and that the "transformation" of energy could be more correctly described as the transference of kinetic energy from one home to another, the effects it produced depending on the nature of its home. This had been recognized in the case of the transformation of the kinetic energy of a moving body striking against a target into heat, the energy of the heated body being the kinetic energy of its molecules, and it seemed to me that the same thing might apply to other kinds of energy.

These remarks illustrate that normal attitude in inquiry which does not involve *toto coelo* distinctions and an ultimate dissolution of discourse. They may cause one much trouble and lead to a demand for more light on the subject, but the light demanded is of the same

[6] New York, Macmillan, 1937, p. 21.

sort that has been shining on the path of knowledge up to the point reached. It is not a demand to read Locke's *Essay* in order to proceed with confidence or the lack of it. We may ask where the homes of energy come from, but wherever they come from they are homes of energy, and when we consider those which are open to examination we can be quite sure that there is no home which would be *toto coelo* different from any home such as those we now name. A *toto coelo* different home reduces energy to a mere "it," and to find out what "it" does we must acknowledge it to be in an accessible home. Shall we now debate whether energy exists or does not exist? If the *habeas corpus* principle does not apply to it by itself, shall we throw "energy" away as if the name named nothing or were only a term in discourse signifying an experimental procedure? What, in principle, is the difference between a home with energy, being "at work," and a man with a mind, being "conscious"?

There are homes for energy, but energy is not a home. There are bodies for mind, but mind is not a body. With its home, energy is at work; with its body, mind thinks. Such is Nature's pattern of existence, and it is that pattern which makes the *habeas corpus* principle intelligible in identifying existence. One cannot help asking: What now is the difference between energy and mind besides a difference of residence? "Mental energy" becomes as valid as "heat energy" or "radiant energy." "The conservation of energy" begins to become meaningful, and its "transformations" intelligible. *But one must now remember that the mind has not been dethroned by this reduction to energy.* All the specific kinds of energy have been equally dethroned, for energy without a home is not at work. In other words, energy has no privileged home. To claim that it has is to claim privilege for a specific kind of energy. If that is done, the conclusion seems inevitable that mental energy is that specific kind, for without that kind the book from which I quoted could not have been written; there would be no pursuit of knowledge and no formulation of knowledge in equations of energy.

This section, however, is not concerned with the principles of energy. "Sense and Intellect" is its theme. The two illustrations just used exhibit how that distinction and intelligible discourse disintegrate when, relying on experience, Locke writes about the provinces of the intellectual world and that disintegration does not occur when, with the same reliance, Sir J. J. Thomson writes about energy. Three intellectual provinces so absolutely separate and distinct that "from sense to intellect and back again to sense" is wholly unintelligible; many energies understood as transformations of energy measurable and formulated in a world where a missile hits a target—the difference is profound. The provinces have no intercourse with one another, but, as Leibniz pointed out, they must have if there is to be any actual and effective exploration of them. The homes of energy may leave us puzzled, but there are the homes in the visible world before our eyes, and there also is discovered intercourse between them which can be developed and expressed in language. Here the only danger is that someone may regard energy itself as a home. When that is done, the home is beyond any conceivable discovery. Energy conceived as moving, as one body moves into another body, so that it can be arrested on its way and locked up until somebody furnishes bail, makes nonsense of energy. Energy does not exist like that. Yet it is so real, so important, so precious that we want as much of it as we can get.

Now, the propositions of existence in intelligible discourse declare precisely that sort of arrangement to be Nature's arrangement. Sense and intellect are that sort of arrangement. It is that sort of arrangement which is expressed in the distinction between the sense world and the intelligible world, in the distinction between body and mind, and in the distinction between Nature lived with and Nature understood. The distinction can be analyzed only as it is used in the analysis. If there is any problem here it is whether one is competent to say in words what things are, and that problem can be solved only by saying in words what they are.

Of course we may say that we *assume* that competence. But when we try to *prove* that we assume it, the result is that discourse degenerates into unintelligibility. That disaster may be concealed by the use of sentences which have the semblance of intelligibility, but leave nothing in sense to be grasped by the intellect. If there is an assumption, it concerns Nature rather than us. She has made a universe of discourse essential to the understanding of her. If she is not such a universe in her own right, is not herself articulated, articulate speech is incompetent to say anything at all. Nature is not *a* body with *a* mind. She is what the distinction between body and mind is. I do not mean that she perceives, thinks, remembers, imagines, and pursues happiness, but I do mean that we are not deceived when we speak of her qualities, her quantities, her places and times, her histories, her continuities, her promises and potencies, her predictable events, her teleology, her order, her linkages of pleasure and pain. So speaking is evidence of her discursive character, and our language is a translation of hers. We have to learn how to translate if her utterances of heaven and earth and sea are to be transmuted into those of our vernacular.

Chapter Five ✳ THE PURSUIT OF HAPPINESS

Justification of Nature

IN THE preceding chapters I have repeatedly emphasized the difference between knowledge of Nature
and attempts to justify her ways. So important have I
found this difference to be for the integrity of knowledge that I may have needlessly elaborated it in the
several contexts in which it has appeared. Ways and
means of improving our knowledge of Nature consti-
tute the only problem of knowledge I can find worth
while. I hope that my repeated assaults upon suggestions of a problem of a different kind have made this
clear. The limitations put upon knowledge by the personal pronoun "our" are not limitations of its character.
This attitude, however, does not warrant the conclusion that all the questions we put to Nature can or
would be answered if our knowledge were sufficiently
improved. Knowledge is not adequate to answer them.
We answer them in other ways. I would now consider

some of these ways because of their persistence in human history.

Some of the questions we ask about Nature are either absurd or irrelevant, because the circumstances under which they are asked afford no clue to circumstances under which they might be answered. Such, for example, are the following: Is Nature herself large or small? What is her weight? Is she three-dimensional—her space curved or rectilinear? What is her age? How would she appear if no one regarded her? She defeats the attempt to answer such questions. Other questions she answers as we increase our knowledge. What nourishes the human body and how? What is the moon's distance from the earth? How far can materials be analyzed and synthetized? In accord with what formulas do events occur? Then, as already indicated, there are questions which ask for a justification of what she is and does, the "why should" questions, which all of us seem ultimately driven to ask, but which she seems never to answer. Why, then, should we ask them, and what sort of answer do we make? How are they and their answers justified? The question of justification has now become crucial, and I would illustrate its searching character by quoting the words of Vernon Kellogg:

The biologist is a homely and practical-minded person, who is little given to over-refined logic and debate, but much given to observation and experiment. His laboratory tells him what a precarious and fragile thing life is, how material and condition-ruled and circumscribed a living creature is. But his wife and child and his own consciousness tell him much more, how immeasurably more, there is in life than he learns in his laboratory. It is this extra-laboratory observation and realization of the possibilities and actualities of human life that make it, even to the biologist, the vivid, many-colored, suggestive, and thrilling thing it is—the thing so full of occasionally realized great moments and of glimpses of infinitely great possibilities, that sometimes it seems all mystery, all something more than of this world, and hence all something quite hopeless to study by the methods of his science, indeed quite hopeless even profitably to wonder about. Why not take it and make the most of it?

And then comes the insistent question: Ah, *how* make the most of it? And he becomes again the patient, struggling student of biology, the student of the laws or conditions of life.[1]

I find neither defeat nor despair in those words. Every sincere laborer in the vineyard of knowledge has moments when his wages seem wholly inadequate. What is to be done about it? How make the most of the possibilities which those moments reveal? He turns to his work—his wages the same whether he has worked for an evening's hour or born the burden and heat of the day. He has not stoically justified himself. He has let Nature justify his labor.

In other words, we do not have to justify the pursuit of knowledge. If we raise the problem of justification in

[1] *Vernon Kellogg, 1867–1937*, p. 159, Washington, D. C., Belgian American Educational Foundation, Inc., 1939. Reprinted from *The Atlantic Monthly*, CXXVII (June, 1921), 785–86.

this connection, we have overlooked Nature's own moral character. She *as inclusive* of us, not we as exclusive of her, defines ultimately what morality is. I am not turning Nature into a moral philosopher and asking her to write a textbook or a guide to the perplexed. I could give her wisdom and the love of it, because she does not idly speculate about the good. She makes much of our moralizing look absurd, even such sublimities as Kant's categorical imperative and such banalities as the utilitarian's greatest good of the greatest number. Although, when personified, she is our mother, she is clearly not a humanitarian. All this is plainly written in her book and read before we invent explanations of morality by appealing to the dawn of conscience, to an innate sense of duty or a moral intuition, to sympathy, to a natural altruism, or to an egotism refined in its own interest. All these explanations are attempts to explain the fact that explains them and gives to them whatever justification they may have. The fact is that the pursuit of knowledge apart from the pursuit of happiness has no justification whatever and eventually becomes meaningless. This is a circumstance for which *we* are not responsible. It defines what a moral order is. That Nature in her own being determines what a moral order is, is not a hypothesis to be proved by argument. In a case like this, argument is of the kind that first assumes conditions

contrary to fact and then proceeds to furnish evidence
that shows that conclusions from these assumptions are
themselves contrary to fact. The force of such arguments lies in their illuminating, rather than in their
probative, character. Examples are found in every
branch of knowledge, even in mathematics. In the interest of rigor, we would prove that the lines a and b
are perpendicular to each other; we assume that they
are not and then show that the assumption requires
that two other lines c and d are unequal; but these lines
are equal and so the assumption is absurd. Our sense of
the importance of rigor in mathematics is thereby
heightened, and the integrity of geometrical relations
clarified. In cases like this, arguments from conditions
contrary to fact are at their best. Their danger lies in a
tendency to degenerate into so-called laws of pure
logical thinking, as if we began by postulating x and y
and then affirmed that x either is or is not y. We evidently acquire no knowledge thereby, for x and y, if
they are to lead us anywhere, must first be symbols for
something else than anything whatever.

Yet the specious argument may be risked in the interest of some clarification of Nature's integrity. Let us
suppose that she does not determine what a moral
order is. Consequences flow from that supposition.
Among them is Spinoza's dictum that events are not
good or evil in themselves, but only as the emotional

nature (*animus*) is affected by them. With him the pursuit of happiness was a matter of falling in love, for in that pursuit men are made or marred by what they fall in love with; it controls their happiness and unhappiness. In love with riches, personal distinction, or the lusts of the flesh, men are a prey to envy, hatred, and malice, to anxiety and disease, and to all sorts of mental disturbances. They are unhappy, not happy; discontented, not contented. But men cannot help falling in love with something or other. The sort of unhappiness from which they suffer through their bondage to what they love would vanish and they would be free, if they were in love with an object which provoked no jealousy and no disturbances of the mind. Such an object can be found only through the discovery of the connection between the mind and Nature entire. But what is Nature entire? It is either "God or Nature" or "God and nature." As the latter, nature is God's creation following from him out of the necessity of his own being, but not because he is willful or provident. We belong to his created nature, and our emotional nature belongs to it. Good and evil, mental disturbances, and the pursuit of happiness follow as a matter of course. What now, it may pertinently be asked, has become of the assumption that Nature does not determine what a moral order is? How much has the use of a big letter or a little one to do with the matter? Suppose that there is no

God; Nature, as we analyze her, is not dependent on that supposition or its contrary. Because this is so, Spinoza was called an atheist, in spite of his passionate declaration that even by human minds an object can be found so powerful in the love it imparts that jealousy and disturbances vanish and man's soul is free. That which has kept Spinoza remembered is, not his contributions to the advancement of knowledge, but his demonstration *ordine geometrico* that it is absurd to suppose that what a moral order is, is not determined by Nature. Such a supposition violates Nature's integrity.

Spinoza is here cited, not as an authority, but as an example of a line of thought repeated through centuries of reflection on morals. "Morals" and "morality" have not an equivalent effect in the universe of discourse. The former suggests folkways and codes of various sort, while the latter suggests an order to which these ways and codes are ultimately relevant, an order in which the pursuit of happiness and the pursuit of knowledge are linked or like contrasted poles in a common field of activity. Suppose that this is not so. What follows, then, in any analysis of Nature? Every shred of Nature's teleology would vanish or be turned into a monstrous absurdity. Nature, then, could not be usable for any purpose. She could neither let nor hinder. We try in vain to obviate this conclusion by introducing purposes from without; for in what conceivable way can she be arranged so that when purposes are introduced she lets or hinders their realization? Must we first be sick in order that her chemistry may yield a pharmacology? Must we first be hungry in order that we may have digestive organs which, although composed of her materials, transmute her materials into food? Must we first want to see in order that eyes from her may come into being bringing a vision of her along? Do we first want to be adapted to her environment in order that her environment may permit that adaptation? Our needs and purposes are what they are because they are linked with Nature's teleology. They do not create that teleology in order that they may be let or hindered in their satisfaction.

It is also contrary to fact to suppose that Nature intends a moral order. She subtends one, rather, like the arc of a circle its cord, illustrating thereby an incommensurability between events in their happening and events in their value. Does she intend spinning spiders and, for their food, flies caught in the web, intending also that spiders should be food for wasps? Does she intend that women should bear and suckle children and also that they should die in childbirth? Does she intend the sun to be eclipsed? Does she intend anything whatever? It is just because she does not, that she is found to be reliable. Were she whimsical, or did she exhibit a preference for some events over others, she could not be trusted. So essential are her indifference and necessity that one is tempted to say that they are precisely what they are in order that events may have the chance to run their course and fulfill, however incompletely, their forecast of possibility, and that that is her intention. The "in order that" may be set aside, but the fact remains that the pursuit of knowledge in the presence of necessity and indifference is essential to the pursuit of happiness. Thereby a moral order is defined. No other definition ultimately fits the facts. Nature clearly exhibits a moral order, not because we distort her or willfully accommodate her to some antecedent definition of our own of what a moral order is or ought to be, but because we have acquired from her the idea of what such an order is. We are not free to make arbitrary definitions. The more clearly this is recognized, the more certain becomes the knowledge that moral problems can cease to be only with the cessation of Nature. If that seems to be too extravagant, let it be said that so long as there is the pursuit of happiness, moral problems will arise—problems of good and evil, of just and unjust, problems of virtue and character. Knowledge cannot get rid of them.

The supposition that it could is again a supposition contrary to fact. One has only to try the matter out. Freed from the hauntings of conscience, untroubled by the sense of duty, with no occasion for sympathy, with no burden of responsibility, with no chance to be altruistic or egoistic, with Nature's necessity and indifference so completely mastered by knowledge that what ought to be done is so clear that it will be done, how could happiness be pursued? Could it then be said to have been securely attained? Would happiness mean anything in a world without morality? We answer the question negatively when we deny both happiness and the pursuit of it to the stars and the seasons, but hesitate to include the swarm of animals, the spectacle of birth and death, of cities and wars—public experience. Such hesitation ought both to astonish and instruct us. It seems very strange indeed that the swarm of animals should introduce a "struggle for existence." It seems stranger still that an animal, having learned all that there is to know, would then have no struggle in its existence. It seems far more likely that such an animal would have a vision of possibilities so overpowering that the insistent question would come: How make the most of it? Unfortunately he would have no laboratory for an asylum wherein he might become "a homely and practical minded person." It is instructive to carry absurdities to their limit.

Nature, then, may be said to justify a moral order so far forth as she is that kind of order herself and the source of our idea of it. In attempting to clarify this I have been more embarrassed by personification than in other parts of this essay. A literary preference or affectation has, perhaps, the look of trying to force an issue by using a capital letter and personal pronouns in a context which seems to demand their exclusion if clearness is to be attained. The exclusion is, however, difficult. The difference between a personal and impersonal style of writing turns out to be more than a literary difference. I have already given illustrations of this. When, for example, the impersonal pronoun "it" has for antecedent nouns like "mind" or "consciousness," that which is ultimately identified in discourse is a mindful or conscious being and, conspicuously, a "man" or "human" being. He, not his mind or his consciousness, is the agent in his behavior within his surroundings. The personal note is struck in that identification of an agent. Something similar is to be said whenever there is required the identification of an agent. Agents do whatever is done in Nature, and what they do is not an agency which does it for them. Nor are the circumstances under which something is done the agent of the doing in any other sense than that there are agents among the circumstances. Switching to the passive voice of the verb does not alter the facts. Only a superficial and literary positivism is thereby gained. The passive voice suppresses the agent by turning what he does into what is done by him under the circum-

stances of his doing it. The neuter pronoun is fitting
for what is done after it is done, but all doings involve
agents and are generative; they give birth to consequences. There is a native animism in all of us which
renders the distinction between personal and impersonal writing much like the rhetorical distinction between poetry and prose. "There is relentless necessity
in Nature," is poetry. Is nothing but the impersonal
left by striking out the adjective "relentless"? What,
pray, is the "need" in necessity?

Nature has been personified in this essay, not, however, to prepare the way to prove that she is a person. I
said at the beginning that my personification was a
confession of piety. She is neither active nor passive, although time and again I have written as if she were.
She is not an agent, but such an integration of agents
that knowledge and happiness are linked together. I
could say, in an attempt to be as impersonal as possible, that she is a polarized circumstance, one pole
being an environment and the other an individual
agent of some sort, and all so integrated that the polarized duality cannot be a dualism of original opposites,
magically interacting. All that might sound to some
ears like a jumble of words and to others like a contribution to philosophy or metaphysics, possibly profound
and worthy of a distinguishing name. I dislike esoteric
language. It is as much a figure of speech as any other.

I am not concerned with the question whether Nature ought to be personified or not, but with the difference between a person and being personified. We, as among Nature's agents, do not escape the personal emphasis. We do not need to be told that we pursue knowledge for the sake of happiness and that if the pursuit of knowledge is to be effective it must be disinterested. That effectiveness confronts the pursuit of happiness with a complete indifference. Then we find ourselves in a moral order where risks are run and responsibility is incurred, and there are rewards and punishments whether they are intended or not. Being personal is driven home. Nature known as "impersonal circumstance" becomes Nature embraced by persons, and personification mounts.

How far other agents in Nature are similarly circumstanced is a speculative question. Is the Sun doing his duty by shining, and doing it to the best of his ability under the circumstances? Playing with the supposition that he is may be instructive. I can imagine him indignant at Earth's complaints for parching her foliage and drying up her springs, even if she blesses him for storing up heat in the coals in her bosom. Will she never be satisfied? She complains of the heat, although she knows that he shines on the Moon, who keeps cool. She knows too that as her offspring ascends toward the Sun by climbing mountains or inventing machines, the colder it gets. The Sun may be both amused and annoyed by scientists who look upon him as a mighty agent and yet he may transform what he does into what is done under the circumstances. It is now fantastic to talk about the sun in the foregoing manner, but such fantastic talk reveals us to ourselves, for it was once the way we talked in the pursuit of knowledge. It is an ultimate sort of self-justification—inverting our personality into a personification of Nature and then purifying ourselves by reducing our agency to circumstance.

Again the moral order confronts us, but like an order of personal agents pursuing happiness in a world of circumstance which they must know as indifferent to their own interests if those interests are to be served by knowledge. When and how did such an order historically arise? It is beyond dispute that we live in such an order now, come into it at birth, and pass out of it at death, and that we find it essential to the kind of life we lead. That we never did nor could create it is a conviction which steadily grows with increasing knowledge. In moments of personal revolt we often declare that we would never create such an order had we the power, forgetting that we are then passing a moral judgment on that order itself. When we try our hand at re-creating and are rigorously thorough, fully awake to what we would and would not have, we end where we began—with the pursuit of happiness in a world of in-

different circumstance. The personal attitude dom-
inates us in the end, whether or not Nature is personified in the beginning. It is this fact, not any obscurity
about what a moral order is, that leads to attempts to
justify such an order otherwise than by accepting its
natural status as sufficient.

Now the desire arises for the personal possession of a
knowledge which would give us security, only the
knowledge must not be like physics, biology, or history.
They and their like do not deliver the kind of security
desired. They are natural knowledge, and such knowledge pushed imaginatively to its limits does not approach a justification of the kind now desired. No
"in the beginning" of a historical sort will now suffice
for the search, for history discloses that there is no
"beginning" of "in the beginning" and that the search
for one can do no better than end, through fatigue, in a
chaos of darkness illuminated only by a cry for light
which would bring back heaven and earth and sea with
all that in them is, if there is to be anything to explore.
The desired knowledge requires a light which would
reveal something totally different, something that
would satisfy personality instead of cognitive curiosity.
With emphasis primarily on *the person*, human nature
seeks kinship, not with animals and the rest of Nature,
but with divinity. Knowledge of divinity would be, not
natural, but supernatural knowledge.

The substance of the preceding paragraphs has been

expressed in many different ways, in many different places, and by all sorts and conditions of men. The language may vary, the circumstances may vary, certain emphases may vary, but the substance does not. The language varies most, because the words for the supernatural are the words for the natural. Their use is, consequently, relevant to the personal circumstances of their uttering and to the social institutions devoted to the cultivation of religion. My insistence that the natural, or Nature, is the only object of knowledge is not a stubborn clinging to a particular use of a word, but a recognition that the supernatural is something confessed and that the word "faith" suits it better than the word "knowledge." This is both orthodox knowledge and the confession that faith is a force. It is not a force which removes mountains, but one which gives to the pursuit of happiness a character beyond the moral order. The evidences of its power are abundant. This power we may be said to know, for the illustrations and works of faith are abundant.

The Supernatural

Appeals to the supernatural neither explain nor justify Nature. They may explain a good deal about ourselves and confirm the doctrine that we, not Nature, are justified by faith. We are not justified by our good works. The doctrine has been disputed time and again.

Disputes about it, however, as disputes about similar doctrines, end either by suppressing what has been taken for granted from the start or by changing the subject in such a way that an apparently new dispute will engage attention. We may drop justification and switch to justice. Then we would have the just judge merciful. Soon we are equating justice with mercy— and we ask not to be judged by our deeds, but by our faith, praying that the court will be liberal and decide, not according to the law, but for the general good. Is war a good deed? Is it the road to justice? Turn it into a crusade for righteousness and mercy, and it becomes justified by faith. Who is not familiar with all this? How easy it is to make it look ridiculous, to stand aloof and wear the cynic's smile. Cynicism is the refusal to have a faith which justifies.

Faith and its consequences are acknowledgments of the supernatural. I am quite willing to add to that affirmation the qualification "in human experience," for it is that experience which is now under consideration. So I repeat that faith is a justification, not of Nature, but of ourselves. I would now add that we want to be justified ultimately, not to Nature or even in our own eyes, but in the eyes of one to whom we might pray, "Thy will be done," and who might say in judgment, were speech possible, "Well done! Good and faithful servant." There the supernatural is acknowledged.

Let Nature have a will; her will will be done whether asked or not. That is found out without difficulty. The sort of will which is also done whether asked or not and yet is asked to be done with judgment following is not the will of Nature or of her laws combined. It is not a natural phenomenon. It is rather a definition of the supernatural, a will past human understanding, one which natural knowledge does not disclose. Nature may suggest it because we are residents in her domain, and in that sense the supernatural is as natural as the natural. The trickiness of words ought to cause no deception here. Religious behavior can be studied as well as any other kind of animal behavior, and to make it wholly nonnatural, in the full sense of that logical negative, is to turn the animal man, partly at least, into a supernatural being. The supernatural is encountered in spite of all the dialectic of words. Since religious behavior occurs in Nature and, in occurring, is an acknowledgment of the supernatural, it sounds rather odd to affirm that "there is no such thing as the supernatural." The supernatural may not exist, but it is easy for a dialectician to turn its nonexistence into a definition of its existence. These warnings against the misuse of dialectic have become wearisome. My excuse is that I would try to clarify the acknowledgment of the supernatural in its evident association with human behavior. It thereby receives its definition in unmistakable terms.

There are factors in the pursuit of knowledge which hint, so to speak, at the supernatural and which are often employed as arguments for the existence of God. Examples are, Nature's teleology, the contingent character of events when arranged in causal sequence, the incommensurability of mechanism and life, of mind and matter, of body and soul, the disciplinary character of the moral order. These arguments are recurrent and usually produce recurrent confusion. For many they are confessions of faith, rather than proofs of the supernatural. For others they may prop a tottering faith or help to recover a lost one, but their convincing power is very far from being the convincing power of knowledge. They do not prove the existence of a supernatural agent who interferes with Nature. Only miracles can do that, and it is very difficult to identify a miracle without admitting that the laws of Nature adjust themselves for its occurrence. The arguments are, in effect, indications of the kind of being God is expected to be, rather than proofs that he is an agent exercising the functions of government. To the deeply religious, such a conception of God seems almost blasphemous, although they praise Him as holy and almighty and pray that His will be done. With Him, doing His will is His will being done. Both life and death are His will, although He does not will them. That confession has been written time and again in religious history.

But that is not a final word about these arguments for the supernatural. They express the fact that Nature, entire and integrated, wears yet an unfinished look. She never *is* what she *was* or what she *will be*. She refuses to be included in a calendar, and yet from hour to hour she tells a tale, and that tale is not finished. This incompleteness seems to cry for completeness, this imperfection for perfection. The consideration of the concrete and definite tends to turn into a consideration of the abstract and indefinite, and categories tend to take the place of events. Something of this has been indicated in Chapter III. There were emphasized the dependence of the analysis of events upon their completion and that matter is the changeless in changing materials. There is a clear and understandable sense in which the perfect is prior to the imperfect and the changeless prior to the changing—a priority which keeps thought from becoming blocked in its progress and holds it to an identifiable track. From this priority categories such as "being," "substance," "essence," "idea," and "power" derive such meanings as they have in discourse. They are very intensive terms. They steady discourse and keep it from disintegrating. They are *essential* to it—and there I have used an adjective derived from one of them. Their authority is so great that, in spite of the fact that they identify nothing when independent of the concrete, it is repeatedly affirmed that what they identify independently is un-knowable, but that if it would be known, it would be unified and would explain Nature's incomplete, im-perfect, and unfinished look. She would be the adum-bration of an already perfect scheme. Arguments for the existence of God illustrate the line of thought thus briefly sketched. They are generalizations of the pri-ority of perfection. They would finish Nature's un-finished character and complete her incompleteness.

Such reasoning, and doctrines like justification by faith are characteristic of a very advanced theology. That is why they have been chosen to illustrate the acknowledgment of the supernatural. Religious cults, often heavily burdened with superstition, obscure the matter. When "God" ceases to be the singular of the plural "gods," something quite different from the sub-stitution of one god for many has occurred. The at-mosphere of reflection has changed. There is now found something almost akin to knowledge; almost, but not wholly, for doctrines take the place of formu-lated discovery. The apparent kinship lies in a simi-larity in reasoning. No theory is free from the abstract or from categories which keep it intact and render it intelligible and communicable. "Idea" is a good example. Every theory is a synthesis of ideas. The ideas are not their objects. They are in their objects and when drawn out from them are called "ideas" of those objects, so that ideas are not concrete as their objects are. A psychologist can make them subject matter of his science only by accepting their objects along with them. Indeed, taking objects along with their ideas is characteristic of the whole pursuit of knowledge, and the source of error lies in letting ideas exceed the limits which their objects set. This matter could be extensively elaborated; but for one not too violently choked by an unconventional use of language it may be sufficient to indicate that "heat" is the idea of hot and cold objects, "motion" the idea of moving bodies, and "energy" the idea of working bodies, and that the danger of error lies in allowing heat to heat objects, motion to move them, and energy to make them work.

Doctrines or theories of the supernatural adopt the pattern set by the pursuit of knowledge. Their apparent kinship with knowledge is thereby accounted for. Superficially there is no difference in methodology or rational procedure. There is, however, a profound difference. Whereas in theories of the natural, objects generate ideas, in theories of the supernatural, ideas generate objects. Putting the matter that way may sound a little too rhetorically neat—an oversimplification of a procedure inherently complex. It is risked for the sake of emphasis. The inversion of "from objects to ideas" into "from ideas to objects" occurs frequently in the pursuit of knowledge and has often proved fruitful. A conspiracy of ideas, as it were, suggests an object which would turn out to be their source were that object available in its own right. The "ether" has become a classical example. That "matter" of which Tyndall spoke so eloquently is another. Such objects are styled "hypothetical" instead of "supernatural" because of their connection with the development of natural knowledge. Objects called "supernatural" are also approached through a conspiracy of ideas. They might, therefore, be styled "hypothetical," only they are connected with the pursuit of happiness and attempts at self-justification. Were they equatable in status with the hypothetical objects developed in the pursuit of knowledge, they would lose their significance. Neither the religious nor the antireligious, neither theist nor atheist, will have God's status equivalent to that of the "ether" or "matter." With such equivalence, the one has nothing to worship and the other nothing to discover. And without the supernatural emphasis pantheists say nothing at all when they say that Nature herself is God. In worshipping her they worship a divinity *in* her, which is not a natural object. Theories of the natural and theories of the supernatural appear alike in their procedures and reasoning. They are conspicuously different in their connections. "God," "ether," and "matter" may in a sense be objects of faith; but not in the same sense, even if they are approached in similar ways.

The acknowledgment of the supernatural and the

device for justification are pointedly expressed in the words of the Psalmist, "When I consider thy heavens, the work of thy fingers, the moon and the stars which thou hast ordained, what is man that thou art mindful of him?" That question, though ancient, is also modern. Increased consideration of the heavens by man increased his wonder whether there is any mindfulness of him. The evidence of the heavens is negative. The evidence of man—*that* is something quite different. In considering Nature, why *should* he ask a question which he *does* ask? Let the "does" suffice for the "should" and the whole matter be "psychologically" explained. Then man does appeal to the supernatural and try to justify himself by faith in it, the faith that the supernatural is or can be mindful of him if he makes himself worthy by prayer and praise and sacrifice and by confessing that he and Nature belong, not to himself, but to God. Probe the matter in its natural setting and the source of both religion and superstition is disclosed. These two leave Nature still the vineyard wherein the work of knowledge is done. Her own inherent integrity has not been changed. To the faithful, however, she has become something additional, a scheme of things incidental to a different scheme. That different scheme cannot be explored as Nature is explored. The language used in descriptions of it is perforce the language of Nature, but that language then reveals its heavy

load of ambiguity. It looks much like a primitive, animistic language when compared with the language of
science, until the terms of the latter are thoroughly
searched and found to be suppressions of a primitive
animism which lends them much of their meaning.
"Gravitation" has not yet quite ceased its "pulling"
and "drawing." And both languages in the end seem
to be driven to the same sort of categories. It would
seem, therefore, unprofitable to declare a war between
the natural and the supernatural. Nature as a scheme
of things, with an inherent integrity of her own, and
Nature as incidental to a wholly different scheme of
things can hardly summon their hosts to battle with
neutrality observing them from afar.

The Cult of the Supernatural

To the pursuit of knowledge in the interest of the
pursuit of happiness must be added the cult of the
supernatural. Anthropological studies are thereby suggested, for the cult is conspicuously human. It may be
that only to human eyes is Nature a manifestation of
God's glory and an exhibition of his will done. One
may note, however, that our ascription of instinct to
animals and of something like it to all living things
amounts to little more than admitting that we think of
them as under the control and even the guidance of
powers which they cannot help obeying and to which

they "instinctively" submit as if their blind obedience were their mode of worship. I would avoid speculations about such matters, but I find it difficult to avoid recording impressions received from attempts to analyze currently accepted opinions and beliefs. After reading, for example, in the early nineties Huxley's essay on *Morals and Evolution*, a commonplace of the "evolution" of my student days ceased to be impressive as a scientific dogma and became mysterious. What sense could "the struggle for existence and the survival of the fittest" possibly have if the only test of fitness were survival? I could find no increment in knowledge of any sort in being told that "survivors are those who survive." Are survivors the fittest? Questions like those multiplied until I found myself asking: Why not say that "there's a divinity that shapes our ends, rough-hew them how we will" or "what is man that thou art mindful of him"? Is he fit to survive? What *is* the use of speculating about such matters when biology frequently gives expression to the cult of the supernatural? It is more profitable to study that cult when it is less ambiguously exhibited.

Here the cult is taken as the ceremonial expression of the acknowledgment of the supernatural and religion as the personal acceptance of that acknowledgment as a principle of stability in the pursuit of happiness. I do not think that I misread the facts. If the word "vulgar" had not acquired a sinister implication which the word "common" does not wholly remove, I could say with the vulgar that the religious are those who have a sense of the need and possibility of salvation. Only the saved can be genuinely happy and at peace. And what are they saved from? The vulgar answer is "their sins." And what are their sins? Pride and the rest which may be forgiven because of human frailty. But there is one sin which is unforgivable: the refusal of allegiance to the supernatural. One may be converted from that sin, and then there is salvation and the possibility of forgiveness for the others. This view of religion is not confined to Christendom nor to the Roman Church. It is implicit in all cults of the supernatural and is the reason why the Christian Mission has spread to so many peoples the world over. I am not writing apologetics, but appealing to history and to the language of the vulgar.

The cult of the supernatural is, therefore, not itself evidence of religion on the part of those who practice it. This also is vulgarly recognized. The cult may be studied with religion left almost wholly out of the account. There is advantage in so doing, for rites and ceremonies are indications of attitudes toward Nature and human life with implications of the supernatural or something like it in them. That there should be ceremonies at all can become an arresting fact, especially when man forgets his own and turns to Nature to see if any are then left. A poet, even a Lucretius, has little beyond versification to do with the ceremonies of the spring. Materials of poetry are expansed unto his eyes. What he reads into the scene and out of it are almost indistinguishable. A native animistic attitude toward Nature is disclosed. In a way the language of animism comes first and that of knowledge afterward.

There is danger here, however, of an overemphasis. The attitude of the savage or primitive man is sometimes regarded as quite different from that of the civilized and the birth and growth of scientific knowledge is sometimes found in a progressive reduction of animistic powers to natural causes. This looks like a misreading of the facts. Science and ceremony have been and are coeval, and both have had their historical developments. The primitive man ought not to be expected to discriminate after the manner of the sophisticated. He discriminates in what he does, and he knows well what is and what is not within his own power. Nor, when the circumstances and ways of his living are considered, can he be expected to formulate his knowledge in communicable equations. He learns, quite literally, by experience and teaches by having the young repeat the experiences. His husbandry, his arts and crafts, and much of his medicine are matters of experience and teachable in their own terms. He counts and measures, notes the seasons, invents markers for remembrance, keeps some account of time. He is not ignorant of the law of the balance when he makes or throws a weapon or of the refraction of light when he spears a fish. He poisons and barbs Nature's arrows, well knowing what he is doing. All such knowledge of Nature is his without any appeal to the supernatural. It is entitled to be called "science," even if it is science in its historically primitive stages. The beginnings of science go back to the beginnings of man. One may say that there has always been in human history a "natural philosophy," summing up from generation to generation what has been learned through that sort of observation and reflection which characterizes the pursuit of knowledge generally. There has always been lore free from legend.

In the life of primitive man, however, there is much ceremony and secrecy. Part of this is ornamentation or decoration of what he does, in order to enhance its value; part of it is an attempt to control circumstances which his knowledge does not help him to control. That which gives to him the appearance of a lack of scientific interest is his habit of looking upon Nature as peopled with friendly and unfriendly powers. Many a civilized man can recover this attitude by trying to sleep on the ground for one night in the wild. That can be an awful experience. Nature then is not an object for scientific research, but a brooding and enfolding mystery. Dull would he be of soul who, lying under the stars in the Big Basin of California and with human companionship at call, did not feel that those giant trees were regarding him with a little contempt for his youth and egotism. The savage is used to it. He takes it all as a matter of course and in its own terms, with the ceremonies of friendship and enmity. He prays, worships, sacrifices, propitiates, dances, gives personal names to the forces of Nature, makes up stories about them, and even tries to frighten them. Those mysterious but friendly and unfriendly people of earth and sky are like the familiar people of neighboring tribes with whom he is at peace or at war, and they should be approached with like ceremonies. The gods are born. They are natural beings because they dwell in Nature; they are also supernatural in that they are somehow Nature's ultimate possessors and have her in their control. One may say, therefore, that the attitude of the savage toward Nature is fundamentally religious in the sense that his reflective living and thinking are governed more by his ideas of supposed friendly and unfriendly powers operating in Nature than by the discovery of her laws. He is more given to the cult of the supernatural than to the pursuit of knowledge. Medicine is the combined art of caring for the body's well being and for the keeping of secrets. To get instruction in medicine is like going to school for an education—

going from the family and homely remedies to the priest and his professional craft.

Such, in general, is a sketch of the attitude of the savage toward Nature as disclosed by students of anthropology. It is far from being an imaginary reconstruction of a vanished past. Primitive people have survived and can be studied without attempting to reconstruct a long lost past out of meager data. If the sketch represents the childhood of the race, that childhood is still with us, and the study of it as a living present rather than a survival of a dead past has shattered many imaginary reconstructions of primeval society. Anthropological material is now found nearer home. Many "conventions" which were once disposed of as "survivals" are found to require a different disposal. Their persistence has become so impressive that it is easy to believe that ancestry has little to do with them and that they are products of current circumstances even if they wear, as it were, buttons which serve no buttoning purpose, but are reminders, to the historian of fashions, of buttons which once were useful. The zipper may survive as an ornament. I have used a trivial example to suggest something far from trivial. Anthropology, although still mainly occupied with what is called primitive society, seems to be becoming more and more occupied with human ceremonies, customs, habits, institutions, and languages generally.

It has greatly enlarged the range of its source materials, so that the idea of "primitive society" is becoming less significant in the study of man. Man in civilized society is still a man, often so behaving that his ancestry is largely irrelevant. In other words, many of his ceremonies are due to a continuity in the natural circumstances of human experience and are traditional only because they exhibit vestigial survivals of the past. Government, for example, is a natural product of neighborhood living. The seed of it is sown where two or three are met together. It is not long before that seed flowers into some sort of pomp and circumstance of which some portion may be kept up without serving any other purpose than the adornment of an institution.

It is with the significance and effect of ceremony that I am here concerned. What is a ceremony? Washing one's hands simply to get rid of blood stains is not; Lady Macbeth's washing of her hands, even in sleep, is. There is here no need of instruction from a teacher to help one to see the difference. When, in the washing of hands, does the washing become ceremonial? If I must answer, I must descend to the trivial—the moment the water is perfumed. With that descent I hear over the radio much advertising of ceremonial cleanliness; I am taken to the bathtub and to the mirror before which I shave. The bathroom has ceased to be a convenient sanitary device and has become a shrine for ceremonial purification. Leaving the trivial, where can Lady Macbeth wash her hands clean? One can follow the road from the perfumed water to the sacrament of baptism. The water remains water, but the perfume changes from an odor for the nostrils to words which evoke the supernatural, "Sanctify this water to the mystical washing away of sin." With something not aqueous to enhance the washing, cleanliness begins to become next to godliness. Such illustrations expose the truth about the significance and effect of ceremonies. When the multitude and variety of them are considered and then a comparison is made between the civilized and the savage, I doubt if the ratio of ceremony to the pursuit of knowledge would be found higher among the latter than among the former. From birth to death, no matter when nor where, there is more ceremony than science in the conduct of life.

There are few ceremonies that cannot be made to look ridiculous when their significance and effect are disregarded. Caricature is often a favorite literary sport. It is tempting to indulge in it, for it is itself a ceremony exposing the kinship of comedy and tragedy and of laughter and tears. Of this exposure, Plato's *Symposium* is an example hard to match. I have often thought that a more appropriate name for that piece would be "Agathon's Dinner"—that dinner of men, most of whom had been drunk the night before, where love was the theme and where that theme was carried to the heights of an unutterable ecstasy freed from all sensuality and then allowed to degenerate into a riot of drunkenness, with Socrates and Aristophanes discussing comedy and tragedy at the end until Aristophanes slipped under the table and Socrates, still sober, departed to take a bath. To cite Gilbert and Sullivan's *Yeoman of the Guard*, is not to wander far afield.

> I have a song to sing, O,
> Sing me your song, O.

The audience goes away a little troubled to discover that the merriment of man and maid should end with that song sung in the key of tragedy. The ceremonies of love—who has done them justice? Launcelot and Guinevere, the policeman and the cook, the Divine Comedy.

Caricature, although tempting, is out of place when the significance and the effect of ceremony are under consideration. Some flavor of irony may be permitted, for seriousness can become unhealthy when it cannot wear that smile which indicates neither ridicule nor contempt. The significance of ceremony lies in a lifting up of what is done to a status not essential to the simple doing of it. Or, stated differently, it is the recognition of mounting levels to which what is done can be carried and receive thereby a value increasingly less utilitarian, without, however, the loss of utility by the way. Since the value is a heightened sense of perception of a deed done or in the doing, it might appropriately be called "aesthetic," but that adjective is misleading because of its current association with the appreciation of beauty. Yet ceremony and beautifying are often identical. A ceremonial dance may be entrancing to behold; a well-laid dinner table with all its ceremonial implementation may appear too beautiful to be disturbed by eating, drinking, and chatter unless gods and goddesses are seated about it. Perhaps illustrations like that go pretty much to the roots of the matter. Hospitality is far more than simply taking in the casual wayfarer. It is the acknowledgment of expected guests. It has long been regarded as a sacred thing and has its sacramental obligations. In breaking bread in his own cottage with a stranger the peasant may entertain the prince. In many a land this legend is told, often springing up, as it were, from the native soil. The ultimate significance of ceremony lies in the recognition of the sacramental. Without that it is formal etiquette. Then the spirit has gone out and we subscribe ourselves, "Respectfully yours," as the most noncommittal of subscriptions.

The distinction between man and other animals is almost exclusively in terms of ceremony. By using what

he names his "reason," he makes his sublime egotism
look fantastic. His "natural desire to know" and the
"natural rights" with which he boasts to have been
"unalienably endowed," are reduced to exhibitions of
"a natural instinct for self-preservation," which in its
turn is generalized into a universal principle that
everything has a *conatus in suo esse perseverare:* the natural
habit of all moving bodies to maintain their own status
unless interfered with. Preserving man's status is preserving the pursuit of knowledge in support of the
pursuit of his own happiness. "His own" is rationally
necessary to preserve his own egotism. Man finds that
he cannot live "rationally," that he must live "reasonably," motivated as he is by that instinct for self-
preservation, "the first law of life." Having broken rule
after rule of logic, he turns to ceremony and then finds
a ladder up which he can climb carrying on his back
his load of animality to be dropped when he reaches
heaven's gate.

I have not made all that up. It is all found in the
books and voiced and practiced by learned and un-
learned alike. It is confirmed by experience. "Re-
forms," "movements," "causes," "crusades," "revolutions," "societies for the prevention, promotion, or
preservation of this and that" exhibit it with emphasis.
The assemblies, the processions, the bands, the march-
ing songs, the emblems—flags, pins, buttons, ribbons—

the dogmas, the salutes, and, above all, the pledges, the covenants, the vows, the oaths, and the sacraments! How irrational it all is, and how reasonable! Psychological theories invented to explain it usually end by making "human nature" so responsible for it that without "human nature" Nature would be devoid of both science and ceremony. This is very much like making "human nature" itself supernatural or at least so dualizing body and soul that the body comes from a wholly material world while the soul comes from a spiritual one to assist the body, already mechanically equipped with organs for the purpose, in adapting itself to its environment. I must confess that this seems to me like turning the significance of ceremony, along with the pursuit of knowledge in the interest of happiness, upside down.

The distinction between the "rational" and the "reasonable" which I have drawn is of that tenuous kind which is apt to break down under strain. It is like that between "mind" and "soul," suggesting an accent or emphasis rather than a partition. When the soul thinks, it is mind; when the mind feels, it is soul. To love with all one's heart, with all one's soul, with all one's mind, and with all one's strength is not to set up four compartments in which love may be exercised. It is more like the tonic discriminations of a musical scale exhibited in a melody. So it is with the rational and the reasonable. The rational is rigorous, impersonal, and averse to compromise; the reasonable is yielding, personal, and makes compromise a virtue. The rational entertains causes, the reasonable seeks consequences, so that a man is not rational unless he is reasonable or reasonable unless he is rational. In the light of this tenuous discrimination, the effect of ceremony may be said to be the exhibition of reasonableness rather than rationality. Consequently, in the dry light of reason ceremony is absurd, while in the mellow light of reasonableness it is absurd only in caricature. Even so, it is not wholly absurd. Young lovers in their adolescent ecstasy are sorely offended when ridiculed face to face, but they will hold hands in delight when watching young lovers caricatured on the stage. They know what it is all about. They can call one another silly without offense. This is quite irrational.

It is also quite reasonable. When the extent and variety of ceremonial living are not allowed to obscure the main point, the effect of ceremony is its significance utilized in support of living reasonably so that the inevitable friction of associated living is eased. It is like oil to grinding wheels. The "polite" is the "polished." The effect of ceremony ought not to be confused with its significance. The latter goes down deep into the springs of life to burst out or to flower in exhibitions of desire and aspiration, becoming devotional, dedicatory, and sacramental. Its effect is the formation of habits, customs, and conventions which are stabilizers in the conduct of life even when ceremony has lost its significance. If men rise when women enter their company, an atmosphere of ladies and gentlemen is created although neither ladies nor gentlemen are present. Our century, having inherited from its predecessor the beginnings of a revolt against conventionality and having increased the extent and velocity of the revolt, finds us nevertheless shocked today when nations make war without first declaring it. Unconventionality is itself a convention of the most inconvenient sort. When there are no generally accepted modes of behavior, one is driven more and more to decide momentarily how to behave and becomes more and more a prey to those clever enough to turn unconventionality to their own advantage. The habit of buying what you want tends to transform itself into the habit of buying what you're sold. Many habits are similarly transformed—living in terms of one's own criticized experience into living under the seductions of advertising; going to worship into going to church; preaching salvation into preaching reform. In all this a satirist finds material enough to keep him busy for life. A moralist must take it seriously.

This book, however, is not an essay in morals, but one about Nature. It may often appear like the former.

An analysis of Nature which finds her setting the pattern of a moral order can hardly fail to carry with it practical implications. If ceremony, regarded as something natural, with sources that are not restricted to "human nature" alone, is not a freakish artifice, if it has the effect of stabilizing the pursuit of happiness and tends to lend some security to that pursuit, a moral is obviously suggested. There is a difference between pointing out what *is* done and preaching what *ought* to be done, but that difference itself is one of the circumstances to be pointed out. It may properly be said that the pursuit of happiness is not a duty. It must also be said that in the pursuit of happiness duties are inevitable. One may bring this home very effectively to oneself by reaching first the conclusion that there is nothing whatever that ought to be done and then realizing that that conclusion is itself the beginning of moral wisdom, for now comes the insistent question: What ought to be done about it? You can end the pursuit of happiness when you will. Is that what ought to be done about it? Is that happiness attained? The most hard-headed analysis ends with moral questions acknowledged. The significance and effect of ceremonies make it clear enough that any salvation in the pursuit of happiness is bound up with them. The moral is clear enough. The great institutions of mankind and the crucial events in the lives of individuals ought to be recognized as sacred—the family, the government, the school, birth, marriage, and death. It is trivial to meet the word "sacred" with the reminder that *this* family, *this* government, *this* school, *this* church, *this* birth, *this* marriage, and *this* death are all monstrous and ought not to be tolerated. The reminder is but a reminder of duties to be performed if the number of monstrosities is not to be multiplied. Duty is not done by becoming disgusted with the obligation to do it. Without ceremony and duties the pursuit of happiness would be well-nigh inconceivable.

Ceremony has been linked with the cult of the supernatural because both acknowledge a kind of superiority which the pursuit of knowledge for its own sake does not deliver. Knowledge so pursued can deliver a prospect of boundless possibilities without freeing Nature from that indifference necessary to her teleology. That same teleology, although the source from which the idea of moral order is derived, may, when reflectively considered, engender an attitude of positivistic or stoical acceptance. This attitude, however, in spite of exhibitions of nobility of character, is uneasy, sad, and unhappy. It is a kind of courageous adolescence sophisticated and matured—the dauntless soul, habituated to the changes and chances of mortal life, no longer surprised by them, but comforted by the ultimate recourse, "you can end it when you will." This sad happiness does not commend itself to the majority of those who reflect on the moral order. They want the antithesis of stoicism—not sad happiness, but that peaceful happiness which attends surrender and devotion to something superior to their own individual fortune and to which they natively belong. That something may be conceived in different ways, but it is always "the ideal," something which is a completion of incompleteness—and death is never that—for which it is really worth while to die whether one dies for it or not. There are degrees of exaltation in the ideal. It expands with its exaltation, ultimately embracing Nature whole and entire. At the last it makes human life so sacred that suicide becomes self-murder and both the judicial and merciful taking of life are regarded as forgivable rather than justified. All ceremony is testimony to faith in the ideal, faith in the ever-superior, ending in faith in the superior-to-Nature.

Rites and ceremonies are, then, acknowledgments of the supernatural. They are, as already indicated, dubious and inconclusive proofs of its existence. Obviously that which is acknowledged to be superior to Nature cannot be proved to exist in the way existence is proved or disproved in Nature. Could it be, it would cease to be supernatural. Its existence must be supernatural existence like that of the fires of hell, which burn without consuming that which they burn, or like the streets of heaven, paved with gold that was never mined. Affirmations and denials of existence are in the acknowledgment of the supernatural both refuted, for what is affirmed is a profound incommensurability. The principle here involved is a commonplace in philosophy whenever the attempt is made to define categories in an ultimate significance irrespective of what they categorize. "Appearance and reality" is an excellent example. The distinction here is not troublesome when we affirm that a scene in a mirror appears to have depth, but in reality has none, or that a straight stick appears bent in a pool, but in reality is not. In general terms, whenever the distinction is relevant to the same context there is little, if any, ambiguity. Let it, however, be a distinction between ultimate contexts—then it becomes impossible to affirm of the one what is affirmed of the other. Each context has an existence of its own, but existence has now become ambiguous, for the existence of the one is not the existence of the other. The existence of the supernatural in Nature may be likened to the existence of depth in a mirror and be named a "perspective" in accord with a philosophical usage having some present currency. Its effectiveness and power are not thereby removed. The mirror perspective is of consequence in optical instruments, and the supernatural perspective is of consequence in human life.

Sacred Literature

The classification of the writings of mankind into the literary and the scientific, although ambiguous, emphasizes a contrast which illustrations disclose before any need of definitions arises. The difference between the plays of Shakespeare and a learned commentary upon them is unmistakable. If a treatise on chemistry is added for further comparison, the difference is magnified. "Literature" and "science" become names for a classification, and definitions are framed to embody the distinguishing criteria. Thereby all writings tend to fall into one or the other of two mutually exclusive classes in spite of ambiguous instances. According to this procedure, the classification of sacred writings with science is clearly improper. The book of Genesis has more evident kinship with Shakespeare's plays than with the commentary, and none with the treatise on chemistry. No question of comparative value is here involved; nor is the matter wholly one of convenient classification. The significance of the classification lies in the recognition that the promptings to write literature are different from the promptings to write science and that consequently it is more fitting to speak of "sacred literature" than of "sacred science." One may hold science sacred and write about it in that spirit without making any contribution to science whatever.

But sacred literature is also distinguished from the secular, and this distinction is double edged. It divides sacred literature from all other literature and also brings science within the scope of the secular. We now have two classifications of writings: one into the literary and the scientific, the other into the sacred and the secular. They are not mutually exclusive. Taken together, they indicate a natural tendency to associate the sacred with the literary when the contrast with the scientific is emphasized, and to isolate it within the literary when a contrast with the secular is relevant. Sacred literature, without ceasing to be literature, has a character of its own which generates a far-reaching discrimination between the sacred and the secular. All this becomes more evident and impressive when the general types of literature are considered, such as prose, poetry, the drama, the story, the fantasy. Sacred literature exhibits them all, but with a special intonation. Even theology, which may claim to be supreme among the sciences, rests its claim on a character of its own rather than on the superlative possession of a character in which other sciences comparatively share.

These labored remarks about classification are of little value without illustrations to illuminate them. They have seemed worth making out of respect for the natural tendency repeatedly exhibited by the human animal to try to reduce to some ordered distinction the chaos of affirmations and denials he makes about himself and his circumstances. He never talks about them in a unified and consistent way. He himself recognizes that his expressions vary with his circumstances and that the manner of expression under one set of circumstances is often wholly inappropriate under a different set. If in his reflective moments he is rigorously critical of his language, he must admit that his "technical terms" are products of his attempts to free his speech from its native and inevitable animism. He is a living being who cannot help speaking the speech of life. As indicated in the preceding chapter, when his language is considered the universe becomes a universe of discourse in which things are what they are said to be—as if Nature herself were polarized in a manner congruent with the subjects and predicates of his own propositions, making his speech an instance of her own universal metabolism. Otherwise, how could a living being say what things are? Since he addresses Nature variously, he ought to be a little amused at his own efforts to explain why. When he is most serious he ought to remember both his laughter and his tears, for without them there is nothing to be serious about. If, then, the secular and the sacred are to be considered seriously, classifications, in recognizing their difference, ought not to lead one to put them in opposition as competitors for allegiance. That would be to forget laughter and tears. Nor are they opposed as sense and nonsense, for the secular does not contain less nonsense than the sacred. Such opposition as they have lies in contrasted attitudes toward Nature. In secular literature Nature is primary no matter how she is rendered; in the sacred, Nature is secondary. Sacred literature intones, one may say, what has already been said about the supernatural.

The few illustrations which follow have been deliberately chosen in order to bring out this intonation with a high degree of freedom from disturbing dissonances. There is so much apparent puerility and absurdity in the great bulk of sacred literature that its mature significance can be easily obscured. Its language contains propositions which when strictly construed in accordance with the canons of the secular are either quite incredible or so fantastic that even symbolism and imagery are excluded. The behavior of gods and God and the relations between the divine and the human are often so preposterously recorded that those of us sensitive to decency and justice are often shocked, until we attentively consider the millions who are not shocked at all and that they, too, unless extraordinarily stupid, would be shocked if the supernatural were not involved. Their normal attitude is akin to that of children listening to fairy tales and finding them venturesomely illustrative or instructive rather than credible or incredible. When the language of the sacred has been subjected to the discipline of reflection, its intonation is clearer. Perhaps it is most clear when it comes as an interruption of the secular. Conventionally, from the savage to the civilized, religious exercises come as interruptions in the daily round, like grace before meat, going to church on Sunday, or opening a wholly secular meeting with prayer.

The Old Testament is largely a narrative of the fortunes of an ancient people who early in their history came to believe that they had been chosen by the Maker of heaven and earth to walk in His ways and obey His commandments. It has been numbered among the great sacred books and incorporated into Christendom. There is no need here to review what scholars have learned of its own history. Considerations of its source and origin are usually unnecessary when reading it as an expression of human experience. A reader finds it very uneven and yet producing a total effect which in its turn acts like a principle of criticism for what the book contains. Obviously, there are other books which might have been selected for illustration. My own choice is largely arbitrary, except for the reason that I want my illustrations to be familiar and to be as free as possible from the contrast implied by the division of the Bible into the Old and the New Testaments.

Judge me, O God, and plead my cause against an ungodly nation: O deliver me from the deceitful and unjust man.

For thou art the God of my strength; why dost thou cast me off? Why go I mourning because of the oppression of the enemy?

O send out thy light and thy truth: let them lead me; let them bring me unto thy holy hill, and to thy tabernacles.

Then will I go unto the altar of God, unto God my exceeding joy: yea, upon the harp will I praise thee, O God my God.

Why art thou cast down, O my soul? and why art thou disquieted within me? hope in God: for I shall yet praise him, who is the health of my countenance, and my God.

This appeal to judgment other than human intones the sacred note. Of course one may doubt whether there is such judgment. That, however, is not the point. The psalm itself expresses doubt and bewilderment, but it also confesses the faith that only a superhuman judgment can be adequate and finds in that confession the reason for continued praise. One does not need to know who wrote the psalm or when.

In the light of that psalm the story of Esther looks wholly secular from start to finish. It is the story, many times told, of intrigue lodging the intriguing woman in the home. It may be a true story, for that sort of intrigue has been practiced again and again, and judgment of it is human judgment. It confesses no faith and is not an inspiration to continued praise. Although accepted as canonical in the scriptures of Jews and Christians, there are additions to it relegated to the Apocrypha. The story of Job presents an impressive contrast. That there was long ago a man of that name who maintained his integrity in spite of misfortunes and would not admit that they were punishments for his sins is credible. The story as told is not, unless one believes that Satan conspired with God to put Job to the test. Credibility, however, is not essential to the story's power. That summons from the whirlwind to Job and his companions to declare where they were when the foundations of the world were laid, before assuming the right of final judgment, stopped all their wordy discussion. After the whirlwind Job's faith became a revelation: "I have heard of thee with the hearing of the ear, but now mine eye seeth thee." The "happy ending" that follows seems like a concession to those who otherwise would not understand—a descent to the secular. New prosperity beyond anything Job had known before, seven sons and three daughters, the latter the fairest in all the land and well-dowered, life extended one hundred and forty years, and the sight of his sons and his sons' sons for four generations make up an ambiguous answer to the satanic question: "Doth Job serve God for naught?" He served for naught, but naught was not his reward.

The sacred intonation is not confined to literature canonically sacred. Shakespeare's *Othello* is a dramatic and tragic rendering of a story of love, jealousy, intrigue, and villainy, written to entertain a varied audience in a theater. There is a scene in it in which

for a moment there is something different—Desdemona's chamber where murder is to be done. She is
asleep, and a light is burning by her bedside. The
jealous husband has convinced himself that he is acting
for a righteous cause. "She must die, else she'll betray
more men." He sees the burning flame and would
quench it, for his deed calls for darkness.

> Put out the light, and then put out the light:
> If I quench thee, thou flaming minister,
> I can again thy former light restore,
> Should I repent me; but once put out thy light,
> Thou cunning'st pattern of excelling nature,
> I know not where is that Promethean heat
> That can thy light relume
> . . . I will kill thee,
> And love thee after.

I have often wondered what would be the effect of
deleting from the play the quoted words. The story of
Othello and Desdemona is much older than Shakespeare. Novelists and dramatists continue to retell it,
varying characters, circumstances, scenery, twists and
turns of the plot, and endings. They have nothing to do
with the plot and do not affect the action. Although
they may indicate something of Othello's character,
that is not an end which they seem to serve. They seem
rather to suspend the action for a moment and to let
two lights possess author, play and audience. Othello is
hardly speaking as himself until, as if coming out of a

trance, he says, "I will kill thee and love thee after," awakening her with a last kiss. The lights bring to remembrance the obvious and commonplace while we wait for murder. There are lights which can be switched on and off at pleasure, and there is a light which can't. The intrusion of the brute fact upon the taking of life does not stop the taking. It leaves the reasons for taking and not taking what they were before, but it gives to giving and taking a setting in which life is turned into a Promethean gift. Where is its Promethean source? Life has become sacred, not because it ought not to be taken, but because it is given. The only justifiable reason for not putting it out is because it cannot be rekindled. Its source has made it so, allowing it to shine among the transitory lights of Nature and be as easily put out as a candle's flame. There is ambiguity here, something like paradox and contradiction. That, however, is characteristic of sacred literature. It expresses paradox, using the resources of language to heighten it and finding them unable to remove it. Knowledge of Nature is not thereby increased, but the pursuit of happiness is profoundly influenced. That pursuit, entangled with death as natural, or in self-defense, or murder, or punishment, or sacrifice, or atonement seems ultimately to demand that the judgment of death requires an independent judgment of life which makes Nature secondary instead of primary.

The myth of Prometheus is old and multiform. Most of us, I suspect, have forgotten that his Greek name is equivalent to our "forethought" and remember him chiefly as the bringer of fire within the power of men to kindle and as their first teacher in the arts that spring from the uses of heat. Zeus, in anger, chained him to a rock and restored his vitals daily after they had been daily devoured by a vulture. Aeschylus portrays Forethought enchained in his "Prometheus Bound." The waves that wash all shores come as a chorus of the Daughters of Ocean to discover the cause of the clangor heard from afar. They find the man in chains and would hear his story. He has angered Zeus. But how?

"I made them that die cease to expect their doom." "Is that all?" Then follows the old story of stolen fire, the arts and crafts of men, and the defiance of Zeus until deliverance comes. One line in a poem has changed the setting of a well-known fable. A god is angry because the first consequence of the gift of forethought is forgetfulness of death; mortals behave as if they were immortal. Death ends them but is not their aim. Arts and crafts, intelligence, foresight, the pursuit of knowledge—all are the consequences of a light that can be put out. Nature has become secondary, and that light primary.

Yet that light is put out by wholly natural means. Again paradox and contradiction become evident. In the pursuit of knowledge the paradox may be recorded when human behavior and attitudes toward Nature are considered, but recording it does not remove it. Equipping man with instincts, faculties, propensities, emotions, and psychoses amounts on final analysis to no more than getting him ready to behave as he does. Examining his bodily organization amounts to killing him piecemeal, so to speak, in order to discover what he loves with; killing him wholly amounts to making it impossible for him to forget that he is mortal. Once dead or missing, his body is in requisition by the living to be disposed of conformably with the ceremonies of society, religion, science, and the law. There are many different ports for missing men.

Again I would stress the caution that I am not arguing for anything. I am trying not to deceive myself or others and am acutely aware how easily both can be done when the pursuit of happiness is under consideration. It is not easy to avoid offending the sensitive and encouraging the superstitious. I have deliberately avoided "defining" happiness. One whose experience has not delivered the difference between "being happy" and "being unhappy" will never learn from the books what the difference is. Such a being would find irrelevant to his existence all the juggling with "pleasure," "contentment," "bliss," "Beatitude," "the good," "peace." With the experience, however, the juggling may become very important, for it is then relevant to a pursuit which it may help to clarify. That pursuit is open to inspection. The greater part of literature is occupied almost exclusively with it, portraying it, criticizing it, and giving advice about it. What shall we do to be happy, and what shall we do to be saved? The second question grows out of the first and becomes ultimately the absorbing question, for happiness is insecure. The more Nature is studied, the more that insecurity is evident. Our own ultimate helplessness becomes undeniable. That conclusion, however, rarely ends the pursuit. We can manage somehow without security, for the promptings of Nature to a little laughter at her sportiveness and a little intoxication with her allurements are not easily suppressed. She, like Prometheus, can still make us cease to expect our doom, even when it hangs like war clouds loaded with destruction above our heads. But where there is life there is hope; and with that wise saw, with its ambiguous "where" and "there," the course of safety begins to alter its direction. There is hope where that Promethean heat is. It lights every fire of Nature, both the relightable and the not-relightable. With it there is safety, because it never puts itself out. Nature with her varied lights and shadows has become subordinate—God's servant, as Sir Thomas Browne called her.

Not a word of this is new. It can all be found in the

literature on the pursuit of happiness. Many confess it as their faith and live by it with a kind of unshakable happiness; many ceremonially confess it and do not live by it; many do not confess it and yet live by it; many neither confess it nor live by it; but nearly all admit that were there no doubt about it the pursuit of happiness would have a charted course. Natural misery might not cease, but natural happiness would be so transformed that no ills of Nature could disturb it.

Nothing originally hypothetical is thereby proved. Yet I think there has been repeated the demonstration that the pursuit of happiness robs Nature of her self-sufficiency. It means nothing to add that this is only a human point of view, unless the addition is supplemented by another point of view which is not human and will thereby clarify the "only." The human point of view has trouble enough in trying to discover the point of view of the salmon and the solitary wasp. It denies a point of view to all that is "purely physical." Philosophers interested in a "first philosophy" should recognize as an obvious dogma that all rivalry of points of view is nonsense unless they are deliverable in the human point of view. A little while ago I was having the Sun complain about Earth's attitude toward him. That is nonsense, but I hope it was instructive nonsense. Indeed, I will confess that I hope there is much of that sort of nonsense in this essay and, further, that I

have thrown into the wastebasket many pages of nonsense so precious that I could not bear seeing it in
print, but rejoiced to see the fire take it in flames to
heaven. I have loved it after. Of course there is a human attitude toward Nature when it is found that she
is insufficient of herself to provide security in the
pursuit of happiness and that if there is to be security it
must be found elsewhere. Demands are now made on
that "elsewhere," and one demand is supreme: it must
be in command of Nature or be somehow her ultimate
source. That "elsewhere" is where there is a light which
is never lit and is never put out and which clarifies all
darkness. When fear is mentioned as the origin of religion it is not ultimately the shrinking fear of fire, but
the reverent or awful fear of being seen through and
through with nothing concealed and with final judgment impending. Of course, a human attitude is involved in all this, but that neither explains it nor explains it away. It does explain, however, why religion,
when historically reviewed, exhibits in its literature and
ceremonies such a mixture of the sublime and the
ridiculous. "Green Pastures" delights a modern audience and sends most of them home a little differently
reflective than they were when they bought their tickets
of admission.

Faith in Elsewhere is the security of happiness, because it is ultimate justification. With sacred litera-

ture in mind, that barren and colorless proposition does not mean primarily that there is what is called "a future life" with rewards and penalties for what has been done Here or "a continued existence" with something still to do. It means that Here and whatever happens Here is for the sake of Elsewhere—for God's glory, not for an earthly purpose. Milton, in the sonnet on the blindness that overtook him ere half his days were done, "fondly" asked,

> "Doth God exact day-labor, light denied?"
> . . . But Patience, to prevent
> That murmur, soon replies, "God doth not need
> Either man's work or his own gifts. . . ."

God needs nothing, yet

> ". . . His state
> Is kingly: thousands at his bidding speed,
> And post o'er land and ocean without rest;
> They also serve who only stand and wait."

Nature in service with her Master Elsewhere is an idea which cannot be derived from an object as ideas normally are. The object has to be evoked by using language in reverse from the logical. It ought not, therefore, to be surprising that the language of sacred literature should so often be fantastic and illogical and yet be ceremonially convincing. One finds the evidence all the way from the savage to the civilized. The Lord does not tend sheep, but He is a shepherd. One is not convinced of this by trying to find Him or imagine Him in green pastures and beside still waters, but by the ceremonial procession with the bishop coming last with his shepherd's crook. The choir may be singing:

> We march, we march to victory
> With the cross of the Lord before us.

There is the cross at the head of the procession. The altar is reached, and there follows the sacrament of hospitality, bread and wine transubstantiated. The faithful Christian is not disturbed by all this incongruity. In the light of his faith it is not incongruous, it is not imagery, it is not symbolism, except as a symbol of a total transubstantiation. That is a reason why an illustration from *Othello* was chosen, with its reference to a pagan hero—the guest for transubstantiated light. Here the myth of Midas becomes instructive. The transubstantiation of everything into gold at a touch or of the elements into hydrogen by a chemical experiment is universally rejected as affording no ultimate security in the pursuit of happiness. No security is preferable. We can end the pursuit when we will or make hay while the sun shines.

The analysis could be carried farther by examining theology or sacred doctrine. The outcome would be the same. Theology is transubstantiated science. Spinoza has expressed this, although not quite in those words. In his *Ethics* he defines God as "substance with infinite attributes, each of which expresses eternal and infinite essence." The definition is somewhat clarified by the fifteenth proposition of the first book: "Whatever is, is in God, and without God, nothing can be nor be conceived." The two parts of the proposition are alternative statements and redefine God as "That without which nothing can be nor be conceived." But "that" is not *a* substance, but "substance only," the transubstantiation of all substances. The words are, of course, troublesome. It is both easy and difficult to make out what they mean—easy when taken to affirm that Nature is secondary, not primary; difficult when we try to deduce the secondary from the primary. Theoretical science is marked by the same ease and difficulty. It is easy to affirm that consequences are secondary, but difficult to make out why antecedents have consequences. With matter primary, it is easy to affirm that its manifestations are secondary, but difficult to make out how the promise and potency of matter make those manifestations. With energy or light primary, it is easy to affirm that their transformation is secondary, but it is difficult to make out why they embody themselves in agents to do their work. Creation and incarnation are among religious doctrines. It is fair to ask whether theoretical science or theology, by using different words, escapes the difficulty of "that without which nothing can be or be conceived." But theology is addressed to Elsewhere, while theoretical science is addressed to Nature. It is in the deductive return from ultimate categories that an intellectual kinship is found between them. The ways of energy are not past finding out by exploring Nature, the ways of God are. That is why theology is relevant, not to the pursuit of knowledge, but to the pursuit of happiness.

A philosopher, therefore, cannot very well dismiss the doctrines of religion as of no importance. He will ask, rather: What importance do they have? There the answer seems to be clear: They supply a metaphysics for Nature secondary, as other doctrines supply one for Nature primary. It is not surprising that in both supplementations similar categories should be used—the commensurable and the incommensurable, the perfect and the imperfect, the infinite and the finite, the necessary and the contingent, the one and the many; the one space and the many places, the one time and the many seconds, the one present with past and future, in the beginning and in the end, the one cause and the many effects, the one substance and the many substances, the one energy and the many energies, the one language and the many vernaculars, the one light and the many lights, the one body and the many bodies, the one mind and the many minds; ultimately, always the one and the many and the commensurable and the incommensurable. Whether metaphysics is secular or sacred depends on the accent of intonations. Accent "knowledge," it is secular; accent "happiness," it is sacred—a laboratory, a ceremony. Precisely where and when the difference in accent begins and ends is not discoverable by voyaging through heaven and earth, the sea, and all that in them is, for the compass is always a needle pointing to a pole—a tendency, a vector.

The second paragraph of the introductory chapter of Santayana's *Reason in Common Sense* begins with these words: "A philosopher could hardly have a higher ambition than to make himself a mouth-piece for the memory and judgment of his race." That memory and judgment include a philosopher's own, for he is one of his race; his home, like theirs, has been Nature. He has no special claim to infallibility. If he ventures to be a mouthpiece for their memory and judgment, he will find that their judgment has always been that Nature is, not only in space and in time, but also in suspense.

Superstition

The practice of witchcraft was forbidden the Israelites. Yet Saul, their first king, having failed to receive a sign from the Lord informing him about the outcome of an impending battle with the Philistines, sought out the Witch of Endor and had her bring back the wise Samuel from the grave. Samuel was annoyed at having been disturbed. He told Saul in plain words that the king was the Lord's enemy, since he had received no sign, and that he and his sons would perish in the battle. They perished. The familiar story is worth attention, for it illustratively defines superstition and exposes a human trait as prevalent today as in the days of Saul. This trait was barely hinted at in the preceding section, but was not forgotten in the writing of it. The temptation to let it creep in was resisted in order to bring out the essential character of the sacred. Seeking signs from the Lord may be just as superstitious as resorting to witches, but the divine sign does not imply witchcraft. This is at least an interesting difference. One who has no desire to pass judgment on practices cannot fail to be impressed by the fact that many people, not convinced by the Christian Church and its ceremonies, turn to societies for psychical research and become convinced by packs of cards and tambourines that there is the supernormal and the supernatural. And it must strike one as a little amazing that the evidence of the Church should so often be labeled superstitious, while that of the séances should be considered scientific. Indeed, when the history of science and religion is critically studied, superstition is abundant in each, and efforts are made to get rid of it.

For the purpose of this essay emphasis should fall on these efforts. The distinction between folly and wisdom is important in the judgments pronounced by one's race. The wise man regards superstition as folly and would remove it if he could. There were many visitors to the oracle at Delphi who left tokens of their visit at the shrine. Plato tells of a visit of the Seven Wise Men of Ancient Greece. They left two tokens, "the first fruits" of wisdom: "Know thyself" and "Keep within bounds." He that does not know what he wants and goes out of bounds is on the road to folly. That road was followed by many visitors to Delphi whose tokens were bribes or payments for services rendered; these believed that the palm should be crossed with a shilling instead of a proverb. Does one know himself or keep within bounds if one counts the wealth of the supernatural in the shillings of Nature? Such counting is superstition. It has its reward. Croesus, having paid much money to be told that if he went to war he would destroy a great empire, went to war and destroyed his own. Saul and his sons perished, their army was defeated, but David saved Israel. Stories of the follies of superstition often seem like examples of it.

If the maxims posted at Delphi are allowed to criticize relentlessly a man's hopes and fears, he is very likely to find that the effectiveness of superstition is something he does not want, that its successfulness would amount to much too much. Affirming this is not affirming what ought to happen, but what repeatedly happens and is supported by evidence. The fortune-teller beguiles us all by arousing an equivocal curiosity about what she will tell us of our future. The effect upon us varies, but in one respect there is an invariable effect. In proportion as we believe her, we prepare for or hasten the coming of fortune if it is good, or we do our best to avoid it if it is bad. We never wholly believe in an unalterable future. Even when we profess to be fatalists our actions belie us. What we find we ultimately need, and what we ultimately want, is Nature's complete indifference to our prayers. Our happiness is not thereby made for us secure, but without that indifference security is left at the mercy of willfulness and whimsicality. So left, we become increasingly insane and fear to take the next step lest the solid earth crumble beneath our feet. He who thoroughly searches his own mind knows that he does not want Nature amenable to his prayers.[2]

[2] I am well aware that this conclusion will be disputed and be regarded by many as the expression of a personal opinion, not of the general opinion of mankind. I would ask, however, for a consideration of the evidence which is too extensive to be reviewed here. It is evident enough that prayer is commonly considered "a last resort" and that in great emergencies men want their prayers answered in the terms in which they are expressed. I am asking for a consideration of prayer when no need of it is felt. I am asking whether anybody who takes time to reflect really wants a god who will make the sun stand still at the request of somebody whom that god particularly favors. What, then, is the use of prayer? I would answer: Consider the pursuit of happiness and try to make clear what would happen to it if prayer were completely left out. Would leaving out prayer carry nothing else along with

The point is that superstition turns out to be self-defeating and increasingly abhorrent. It begets the fear of God which is not clean—which is irreverent, not reverent. Yet like the reverent fear it is evidence that consideration of the pursuit of happiness leaves Nature, as I have phrased it, in suspense. She loses her self-sufficiency in the human view of her. But how shall that in which she is suspended be expressed when it is not available to the pursuit of knowledge? The expression is found in sacred literature. The embarrassment of that literature is its language, for that is the same as the secular. But it has an intonation of its own, whereby in religious doctrine the ultimate categories developed in the pursuit of knowledge are transmuted into categories of the divine.

---

it? Anybody who takes the pains can answer such a question for himself. He does not need a professor of philosophy to give him the answer, so that he can write it down in his notebook, where it will be handy for examination. The professor might suggest that it would be worth while to note that there are shrines to Buddha, to Christ, to the Virgin, to Lenin, to the King, to Democracy, to the Devil, to Victory, and none to Defeat.

CONCLUSION

THE controlling thesis of this essay has been that so far as the pursuit of knowledge is concerned Nature herself is not a problem. She is the field of knowledge, and as that field she is preëminently the familiar visible world. The problems of knowledge are all problems of formulating her coherences. Our ability to formulate them is not a problem. Indeed, the ability of doers to do what they do is evinced in the doing of it; it is not a problem of their ability. How they, with their ability, do what they do is what we, with our ability, try to find out. That is just what the pursuit of knowledge amounts to. Thereby the enterprise of learning is defined, clearly, I think, and without ambiguity.

I am impressed by the very simple illustration of learning which Bacon used when he defended the enterprise against the objections of theologians who claimed that knowledge was condemned by Scripture because the desire of it was the cause of Adam's fall.

To discover then the ignorance and error of this opinion, and the misunderstanding in the grounds thereof, it may well appear these men do not observe or consider that it was not the pure knowledge of nature and universality, a knowledge by the light whereof man did give names unto other creatures in Paradise, as they were brought before him, according unto their proprieties, which gave the occasion to the fall: but it was the proud knowledge of good and evil, with an intent in man to give law unto himself, and to depend no more upon God's commandments, which was the form of the temptation.[1]

The illustration was both a confounding of the objectors and a neat definition of the science of biology—naming creatures according to their proprieties. Such naming began before the fall and has continued ever since, with a blessing rather than a curse the consequence. The possibility of natural knowledge is not a problem, but the advancement of learning is. Man names that which is expansed unto his eyes according to its proprieties. All his *naming* is under the restraint of what he names "space" and "time." That is why the central chapters of this book have been concerned with the visible world, time and history, and the universe of discourse. The analyses begin and end in the visible world and my repeated, varied, and perhaps tedious assaults on "dualism" have been made in order to keep that world from losing its preëminence and finality in the pursuit of knowledge. Nature as the field

[1] Francis Bacon, *The Advancement of Learning*, Oxford, The Clarendon Press, pp. 5–6.

where knowledge is pursued presents no problem of her own being or status. As the field where happiness is pursued, her being and status become equivocal. Then a dualism of the natural and the supernatural arises: hence the final chapter of this essay.

All other dualisms impress me as variants of that one. They all seem to me to follow the pattern of the creation story—a world prepared in faultless working order, then man, so constituted that his presence brings confusion, creating a world of appearance by means of which he tries to work out the constitution of the world of reality beyond. What *have* we with two worlds, one evidently expansed before our eyes and the other inevitably beyond? Does it now make any difference which is called "natural" and which "supernatural"? Let either be called "nature": it is some inadequacy in the one that projects the other. Somehow or other the one is "in order to" the being or discovery of the other and there is no possibility of bridging the gap between them by knowledge. It is bridged "pragmatically," if one will, by procedure, by probability, by faith. The favored word ought not to trouble those who are not obsessed by the superstition that their own professional vernacular alone is orthodox. I choose "faith" for reasons which the context, I hope, makes clear.

The thesis is then that the dualism of the natural and

the supernatural is the dualism of knowledge and faith and that the dualism arises, not because knowledge is pursued, but because happiness is pursued. The two pursuits are not in different worlds; they are in the same world. "Happiness," as I have already indicated, needs no initial definition. If the distinction between happiness and misery is not initially as clear as that between a circle and a square, there is no profit in considering it. The important fact is that the pursuit of happiness leads us to question whether that pursuit is worth while. That is the great question which has haunted mankind for ages. In a way it is an odd question. Nobody ever seems wholly content to take the positive fact that happiness is pursued as an answer. I pursue happiness because I must: I am made that way, it is a natural law of my being which I can't escape; the instinct for self-preservation is deep seated in every living thing and the evidence of it is beyond dispute; even in the organic world everything tends to persist in its own state of being unless interfered with —why, then, raise the troublesome question? If we pursue knowledge because we must, because we are naturally curious and want to know, and are willing to let the pursuit of knowledge go at that, why not be equally willing to let the pursuit of happiness go the same way? Why not be simply positivistic about it? The answer is obvious in positivistic terms—we do not let it go that way, we can't, we are so made that we do not and cannot.

It is the positivistic answer that I have been exploring, approaching it variously in the several sections of this chapter. Its correctness is beyond dispute. It takes little reflection upon it, however, to discover that the two great pursuits of mankind are so interlocked that the pursuit of knowledge without the pursuit of happiness is meaningless and that knowledge is pursued for the sake of happiness, but must be pursued disinterestedly if its service is to be competent. We are made that way, and our being made that way explains what we do about it. What *ought* we to do about a situation like this, is not the question I have been trying to answer. We may do nothing about it, but that does not impress me as worth writing a chapter about. Or I could here turn dialectician and affirm that doing nothing about it is doing something about it, because doing nothing about it under the circumstances is to leave them alone to have what consequences they will. Among the consequences is that although the troublesome question is suppressed we would be the happier if the pursuit of happiness were differently justified.

It is the question whether the pursuit of happiness is ultimately worth while which generates faith in the supernatural, but not knowledge of it, and also "transports" the idea of happiness to lift it above the ordi-

nary. There are other ways of phrasing the same circumstance. There is a current dislike of the word
"supernatural." It has come to suggest little more than
"superstition." The current preference seems to be the
word "ideal." I have deliberately chosen "supernatural," because "ideal" tends to suppress the subordina-
tion of Nature involved. There is great need of more
intellectual honesty these days. Word phobias are not
good guides in the attempt to clarify our opinions and
beliefs. What are our ideals? All of us seem to think
that we ought to have some, that we should not go
through life without any. The latter way of living is
usually regarded with contempt. The cynic, observing
how men fall short of their professed ideals, makes contempt his own ideal and, like a god whose supreme
attribute is scorn, laughs at men with their yearning
bowels of mercy. In ecstasy, an ardent reformer once
told me that he would be willing to see the whole popu-
lation of the United States drowned in the Atlantic
Ocean, if that would be for the Good of Humanity.
Paradise, either once lost, but to be regained, or never
lost, but to be attained, the ideal garden, the ideal
city, the ideal society, ideal humanity, ideal love—
these are not ideas of anything disclosed in Nature's
history, nor does she forecast their realization. She may
suggest, as it were, ideals to the pursuer of happiness,
because he finds her a moral order with pains and

penalties interlocked, with the consequences of deeds overtaking the doer of them, with judgment impending, but never final, with no judgment to follow, but she does not exhibit any preference for human life. The entertainment of ideals is the recognition of that fact, and a faith that there is somehow compensation for it. That means that Nature is subordinate. To be ideal she must be made over completely, so completely that the lion will lie down with the lamb, the lion never hungry and the lamb never food. It is rather difficult to make out in what details lion and lamb would then be lion and lamb. Scientists worried about Promethean heat foresee a rather cold picture of Nature's future.

A future world which would be the ideal has no conceivable date in any calendar. The adjective "future" is irrelevant unless it is given a qualitative, not a temporal, significance. That is my reason for affirming that the use of "ideal" tends to suppress the fact that "the ideal" is an alternative word for "the supernatural." It begets superstition as readily: the ideal can lead to killing men for the glory of the Good in the expectation that the Good will be served and will appropriately bless the killer with a crown of glory.

What, then, *should* be done about it? The final chapter of this essay has not been written to provide an answer to questions of that kind. It has been written, rather, to exhibit by means of conspicuous and familiar examples something of what follows when anything is done. At the last, Nature becomes secondary and subordinate; she is in suspense, and a dualism of the natural and the supernatural is generated. A justification of Nature which she herself does not afford is demanded. She is justified by man's faith that the supernatural is justification, and that faith is the faith that justifies him. For the supernatural he has no other language than that of the natural. This he uses with ceremonial, emblematic, and sacramental effect. It is very difficult to keep his faith free from superstition, for superstition is constantly suggested by his ceremonies. His faith, simply confessed, is that with the supernatural there is salvation. His superstition, simply expressed, is that the supernatural can be diverted by his faith in it and by the ceremonies emblematic of his faith. One can see plainly the difference between Job and Saul— faith kept though one be slain: Samuel called back from his grave by a witch. A philosopher, presuming to make himself a mouthpiece for the judgment of his race, will have been a very superficial student of mankind if he does not discover the judgment that it is faith, not knowledge, that justifies.

INDEX

INDEX